ETHICS and PROFESSIONAL ISSUES in COUPLE and FAMILY THERAPY

ETHICS and PROFESSIONAL ISSUES in COUPLE and FAMILY THERAPY

Edited by Lorna Hecker

Routledge
Taylor & Francis Group
New York   London

Routledge
Taylor & Francis Group
270 Madison Avenue
New York, NY 10016

Routledge
Taylor & Francis Group
27 Church Road
Hove, East Sussex BN3 2FA

© 2010 by Taylor and Francis Group, LLC
Routledge is an imprint of Taylor & Francis Group, an Informa business

Printed in the United States of America on acid-free paper
10 9 8 7 6 5 4 3 2 1

International Standard Book Number: 978-0-7890-3390-1 (Paperback)

Library of Congress Cataloging-in-Publication Data

Ethics and professional issues in couple and family therapy / edited by Lorna Hecker.
    p. cm.
    Includes bibliographical references and index.
    ISBN 978-0-7890-3389-5 (hbk. : alk. paper) -- ISBN 978-0-7890-3390-1 (pbk. : alk. paper)
    1. Family psychotherapy--Moral and ethical aspects. 2. Marital psychotherapy--Moral and ethical aspects. 3. Family therapists--Professional ethics. 4. Marriage counselors--Professional ethics. I. Hecker, Lorna L. II. Title.

RC488.5E87 2010
616.89'156--dc22
                                        2009023509

Visit the Taylor & Francis Web site at
http://www.taylorandfrancis.com

and the Routledge Web site at
http://www.routledgementalhealth.com

Contents

/22/29

Contents

Preface

Primum non nocere—First, do no harm.

Hippocrates (c. 460–400 BC)

You probably chose the field of marriage and family therapy because of a desire to help people, and would likely be aghast at the notion of harming your clients. Yet without proper knowledge, you can make decisions that can indeed cause damage to clients, as well as to your own professional practice. The subjects in this book have been chosen to educate you on the most salient topics regarding the intertwining of ethical, legal, clinical, and professional issues faced by marriage and family therapists. The book has been developed with the American Association for Marriage and Family Therapy (AAMFT) Core Competencies (AAMFT, 2004) in mind. Under the Core Competencies, Domain 5: *Legal Issues, Ethics, and Standards*, the following competencies are specifically addressed in this book:

- Professional ethics and standards of practice that apply to the practice of marriage and family therapy (MFT) are emphasized.
- An ethical decision-making model is provided.
- Emphasis is placed on state and federal laws and regulations that apply to the practice of MFT.
- Situations in which ethics, law, professional liability, and standards of practice apply are illustrated.
- Case scenarios are provided to enable you to recognize ethical dilemmas in the practice setting.
- Readers will be familiar with safety plans for clients who present with self-harm, suicide, abuse, or violence.
- Office policies, procedures, and forms are discussed to be consistent with standards of practice and to protect client confidentiality and parameters of mandatory reporting.

- Mandatory reporting requirements will be outlined.
- The reader will understand self-of-the-therapist issues and how to maintain professional competence.
- Scope of practice will be defined and discussed.

AAMFT developed a *Code of Ethics* (2001) to guide the practitioner, which is included as an appendix to this book. Ethical decision making, however, goes well beyond your professional code of ethics. Education to develop sensitivity to potential ethical issues is part of this process. In this book, the authors discuss the ethical obligations of therapists, which are expected as part of their professional behavior. An ethical decision-making model is provided as a "map" to navigate through complex ethical decisions. Understanding how you think about your values and the values of clients is part of that model. Legal issues are addressed in the context of ethical issues, though legal advice is not dispensed. You should, of course, always refer to your own attorneys for legal advice.

This is a book for professionals who want to understand the context of complex situations in which couple and family therapists find themselves. It is a book for family therapists who, consistent with their systems training, will grasp multilevel problems, grapple with them, and go through a reasoned analysis to find a solution that best meets the needs of the people involved. This is not a philosophical ethics book, but merely introduces the reader to philosophical principles for applied professional ethics decision making. In an ideal world, all therapists would be trained in moral philosophy but that ideal is clearly outside the scope of this book. This book can be utilized as an introductory graduate text in marriage and family therapy graduate programs, by professionals wishing to expand their depth and understanding of the field, or by those who wish to refresh their knowledge of professional issues and ethics for MFT licensing exams.

You will no doubt have quandaries when faced with ethical dilemmas posed in this book. Answers to ethical dilemmas often have a refrain of "it depends." Many variables contribute to evaluation when making sound ethical decisions. A tolerance of ambiguity is necessary for anyone who truly wishes to struggle with ethical dilemmas. You have to be able to juggle many diverging solutions (and viewpoints) at once before the best action can be chosen. Sometimes the best solution is obvious; other times there are competing "best" solutions. Sometimes all alternatives to an ethical dilemma are simply not satisfying or can even be repugnant. Early foreclosure on decisions to decrease your accompanying anxiety can lead to situations (ethical, clinical, or legal) that are worse than the predicament that was initially raised. Although some ethical or clinical decisions need to be made quickly, there are many situations where the therapist can decelerate the process to thoroughly scrutinize the situation at hand.

Therapists see cohabitating couples, dating couples, gay or lesbian couples, engaged couples, and so on. In a movement to be inclusive of these couples and married couples, the book was named *Ethics and Professional Issues in Couple and Family Therapy*. The terms *couple and family therapy* and *marriage and family therapy* are used alternatively throughout the book, with *couple and family therapy* the preferred phrase; occasionally the term *marriage and family therapist* or *marriage and family therapy* is used when referring to the discipline regarding the American Association for Marriage and Family Therapy.

In this book you will find many case scenarios, many based on actual cases to give the reader a sense of the richness of ethical issues that may present themselves in therapy. In some, the ethical or legal issues at hand may be evident, but in others, they may be slight, and you will need to search for the shades of gray that continuously make ethics a subtle but worthwhile pursuit. All case scenarios have had identifying information of the clients and case-specific information altered to protect the anonymity of the clients.

Unfortunately, in my personal experience, I encountered therapists who have not followed the "do no harm" dictate and have hurt people when they violated their professional and moral responsibilities. In some circumstances, there has been egregious harm. I have seen others believe that they are without moral fault, and this alone is a dangerous stance. The person who believes himself or herself to be without moral fault puts himself or herself outside the realm of dialogue, and relationships become secondary to that person's moral agenda. Dialogue is key to resolving most ethical dilemmas, and it is my hope that you have much dialogue as you traverse this book. It is my quest, then, that therapists be educated about ethics for the very positive goal of helping clients, but at the very least, *Primum non nocere*. Therefore, this book provides education, insight, and tools to help you adequately prepare for ethical practice as a couple and family therapist.

References

American Association for Marriage and Family Therapy. (2001). *Code of ethics.* Alexandria, VA: Author.

American Association for Marriage and Family Therapy. (2004). *Marriage and family therapy core competencies.* Alexandria, VA: Author.

Acknowledgments

Many people have helped me in this journey. My parents taught me the true meaning of ethics; they taught me to do the "right thing." They also sacrificed immensely so that I could receive an education. I thank my friends Anna Bower and Kate Sori for their listening ears and encouragement. Thanks to the staff at Taylor & Francis for their support and mutual determination in finishing this work. Appreciation goes out to my inspiring department head Mike Flannery and to my steady colleague Joseph Wetchler. Thank you to Kathy Schultz for all of her help with the "nuts and bolts" of completing the book. Thanks to Julie Ramisch and Sesen Negash for their input and assistance.

No book would get completed without the comic relief of my children, Aaron and Noah. They are the joy of my life. May they grow up to be ethical individuals who understand that being ethical may have a cost that is always worth paying. As always, I appreciate the support and care from my loving partner, Jonathan. Finally, I am thankful for the personal challenges that have been tandem with writing this book, because they have made me aware of what is truly important in life, and have been a reminder of the cost of that "right thing" that one must do. Although it may be temporarily uncomfortable, doing the right thing helps you stand taller, understand goodness, and feel secure. When we do the right thing, we know we are building a better world.

Editor

Lorna L. Hecker, Ph.D., L.M.F.T., is a Professor of Psychology at Purdue University Calumet in Hammond, Indiana, where she is a member of the faculty in the Marriage and Family Therapy program in the Department of Behavioral Sciences. She teaches graduate courses on ethics and professional issues, couples therapy, and trauma and recovery in family therapy. She is also the Director of the Purdue University Calumet Couple and Family Therapy Center. Dr. Hecker is a Clinical Member of the American Association for Marriage and Family Therapy (AAMFT) and an AAMFT Approved Supervisor. Her clinical interests include couples therapy, divorce, and trauma recovery. In 2007, she and Catherine Ford Sori coedited *The Therapist's Notebook II: More Homework, Handouts, and Activities for Use in Psychotherapy*; and in 2008, Sori and Hecker produced Volume III of *The Therapist's Notebook* (Haworth Press). Dr. Hecker coauthored (with Catherine Ford Sori, Ph.D., and Associates) *The Therapist's Notebook for Children and Adolescents: Homework, Handouts, and Activities for Use in Psychotherapy* (Haworth Press, 2003), and authored (with Sharon Deacon and Associates) *The Therapist's Notebook: Homework, Handouts, and Activities for Use in Psychotherapy* (Haworth Press, 1998). She also edited (with Joseph Wetchler) *An Introduction to Marriage and Family Therapy* (Haworth Press, 2003). Dr. Hecker was the founding editor of the *Journal of Clinical Activities, Assignments and Handouts in Psychotherapy Practice*. She has published articles in the *Journal of Marital and Family Therapy*, the *Journal of Contemporary Family Therapy*, the *American Journal of Family Therapy*, and the *Journal of Family Psychotherapy*. Dr. Hecker lives in Munster, Indiana, with her two sons, Aaron and Noah.

About the Contributors

Julia M. Becerra, M.S., is a Ph.D. student in family studies at Purdue University, West Lafayette, Indiana. She is a certified domestic relations mediator in the state of Indiana. Her research interests include family structure, family policy, and sibling relationships.

John Bryant, M.S., is a psychotherapist for Ryan & Ryan Educational Consultants, Inc., and the Lake County Domestic Relations Counseling Bureau in Crown Point, Indiana. Bryant works with individuals, couples, and families, and provides consultation to educators regarding therapeutic issues and their impact upon student learning. He is a licensed educator with 16 years of classroom experience. He has a strong interest in assisting families who are overcoming addiction and recovery issues. He is a founding board member of Journey House, Inc., a not-for-profit transitional housing facility for individuals in recovery; and is also a member of the Jasper County Community Corrections Board.

Jared A. Durtschi, M.S., is currently attending Florida State University's (Tallahassee) doctoral program in Marriage and Family Therapy. He enjoys teaching undergraduates, researching the transition to parenthood, and engaging in clinical work with couples and families.

Jeffrey J. Ford, M.S., is currently employed at Cross Creek Manor in LaVerkin, Utah, as a Marriage and Family Therapist intern.

Chad A. Graff, Ph.D., is the Associate Director of Behavioral Health for the Southwest Institute for Addictive Diseases, Lubbock, Texas. Dr. Graff received a Ph.D. in Marriage and Family Therapy at Texas Tech University and holds an M.S. in Marriage and Family Therapy from Purdue University Calumet, Hammond, Indiana. He earned his B.S. in Family Studies from Brigham Young University, Provo, Utah. He has more than

10 years of experience as a data management systems developer. He currently serves as a consultant to researchers and clinicians on utilizing technology to develop clinical and data management systems.

Kathleen Beck Kmitta, B.S., received her Master's degree from the Marriage and Family Therapy Program at Purdue University Calumet, Hammond, Indiana. She is bilingual and serves both English- and Spanish-speaking clients. Her professional interests include ethics, working with bilingual families, and incorporating play in family therapy.

Nicole Manick, M.S., is a clinician with the Swanson Center in Michigan City and LaPorte, Indiana, doing home-based therapy. She has a strong interest in solution-focused therapy and anger management treatment.

Michelle T. Mannino, M.S., is in clinical practice in Orland Park, Illinois. Her clinical interests include medical family therapy and bereavement, eating disorders, and sex therapy.

Melanie K. McClellan, M.S., is currently employed by Rosemont Center, Inc., Columbus, Ohio, as a multisystemic therapist. Her current therapeutic clientele at the Rosemont Center consists of families who have children involved with the juvenile court system. She has past therapeutic experience working with a diverse population of clientele, including couples, individuals, and families with various therapeutic concerns and backgrounds. She coauthored a chapter in *The Therapist's Notebook Volume II: Finding a Connection* (Haworth Press, 2007).

Sesen M. Negash, M.S., is currently a doctoral student in the Family and Child Sciences Department at Florida State University in Tallahassee. Her research interests include infidelity, high-conflict couples, and sex therapy.

Rebecca A. Nestor, M.S., is currently employed by Nexus Treatment Programs at Indian Oaks Academy, Manteno, Illinois, as a family therapist. At Indian Oaks Academy, she works with male juvenile sex offenders and their families, addressing sexuality, family relationships, cognitive distortions, patterns of abusive behavior, and other behavioral issues.

Denise Netko is currently working as a crisis therapist at the Community Counseling Centers of Chicago. She has clinical experience working in community mental health with children, young adults, couples, and families. Her interests and experiences include eating and body image disorders, self-injury, trauma-related experiences, and mood disorders.

Ryan N. Parsons-Rozycki, M.S., L.M.H.C., is currently employed as a counselor at Purdue University Calumet's Counseling Center, Hammond, Indiana. Parsons-Rozycki has been published in the *American Journal of Family Therapy.* She is a member of Indiana's District One Disaster Mental Health Team and the Northwest Indiana Suicide Prevention Coalition. In addition, her areas of interest include substance abuse, relationships, families, and eating disorders.

Jonathyn Piper, M.S., is currently a doctoral student in the Marriage and Family Therapy Program at Texas Tech University. His interests are queer theory and narrative therapy.

Rhi Anna Platt, M.S., is an intensive in-home marriage and family therapist at Easter Seals in Greenville, North Carolina.

Julie Ramisch, M.S., is currently a doctoral student in the Child and Family Ecology department at Michigan State University, East Lansing. She is a graduate of the master's degree program in Marriage and Family Therapy at Purdue University Calumet, Hammond, Indiana. Her research interests include therapy with individuals with disabilities and their families.

Catherine Ford Sori, Ph.D., is an Associate Professor of Marriage and Family Counseling at Governors State University, University Park, Illinois, and is associate faculty at the Chicago Center for Family Health. Her special interests include training issues related to children in family therapy; family play therapy; children and families facing illness and bereavement, divorce, and stepfamily issues; and integrating spirituality in therapy. Dr. Sori received her Ph.D. in Marriage and Family Therapy from Purdue University, West Lafayette, Indiana. Her publications include numerous book chapters and her articles have appeared in the *Journal of Marital and Family Therapy, The Family Journal,* the *Journal of Clinical Activities, Assignments and Handouts in Psychotherapy Practice,* the *Journal of Couple and Relationship Therapy,* the *American Journal of Family Therapy,* and the *Journal of Family Psychotherapy.* Dr. Sori coauthored or coedited *The Therapist's Notebook III* (in press, Taylor & Francis); *The Therapist's Notebook II: More Homework, Handouts, and Activities for*

Use in Psychotherapy (Haworth Press, 2007); *The Therapist's Notebook for Integrating Spirituality in Counseling*, Volumes I and II; *The Therapist's Notebook for Children and Adolescents: Homework, Handouts, and Activities for Use in Psychotherapy* (Haworth Press, 2003); and *Engaging Children in Family Therapy: Creative Approaches to Integrating Theory and Research in Clinical Practice* (2006). She is on the editorial boards of the *Journal of Couple and Relationship Therapy*, *The Family Journal*, and the *Journal of the Illinois Counseling Association*. Dr. Sori is a Clinical Member of the American Association for Marriage and Family Therapy (AAMFT), a licensed marriage and family therapist, and an AAMFT Approved Supervisor. She is also a member of the American Counseling Association and the Association for Play Therapy.

Ursula Tina Steiner, M. of Law and M.S., is currently working as a coach for an employment agency specializing in victims of accidents and the unemployed in Switzerland. Her interests are intercultural studies, juvenile delinquents, solution-focused brief therapy, and narrative therapy.

Jeffrey M. Stewart, M.S., is currently working as a clinical therapist at a residential treatment facility for adolescent youth in Apia, Samoa. He is interested in helping families heal after residential care, as well as helping individuals find a greater sense of self-worth, self-esteem, and empowerment.

Sara Timmons, M.S., is a doctoral candidate in the Marriage and Family Therapy Program at Michigan State University, East Lansing. Her research interests include intimate partner violence, adult romantic relationships, self-of-the-therapist issues, and therapeutic alliance with couples and families. She is currently working on her dissertation exploring the influence of therapist characteristics on therapeutic alliance; and she is editing a book on the practice of building therapeutic alliance with couples and families for training therapists.

Sophia Treyger, L.P.C., M.S., is currently a psychotherapist at Mt. Sinai Hospital, Chicago, working with chronically mentally ill clients and their families. She is also a volunteer therapist at Chicago Women's Health Center working to empower individuals and couples. Treyger has written extensively for www.RelationShip911.com and is published in the *American Journal of Family Therapy* and *The Therapist's Notebook II.* She has conducted research on factors that promote a positive female queer identity, and her interests include working with disadvantaged and marginalized populations (that is, women; mentally ill; lesbian, gay, bisexual, transgender, queer, or questioning [LGBTQ] and couples), specifically in the fields of sex therapy and education.

Teresa L. Young, M.S., is currently working as a clinical therapist at Choices Counseling Services in Valparaiso and LaPorte, Indiana. Her clinical interests include sex therapy, eating disorders, and couples therapy.

1

Introduction

Lorna L. Hecker

Ethics is about what actions we should take, what rules govern our conduct, what "right thing" we should do, and what we ought not to do. It is
also about how we justify our actions. When making ethical decisions,
couple and family therapists need well-founded reasons to support their
actions. Ethics is influenced by scholarship and evidence and is shaped by
our values, worldview, and context (Roberts & Dyers, 2004). It involves
cognition and affect, and a "moral sensitivity" that includes the recognition that our actions affect the welfare of others (Welfel & Kitchener,
2003). Ethical standards grow out of consistent and well-founded ethical
reasoning; these standards and our own morals and values need to be constantly evaluated to be sure they are based on solid reason. Clients' values
and morals also need to be clearly understood so that empowering, collaborative decisions can be made.

Professional ethical codes provide guidance in ethical decision making. For example, the American Association for Marriage and Family
Therapy *Code of Ethics* (2001) (see Appendix) has eight principles to guide
professional practice: (a) responsibility to clients, (b) confidentiality, (c)
professional competence and integrity, (d) responsibility to students and
supervisees, (e) responsibility to research participants, (f) responsibility to
the profession, (g) financial arrangements, and (h) advertising. Generally,
ethical codes provide guidance to professionals about appropriate practice, they serve to protect the public, and they serve as a basis for sanctions. They often are the foundation on which states, in part, base their
licensure or certification statutes. However, ethical issues do not always
fall neatly within the scope of the code of ethics, leaving the therapist to
decide how to form a course of action.

Reasoning in an ethical way is best not left to emotions or unexamined
personal beliefs or values. An ethical decision-making model is provided

in Chapter 3 to give the reader guidance in this process. When analyzing ethical decisions, we borrow from philosophy and utilize the moral principles of autonomy, nonmaleficence, justice, veracity, beneficence (Beauchamp & Childress, 2001), and fidelity (Nash, 2002):

- *Autonomy* refers to respecting the individual and his or her right to make decisions for himself or herself with regard to his or her own health and well-being.
- *Nonmaleficence* means "above all, do no harm."
- *Justice* means all humans should be treated fairly.
- *Veracity* refers to the importance of truth telling.
- *Beneficence* refers to actions intended to do good for others.
- *Fidelity* refers to honoring commitments and promoting trust.

Sensitivity to potential ethical issues is an additional benefit for any couple and family therapist. Understanding what situations may trigger potential ethical or legal land mines can prevent many untenable circumstances that most of us would rather avoid, presumably including our clients. Couple and family therapists should have a good working knowledge of the situations that may trigger ethical issues; with this knowledge, many difficulties can be preventatively avoided. Those trained in systemic family therapy can have an advantage in making ethical decisions. Ethical issues can involve many stakeholders; family therapists can use their systemic roots to understand the various persons who may be affected by the ethical issue at hand. They can also make hypotheses about how the potential ethical decisions can affect relationships of those stakeholders involved.

When evaluating decisions that may have ethical quandaries, one can evaluate the situation using the following four criteria:

- What are the *ethical* components?
- What are the *clinical* components?
- Are there any potential *legal* issues?
- Are there any *professional* issues to reflect upon?

Ethical components are about how professionals should conduct themselves within the context of the professional relationship and the specific situation. It is the dilemma that is caused when the welfare of people may be at stake. It is influenced strongly by our beliefs and values, our worldview, and the specific context of the ethical dilemma at hand. For example, when a therapist sees a family and he or she suspects that the parents are abusing their child, an ethical issue is posed because the welfare of the child is at stake. However, this is embedded within the clinical issues at hand and is entangled in legal issues due to reporting statutes.

Clinical components relate to the therapeutic context in which the ethical issue is occurring. Ethical issues typically arise out of the clinical context and can affect the therapist–client relationship. The effect of ethical issues may have a positive or negative valence. For example, a therapist who ethically and legally must report parents to child protective services may severely damage the therapist–client relationship, because this violates the confidentiality trust the parents put in the therapist, and they may also feel betrayed and angry that the therapist involved authorities in the therapeutic relationship. Steinberg, Levine, and Doueck (1997) found that 27% of people leave therapy when they are reported to child protective services (as cited in Jankowski & Martin, 2003). Conversely, the parents may understand that the therapist had a legal obligation to do the reporting to child protective services and are interested in bettering their parenting skills so that the abuse never happens again.

There may or may not be legal issues in an ethical situation. In the case of the parents who abuse a child, all 50 states have child abuse reporting statutes. But even though this may be a legal requirement, apparently not all therapists find this ethical in all situations. Jankowski and Martin (2003) found that in cases of child maltreatment, family therapists in Illinois made the decision to report child abuse based on their worldview assumptions, ethical principles, prior clinical and life experiences, situational factors including type and severity of abuse, the amount of evidence presented to them, client characteristics such as age and personal history, and interactional factors including willingness on the part of adult clients to comply with the therapist. Even though they realize they are legally bound, the legal requirement may not appear ethical to the therapist.

Last, there are professional components to any situation. How the therapist conducts himself or herself reflects on the professional as a whole. For example, a therapist who is constantly late to sessions, while strictly not generating an ethical issue, is behaving in a way that reflects poorly on the professional and the profession. In the above example of failing to report child abuse, if the child gets hurt further or dies, it would be a tragedy and would reflect very poorly on the profession of marriage and family therapy.

Consider the following scenario:

> The Lincoln family attends therapy for concerns about their oldest daughter, Elise, who is 15 years old. Elise has been breaking curfew, and the family fears

she is using drugs. Dr. Craig sees all the family members, Mr. & Mrs. Lincoln, Elise, and her younger sister, Macy, age 12. Family therapy focuses on getting the parents to synchronize their parenting efforts in order to increase the parental hierarchy. As therapy progresses, Dr. Craig receives a phone call from Mrs. Lincoln's mother, Mrs. Jackson, stating with concern that the parents are unfit, and that she and her husband would like to try to gain custody of the girls.

Dr. Craig is faced with potential ethical issues. First, she may not speak to Mrs. Jackson without a written release from both parents. This is both an ethical and presumably a legal issue. She must not violate confidentiality, and if she does, she also has the clinical issue of an alliance or coalition developing with Mrs. Jackson that will derail therapy and erode therapeutic trust. Professionally, if Dr. Craig speaks to Mrs. Jackson, she will have acted in an unprofessional manner; confidentiality is the foundation on which couple and family therapy is built. If the public cannot count on it being upheld, there is no reason for them to confide in marriage and family therapists as a discipline. Ultimately, Dr. Craig cannot "confirm or deny" to Mrs. Jackson that the Lincoln family is a client.

All ethical decisions should be evaluated in these four realms. The process of *ethical decision making* is much more complex and is discussed in Chapter 3. A holistic model of ethical decision making is presented that takes into account a theory of values from which to evaluate both the therapist and the client. Cultural context and worldviews are inherent in any ethical decision.

What follows are ethical case scenarios that introduce topics that serve as an introduction to the chapters that follow in this book. Most scenarios are variations on actual case events. Names and events have been varied to protect the anonymity of clients.

Martin was a family therapy intern at a university Couple and Family Therapy Center with a young man, Jared, who was referred for anger management counseling. Jared, initially wary of counseling, revealed that he had been involved in a gang, but had changed his ways and was now a father with a partner and two young children. It was clear he had given up his gang activities, and had obtained a job, and stated interest in couples therapy for he and his partner. Jared exhibited symptoms of post-traumatic stress disorder, having witnessed significant violence during his involvement with gangs. While outwardly he portrayed bravado, the more he became comfortable with therapy, the more vulnerable he became with his therapist. Jared began to talk about how he had few friends, and trusted no one. He described a chaotic family of origin, whose members attacked each other frequently, and only availed themselves of Jared when they needed money. He trusted his partner the most, but he was even wary of her. He said he had made a pact with some gang buddies, and that was the deepest trust he had experienced. He began to discuss to the fact that these three friends of his had a secret that they had agreed to tell no one. It became clear to the therapist, over time, that this event was a criminal act. Jared eventually talked in terms that left no doubt to the therapist the men had murdered a rival gang member.

Martin was subsequently subpoenaed to testify in court about Jared's involvement in the murder. Although Jared had thought what he shared was *confidential,* there was an exception to Jared's legal right to *privilege* that was specified in the state statute. Specifically the state statute read: "Matters communicated to the Marriage and Family Therapist (MFT) in the MFT's official capacity by a client are privileged information and may not be disclosed by the MFT to any person, except under the following circumstances: (1) In a criminal proceeding involving a homicide if the disclosure relates directly to the fact or immediate circumstances of the homicide..." (adapted from Indiana Code IC 25-23.6-6). Although this exception had been detailed in the university's *informed consent,* Jared had shared the information anyway, putting Martin in a very tenuous legal position. The judge ordered Martin to testify as to what Jared had confided to him in the therapy sessions. Martin was forced to comply. (Confidentiality and privilege will be defined and discussed further in Chapter 2; informed consent will be detailed in Chapter 13.)

> Mrs. Lee attended therapy with her 10-year-old daughter Rose, stating that she wanted therapy for Rose due to the divorce she had experienced the year prior. Rose seemed to be an outgoing and friendly fourth grader. Mrs. Lee stated she wanted a neutral place for Rose to talk about any concerns she had about the divorce. The family therapist, Dr. Snow, asked for a copy of the divorce decree. Mrs. Lee brought the decree to the subsequent session, and Dr. Snow ascertained that Mrs. Lee had sole legal custody of Rose. Rose lived with Mrs. Lee, and lived with Mr. Lee on alternate weekends and one night per week. Dr. Snow saw Mrs. Lee and Rose conjointly for two sessions, and Rose alone for two sessions. Mrs. Lee stated that she had asked Mr. Lee to join therapy, but he had said that he was not interested. Dr. Snow made no attempt to contact Mr. Lee. During the fifth week of treatment, Dr. Snow received an irate phone call from Mr. Lee, demanding to know why he was not notified his daughter was in treatment.

Dr. Snow correctly assumed that he only needed Mrs. Lee's legal consent to treat Rose because Mrs. Lee had *sole legal custody* of Rose. However, Mr. and Mrs. Lee shared *joint physical custody* of Rose, indicating involvement in her parenting on a regular basis. Mrs. Lee lied when she said Mr. Lee was not interested in therapy; she had never asked Mr. Lee to join them in therapy. Dr. Snow acted within proper legal guidelines, but he was not clinically sound in his decision to exclude Mr. Lee from treatment; this could certainly lead to ethical and legal difficulties. Chapter 4 addresses ethics in therapy with children in families.

> Dr. Stephen was a successful couple and family therapist who treated a young couple who subsequently decided to divorce. He continued to see the young woman, Jill, and the husband dropped out of therapy. During the course of treatment Dr. Stephen often complimented Jill, and told her how no one in her life seemed to appreciate how special she was. He said she was really much more intelligent than what her husband had given her credit for. Jill was flattered by the compliments, as her emotional life was fairly destitute, and she was vulnerable due to her pending divorce. He also sympathized to her feelings regarding her divorce. He seemed like a good friend to Jill, rather than a therapist. He began to sit by her during sessions and hold her hand. Their sessions began to increase in length, and she was often his last client of the day. He eventually began to rub Jill's arms and back, and in future sessions had Jill lay back into his arms so he could hold her. He stated he wanted her to be comfortable and in charge. Jill was confused; she did not think this was part of therapy, but she trusted Dr. Stephen. Eventually, Jill dropped out of therapy. Several months later, Jill reentered therapy with a different therapist. Jill suffered depression and anger, she was suicidal at times, and she suffered flashbacks to the situation.

The American Association for Marriage and Family Therapy (AAMFT) Code of Ethics (2001) Principle 1.4 under "Responsibility to Clients" states "Sexual intimacy with clients is prohibited." What it does not state is the long-term damage caused by this type of impropriety. In Chapter 6, *Sexuality, Boundaries, and Ethics* are analyzed, and in Chapter 5, *Power, Privilege, and Ethics*, the difference between a *boundary crossing* and a *boundary violation* are elucidated for the reader. The need for the therapist to stay in tune with oneself to avoid disastrous situations such as this one is discussed in Chapter 10, *The Self of the Therapist*. The damage to Jill was immense. A therapist must always be in charge of the therapeutic boundaries in therapy. A supervisor must always be in charge of the boundaries between the supervisor and the therapist who seeks supervision with them. Professors teaching family therapy must always be in charge of the boundaries with their students.

> Jasmine and Dorian attend couple therapy citing communication difficulties, often emanating from discussions about Jasmine's waitressing at a local bar. Dorian would become jealous when Jasmine's customers would pay "too much" attention to her. Dorian believed Jasmine dressed too suggestively for work. Jasmine disagreed and thought she received better tips if she dressed nicely. The therapist soon learned that the discussions became loud and included slapping,

pushing, and name-calling, especially when Jasmine had been drinking. Dorian had scratches on his neck. Neighbors had called the police on one occasion.

The therapist is left with the decision as to whether to treat Jasmine and Dorian as a couple or individually. The couple is experiencing intimate partner violence (IPV), and in some cases, couples therapy is indicated, and in others, couples therapy could increase danger. Risk and liability for the therapist is also a consideration. In Chapter 7, distinctions are drawn between *intimate terrorism* and *common couple violence* (Johnson, 2006), in order to aid the reader in making treatment decisions to decrease treatment risks.

> Mr. Albright brought his 72-year-old father to therapy because of his growing concern for his father's depression after the death of the elder Mr. Albright's wife. The therapist, Dr. McDonald, saw Mr. Albright for six sessions, and then Mr. Albright dropped out of therapy. During those six sessions, he stated to the therapist frequently that he simply wanted to join his wife. Mr. Albright did not improve in therapy, and Dr. McDonald made a referral to a psychiatrist for an evaluation for an antidepressant. Dr. McDonald did not attempt to contact the psychiatrist, nor did he inform the elder Mr. Albright's son of his suicidality. The elder Mr. Albright took an overdose of sleeping medication prescribed by the psychiatrist and died. His son sued Dr. McDonald for malpractice.

Dr. McDonald did not follow an appropriate *standard of care* when treating the elder Mr. Albright. He would have been on solid ground to breach confidentiality and tell Mr. Albright's son of his father's suicidality (although he may have needed to simply ask him permission to do this). He also did not contact the other treating party to provide important information regarding the client. It may have also been useful to contact Adult Protective Services. It is likely his care will be seen by the court as *malpractice*. In Chapter 8, risk factors and suicide are discussed in more detail.

> Amisha, a licensed marriage and family therapist, was seeing Harold, who was separated from his wife, Laura. Harold had been despondent about the separation and was hoping the separation was temporary. He wanted to move back in with Laura and their two children. Laura, however, seemed to have other ideas. She taunted Harold and said that he was "no man" and that she could find a better man than he was, citing his difficulties earning a decent wage, and the drinking he did that she thought was in excess. Harold began to suspect that Laura had a boyfriend and frequently ranted about it in therapy with Amisha. He said that if he ever caught her with this man, he would kill them both. Amisha asked Harold if he was serious, and he said he was "half-serious."

Two weeks later, Harold came to session, and it was clear he had been drinking. He stated that he had caught Laura in bed with a man, someone Laura worked with, and he was going to "settle the score" with Laura and this man. He thanked the therapist for her help, and he left the session abruptly before Amisha could intervene.

Amisha is now faced with a dilemma. She has promised Harold confidentiality, but she is fearful for Laura's well-being, as well of that of the other man. In addition, according to her state statute, she has a *duty to warn* the intended victims. Had Amisha done a violence assessment on Harold? Had she been able to predict if Harold was likely to be violent? Did she have contact information for Laura? Should she call the police? Should she call Laura? These issues will be addressed in Chapter 9, *Managing Risk With Potentially Dangerous Clients*.

Leslie, a licensed marriage and family therapist, was seeing Chitra and Gopal, a young Indian couple who grew up in the states and was living with Gopal's parents who had immigrated to the United States from India. Chitra and Gopal's marriage had been arranged. The couple's biggest stressor was that Chitra did not get along with Gopal's parents and felt that they treated her unfairly. She was expected to do all of the housework as well as the majority of the cooking. Gopal felt caught in a loyalty conflict between Chitra and his parents. Leslie surmised that the situation seemed like a "pressure cooker," and the couple agreed. Leslie was concerned about the patriarchal and sexist nature of the environment Chitra was living in. She suggested that Chitra move out for a short amount of time to give the family time apart in order to relieve some of the pressure.

Subprinciple 1.8 of the AAMFT Code of Ethics (2001) stated:

Marriage and family therapists respect the rights of clients to make decisions and help them understand the consequences of these decisions. Therapists clearly advise clients that they have the responsibility to make decisions regarding relationships such as cohabitation, marriage, divorce, separation, reconciliation, custody, and visitation.

Leslie clearly violated Subprinciple 1.8 and was letting her Western values guide therapy. She was not respecting the rights of Chitra and Gopal to make decisions for themselves. Chitra would likely have suffered disastrous consequences for the decision Leslie was suggesting. In Chapter 10, the *The Self of the Therapist* and the *therapist's values* are explored in order to understand how we affect therapy and how therapy affects us.

Dr. Moonstone has a private practice that is quite successful. He has a cleaning woman, Ms. Ingrid, who cleans nightly, and he sees her every night as he finishes up with evening clients. Over the years, they have become friendly, and he has come to know her family situation. Ms. Ingrid cleans for a living, and her husband works as an auto mechanic. One evening, Ms. Ingrid relates that her teenage daughter, Iris, is getting in trouble at school and has recently been arrested for using marijuana. Ms. Ingrid turned to Dr. Moonstone for help. She begged Dr. Moonstone to see Iris, and Dr. Moonstone, though uncomfortable with the arrangement, agreed to just one session of therapy to assess Iris and then make a referral based on her needs. Ms. Ingrid and her husband, David, attended the assessment session as Dr. Moonstone requested. During the family assessment, Ms. Ingrid, David, and Iris had a major altercation with which Dr. Moonstone had to intervene decisively and firmly to gain order in the therapy room because the fight nearly turned physical. Dr. Moonstone made the referral, but the next time he saw Ms. Ingrid, she refused to speak to him.

Dr. Moonstone learned the hard way not to engage in a *multiple relationship*. Although Ms. Ingrid's request may have seemed harmless, to mix business with someone with whom he already had a prior business relationship created an untenable situation. Dr. Moonstone is in the more powerful position; thus, he is in charge of guarding the boundary around engaging in an inappropriate relationship. Power, privilege, and multiple relationships will be discussed in more detail in Chapter 5.

Simone, a licensed marital and family therapist, worked in a state-funded agency. She was working with a married couple, Jerrick and Tameca, who had lost their baby to sudden infant death syndrome. Jerrick and Tameca both came from homes with strong religious traditions and utilized prayer as a major coping mechanism for managing their loss. Simone was not particularly religious or spiritual but respected and admired the couple's strong faith. On the first anniversary of the loss of their baby, the couple was grieving. When Simone asked the couple what they thought would help them most on that day, they asked if Simone would pray with them.

The difficulty Simone encountered is that Jerrick and Tameca requested spiritual intervention in therapy, however slight it is, and Simone has never explicitly discussed this or her own spiritual values with Jerrick and Tameca. Thus, she is put in what she perceives to be an awkward position. If she declines to pray, she risks alienating her clients. If she prays, she risks sounding insincere or awkward and going against her personal values. She must also perform therapy within her *scope of practice* in order to be ethical. In Chapter 11, understanding spirituality and religion as a multicultural issue is discussed, as well as the ethical issues that surround spiritual or religious interventions with clients, and informed consent surrounding this type of intervention.

Dr. Rodriquez worked in San Antonio, Texas, and helped divorced parents. He worked with Bob and Linda, who were court ordered to see him; the courts had all but given up on intervening with them due to their acrimonious nature and repeated visits to court to fight over the smallest of details. Dr. Rodriquez helped Bob and Linda to come to an agreement about their parenting plan, and he even worked with them to develop a method for exchanging the children's clothing that both agreed upon. He often acted as a coach and referee because Bob and Linda were so acrimonious at times that they could not communicate directly with each other without third-party intervention. When the couple could not communicate without toxicity, he would have them e-mail each other and copy him in order to decrease the conflict. Dr. Rodriquez worked with them on solving problems relating to the children's homework, and issues surrounding holidays. Dr. Rodriquez was assigned by the court and had authority to make decisions for the couple on some issues, excluding custody, that the couple could not agree on.

Dr. Rodriquez lives in Texas where there is legal provision for therapists to become *parent coordinators*. Couple and family therapists are expanding their roles into other arenas where they can be useful to families in need. These roles with families in distress that interact with the legal system are discussed in detail in Chapter 12.

Karen Ames, a licensed marriage and family therapist, saw the Kramer family for 12 sessions. The Kramer family was concerned about the depression of their 16-year-old son, Darnell. Karen saw the family regularly and she also saw Darnell separately for part of each session to evaluate him for depression and suicide ideation. She methodically and consistently evaluated him for the signs and symptoms of depression, and although he initially showed evidence of depression, as family therapy progressed, his symptoms improved. She also taught the parents what to watch for with regard to Darnell's depression and asked them to let her know if his symptoms worsened. However, the parents agreed, Darnell was improving. The family terminated therapy after the twelfth session, considering therapy to be a success. Three weeks later, Darnell killed himself. Some time passed, and Karen was surprised to be served notice that she was being sued for malpractice in the case. It was being alleged that her treatment fell below the acceptable standard of care. Her records were being subpoenaed as well. Unfortunately for Karen, she recorded only that she had family therapy, not that she met privately with Darnell. She never recorded that she individually assessed him for depression and suicide ideation.

Karen is in trouble. She did not properly document her treatment of Darnell. Simpson and Stacy (2004) noted that whether or not malpractice action goes forward can be determined by the quality of documentation. Karen, essentially, had no documentation to speak of; just the family therapy sessions were documented. She also performed no formal suicide assessment because Darnell's depression improved, and she did not see it as necessary, but her justification for not doing this was not documented either. Documentation will be discussed in Chapter 13, and *Risk Factors and Suicide* are discussed in Chapter 8.

> Lawson Marks is a licensed marriage and family therapist in the state of Wisconsin. He decided to augment his practice by offering an e-therapy practice. He established a Web site, which he was careful to encrypt. Potential clients e-mail directly from the site, and his secretary then sets up a phone therapy session for him with the client. Even though he is relatively new to his e-therapy practice, he had a session with a client in Idaho. During the session, the client reveals that she took an overdose of sleeping pills.

Lawson now has several challenges. Has he received accurate contact information so he can quickly locate the client to send the person emergency care? Has the client given informed consent so he or she knows that this is going to happen? Could the client have lied about his or her contact information, leaving Lawson helpless to intervene? If he does intervene, is his license applicable across state lines? If he is not practicing what is "usual and customary" therapy practice, does his malpractice insurance cover him? These issues will be discussed in detail in Chapter 15, *E-Therapy: Developing an Ethical Online Practice.*

Summary

On some issues, couple and family therapists have exquisitely clear direction from professional codes of ethics (e.g., AAMFT, [2001]), such as the fact that therapists should not have sex with their clients, but others often fall into gray areas that rely instead on therapists making reasoned ethical decisions. Therapists need to develop an ethical sensitivity to potential ethical issues in order to decrease their risk in practice and increase their maneuverability in the therapy room. Protecting the autonomy of the client is of utmost importance, and the foundation of trust of the therapeutic relationship is put forth in the ethical dictate of nonmaleficence—"above all, do no harm." Therapists are responsible for protecting clients and preserving the sanctuary of the therapeutic relationship. Trust is the foundation of any therapeutic relationship and must be carefully guarded in order for the profession to survive and thrive. Couple and family therapists are in a unique position to understand the complexities of ethical situations, which can include ethical, legal, clinical, and professional components, because of their training in family systems theory. They are best able to hypothesize the many potential scenarios that could occur if they took the many possible courses of action they need to consider when evaluating ethical decisions; they can evaluate both the decision, as well as the impact of the decision on the individual, the family, and the relationships between family members and the therapist, and the larger systems involved. Ethics in couple and family therapy is not about moralizing; it is about finding and evaluating one's moral self so that one can understand one's biases, work to understand the worldview of the client, and follow an ethical decision-making model for reasoned ethical choices that best promote good on behalf of clients.

References

American Association for Marriage and Family Therapy. (2001). *Code of ethics.* Alexandria, VA: Author.

Beauchamp, T. L., & Childress, J. F. (2001). *Principles of biomedical ethics* (5th ed.). Oxford: Oxford University Press.

Indiana Code 25-23.6-6 Chapter 6. Social Workers, Privileged Communications. Retrieved October 14, 2008, from: www.in.gov/legislative/ic/code/title25/ar23.6/ch6.html.

Jankowski, P. J., & Martin, M. J. (2003). Reporting cases of child maltreatment: Decision making processes of family therapists in Illinois. *Contemporary Family Therapy, 25*(3), 311–332.

Johnson, Michael P. (2006). Gendered communication and intimate partner violence. In Bonnie J. Dow & Julia T. Wood (Eds.), *The Sage handbook of gender and communication* (pp. 71–87). Thousand Oaks, CA: Sage.

Nash, R. J. (2002). *Real world ethics: Frameworks for educators and human service professionals.* New York: Teachers College Press.

Roberts, L. W., & Dyer, A. R. (2004). *Concise guide to ethics in mental health care.* Washington, DC: American Psychiatric Publishing.

Simpson, S., & Stacy, M. (2004). Avoiding the malpractice snare: Documenting suicide risk assessment. *Journal of Psychiatric Practice, 10*(3), 1–5.

Steinberg, K. L., Levine, M., & Doueck, H. J. (1997). In the service of two masters: Psychotherapists' struggle with child maltreatment mandatory reporting. *American Journal of Orthopsychiatry, 68,* 101–107.

Welfel, E. R., & Kitchener, K. S. (2003). Introduction to the special section: Ethics education—An agenda for the 1990s. In D. N. Bersoff (Ed.). *Ethical conflicts in psychology* (pp. 135–139). Washington, DC: American Psychiatric Association.

2

Ethical Decision Making

Lorna L. Hecker

Nearly all decisions that therapists make have ethical underpinnings, beginning with the first ethical dictate of *nonmaleficence*—"do no harm." Several models of ethical decision making have been proposed in the history of mental health (e.g., Forester-Miller & Davis, 1996; Haas & Malouf, 1989; Kitchener, 1984; Stadler, 1986). Previous models of ethical decision making have been largely cognitive, rational-evaluative models, relying on critical thinking. However, Woody (1990) noted that "In the final analysis we are left with the messy reality that clinical decision-making consists of an unpredictable mix of intuition and rationality" (p. 144).

Hill, Glaser, and Harden (1995) developed a feminist model for ethical decision making that included emotion, intuition, power differences between the client and therapist, and recognition that cultural biases are inherent in value-based decisions. The steps in their ethical decision-making model are relatively similar to those in previous models: (a) recognizing a problem, (b) defining the problem, (c) implementing and evaluating the decision, and (d) continuing reflection. However, in addition to the rational-evaluative process of previous models, they added an evaluation of the therapist's feeling-intuitive process, and the person of the therapist in each decision-making step. Their model was also one of the first models of ethical decision making that included the client in the decision-making process. They believed "one's personal experience and involvement are legitimate and necessary factors to take into account in any analysis" (Hill et al., p. 24).

As one can see, ethical models have been evolving to address the contextual system of the therapist and the client. It is clear the values of the therapist and the client are important but have, as yet, gone unaddressed in ethical decision-making models. In this chapter, a theory of values will be reviewed and integrated into a model for ethical decision making for therapists working with couples and families.

The Role of Values in Ethical Decision Making

Values are fundamental beliefs about what is good and important in life. Morals are values that are attributed to a system of beliefs. Each stakeholder involved in the ethical decision-making process will have his or her own set of values. In family therapy, value conflicts may derive from differences between the therapist's values and the values of the entire family system (Mailloux, 1997) or values between the stakeholders within the system. However, systemic therapists espouse that values and ethics are derived from the dynamics of evolving systems, not individuals (Seymour, 1982; Taggart, 1982). What follows is a presentation of a theory of values that will enable the systems therapist to put values into a systemic framework from which to view families and to aid in ethical decision making.

Evolving Values

Values tend to evolve over time. For example, specific values issues noted by Seymour in 1982 included beliefs about sexism, sexuality, dual careers, abortion and sterilization, minorities, religion, death and dying, and disabilities. Present therapists may pay attention to value issues in these domains, but certainly in some areas therapists have refocused their attention. Why and how do values evolve and change? Although family therapists have been called upon to examine their values and those of their clients, little has been done to understand the origin of the values and how a therapist can understand values in a dynamic, evolving systemic process. In understanding the crux of values in therapy, one must have a meta-theory of values and his or her own personal value evolution which enhance understanding of the therapist as well as the client. Only then can ethical decisions be understood within a holistic context.

Memes and Families

The following explanation of a "theory of values" focuses on *why* people adopt the values they do, not just *what* those values are. It will always be important in therapeutic work to focus on understanding each *individual* family's values, as well as the therapist's own values. The goal here is to provide the reader with a meta-theory of values in order to help make ethical decisions by understanding how clients think about the world. An understanding of values in families can be obtained by looking at the metaphoric "DNA" of values (Wilber, 2000). Don Beck and Christopher Cowan (1996) developed a theory of human development called Spiral Dynamics, based on the work of the late Clare Graves. They hold the belief that humans adapt to their environment based on need and develop new conceptual models accordingly (Beck & Cowan, 1996). The conceptual models are based on value memes, or ᵛ*Memes*. A *meme* is a unit or container of cultural information. A value meme (ᵛMeme) occurs when values are passed from one person to another by nongenetic means. (One way to think about this is that ᵛMemes are the containers for our beliefs that are passed on through the generations, and memes are the actual beliefs we [and our clients] hold). ᵛMemes are self-replicating patterns of information that interact with their surroundings and reflect conceptual schemes, beliefs, and behaviors. They are ways of thinking about *things*, not types of people (Wilber, 2000). What follows is a primer of Spiral Dynamics theory, utilized here to guide the reader in understanding how to think about values, to aid in ethical decision making. For a full discussion of Spiral Dynamics, the reader is referred to the work of Beck and Cowan (1996).

In Spiral Dynamics, there are two tiers of development being in ᵛMemes. First-tier ᵛMemes focus on *subsistence*; second-tier ᵛMemes focus on *being*. Beck and Cowan (1996) conceptualize the ᵛMemes as colors in a spiral, noting individuals or cultures move up and down the spiral, and the colors fade into each other. Individuals, families, and cultures develop and transmit their values through these value memes, or ᵛ*Memes*. People change and forge new systems, which changes personal psychologies, and rules for living, which individuals adapt to. Individuals live in an open system of values, with an infinite number of value modes available. As people (families, communities) evolve, they evolve through increasing levels of complexity in their value systems and worldviews. The Spiral Dynamics model is explained on the NVC Consulting Web site (Spiral Dynamics, 2006):

> The Spiral Dynamics model is about moral or ethical standards: it addresses where those decisions come from and how they are made. Its focus is on *why* people adopt the values they do—not what those values are. It is a deep systems perspective for valuing—not a description of the collections of values held by different individuals, groups or societies since people who can think alike can believe very different things; and people can agree on the very same thing despite vast differences in who they are. (p. 1)

ᵛMemes are organizing principles and may include bio-psycho-social-systems with content such as religion, philosophies, politics, literature, language, music, fads, and so forth (Beck & Cowan, 1996). The Spiral Dynamics model is not chronological or age based (Beck & Cowan, 1996); higher levels are not necessarily more intelligent than lower ones, and vice versa. The model describes variability in thinking, conceptualization, and behavior but does not ascribe the worth or decency of a person (Spiral Dynamics, 2006). Change occurs when life problems are not successfully dealt with at the present level of development; waves of consciousness emerge and flow through individuals and groups along a continuum that forms an expanding spiral.

The eight ᵛMemes are described below and are recognizable in therapists, clients, and client families. They are summarized from Wilber (2000) and Beck & Cowan (1996).

First-Tier Thinking

1. *Beige*—Beige is about the drive to survive; it is when finding food, water, and warmth have priority. It also includes the drive to procreate and stay alive. It organizes small survival bands. *Cultural manifestations and personal displays* include archaic, instinctive, egocentric, conquest, impulse gratification, reflexes, and biological urges. Beige was seen in the first human societies and can be seen in severe mental illness, late-stage Alzheimer's disease, starving masses, and war-ravaged and shell-shocked areas (Beck & Cowan, 1996; Wilber, 2000).

2. *Purple*—Purple is about the value of families or tribes. Goals are safety, protection from harm, and family bonds. It is animalistic. Kinship ties are very important for love, nurturance, and protection. *Cultural manifestations and personal displays* include stressed harmony and safety; family or kinship bonds; sacrifice to the way of the family; preservation of sacred objects, places, events, and memories; and observation of rites of passage and customs. The family or kinship lineage establishes political links and power. It may focus on rites, rituals, curses, blood oaths, charms, superstitions, magic, blessings, curses, or spells that determine events. Purple is strong in Third-World settings, gangs, athletic teams, and corporate "tribes" (Beck & Cowan, 1996; Wilber, 2000).

3. *Red*—The world is a jungle. Feudal lords protect underlings in exchange for obedience and labor. With Red, the tough and strong prevail. *Cultural manifestations and personal displays* include being egocentric, power driven, family tribe, impulsive, excited, person does what he or she wants regardless of the consequences to others, breaks free from any domination

or constraint, expects attention, calls the shots, and conquers and dominates others. Heroic and courageous, Red frees us from restraints of Purple superstition. Red is seen in the "terrible twos," rebellious youth, frontier mentalities, feudal kingdoms, wild rock stars, soldiers of fortune, and New-Age narcissism (Beck & Cowan, 1996; Wilber, 2000).

4. *Blue*—People who have rigid social hierarchies, are paternalistic, and believe there is only one right way to think and act—truth-force, conformists rule. They are obedient to a higher authority who directs the rules. There are predetermined outcomes. *Cultural manifestations and personal displays* include conforming and authority. Groups are concerned with rules, traditions, and obedience. Deferential—guilt is used to control. There is a moral majority and monotheism. Impulsive Red behavior is kept in check through guilt (fear of god or state). There are unvarying principles of right and wrong. The Order enforces a code of conduct. Righteous living produces stability now and guarantees future reward. Laws, regulations, and discipline build moral character. There are rigid social hierarchies and fundamentalism. Blue is seen in codes of chivalry and honor, puritan America, charitable good deeds, religious fundamentalism, Boy and Girl Scouts, and patriotism (Beck & Cowan, 1996; Wilber, 2000).

5. *Orange*—With Orange, the following are seen: strive-drive; scientific achievement; objective, mechanistic, and materialism. Guilt no longer maintains social adherence. Act in self-interest by playing the game to win. Orange seeks truth and meaning in individualistic terms— highly achievement oriented, work especially toward materialistic gains (Beck & Cowan, 1996; Wilber, 2000). *Cultural manifestations and personal displays* include analyzing, strategizing, and prospering; seeking wealth and status; being entrepreneurial and success driven; competing to achieve results; image; mobility; change and advancement; self-reliant; in control; uses earth's resources to create and spread abundant life; optimistic; modern capitalism and marketing; and individualistic. Orange is seen in the Enlightenment, emerging middle classes around the world, materialism, colonialism, secular humanism, fashion industry, cosmetics industry, and Wall Street (Beck & Cowan, 1996; Wilber, 2000).

6. *Green*—Emphasis is on dialogue and relationships—postmodernism; communitarian; relativistic; sociocentric; plants, ecology; sensitive self. Decisions are made through reconciliation and consensus. The human spirit must be freed from greed, dogma, and decisiveness. Sensitivity and caring supersede cold rationality and enrich human development. The Orange materialist way of life no longer answers life's questions (Beck & Cowan, 1996; Wilber, 2000). *Cultural manifestations and personal displays* include egalitarianism, networking, nonlinear thinking,

affiliation, sustainability, sharing, collaboration, fulfillment, affiliation, human bonds, and subjective, nonlinear thinking.

Green is seen in deep ecology, postmodernism, humanistic psychology, Greenpeace, animal rights, Foucault/Derrida, politically correct, diversity movements, and human rights issues (Beck & Cowan, 1996; Wilber, 2000). With completion of the Green ᵛMeme, human consciousness is poised for a jump into "second-tier thinking." (For more information on this process, refer to Beck and Cowan, 1996.)

Second-Tier Thinking

7. *Yellow*—Integrative, flex-flow; systemic; huge varieties of natural hierarchies and forms; chaos and change are natural; knowledge and competency supersede power; mutual realities; people live fully and responsibly as what they are and learn to become; life force; holistic; and existential. *Cultural manifestations* and *personal displays* include existence valued over material possessions; flexibility and functionality are the highest priority; change is the norm; person expresses self for what self desires, but never at the expense of others. Differences are integrated. Builds functional niche to do what one chooses (Beck & Cowan, 1996; Wilber, 2000).

8. *Turquoise*—Whole view; synergy; holistic; transpersonal; spiritual harmony; global view, global community; uses the entire spiral; multiple levels woven into one conscious system; need to control people and situations is gone; sees multiple levels of interaction; self is both distinct and blended as part of a larger, compassionate whole; connections, ecological alignments. There is universal order, not due to external rules (Blue), but rather through group bonds (Green). *Cultural manifestations and personal displays* include search for peace; spirituality; harmony; interlocking of feeling with knowledge; intuitive thinking; cooperative actions; and larger, compassionate whole. Wholeness of existence is experienced through mind and spirit (Beck & Cowan, 1996; Wilber, 2000).

Each person or culture can move up or down the spiral, depending upon circumstances, but tends to have a "center of gravity" (Wilber, 2000) from where he or she acts. A therapist should ascertain where he or she falls on the spiral in terms of their "center of gravity." If a therapist views the world as from the lens of a "Green" ᵛMeme, but his or her client is operating from a "Blue" ᵛMeme, they are likely to have contrasting views on certain topics, perhaps on things such as politics, abortion, and religion. If a cognitive therapist operates from an "Orange" ᵛMeme, treats a client from a street gang who must operate on a day-to-day basis in a "Red" ᵛMeme, their value differences are large. It may also be that a client has a higher-order "center of gravity" than the therapist. The ᵛMemes are the context of culture, social systems, and environment. It is what makes values dynamic and is the fabric of individuals, families, cultures, and societies.

It is important to remember that the ᵛMemes are ways of thinking about things, not types of people. In addition, people in first-tier memes think that their worldview is the correct or best perspective. Only people in the second tier can appreciate the input from the first-tier perspectives.

A Model of Ethical Decision Making

What follows is the ethical decision-making process that is recommended for therapists facing ethical conundrums that occur in practice. A model is presented to guide the therapist through the ethical decision-making process. The first two steps are preliminary steps having to do with therapist awareness; then the therapist is guided into the action phase of decision making.

1. *Awareness of Therapist and Client ᵛMemes*—As stated above, if the therapist is the instrument of ethical and clinical decisions, awareness of one's values is imperative. (To further awareness of one's own values, the reader can engage in the reflection questions in Chapter 10, *The Self of the Therapist*.) Not only should therapists be aware of their values, but they also should be willing to express them openly to their clients. As they learn about their clients, they may learn about value similarities and differences in client families, and between themselves and clients. The therapist should have a good working knowledge of the client's values and ᵛMeme in order to best understand what types of clinical, ethical, or legal situations may arise in therapy.
2. *Awareness of Potential Ethical Issues*—Therapists should be ethically informed and ready. Awareness of the potential of ethical issues that may arise in clinical practice is developed through classes, readings, clinical experience, supervision, continuing education, legal counsel, and so on.
   a. *Know your professional code of ethics.* For example, the American Association for Marriage and Family Therapy (AAMFT) *Code of Ethics* (2001) (see Appendix) covers therapists' responsibility to clients, confidentiality, professional competence and integrity, responsibility of students and supervisees, responsibility to

research participants, responsibility to the profession, financial arrangements, and advertising. Codes are becoming more and more detailed over time (in response to increased attention on consumer protection and because of an increasingly litigious society). Codes generally are designed to provide guidelines for therapists, detail an appropriate standard of care on important issues within the profession, and serve as a basis for professional sanctions.

b. *Know and practice core competencies.* AAMFT has developed core competencies (AAMFT, 2004). The domains include admission to treatment, clinical assessment and diagnosis, treatment planning and case management, therapeutic interventions, legal issues, ethics and standards, and research and program evaluation. Subdomains include conceptual skills, perceptual skills, executive skills, and professional skills. There is a movement toward global behavioral health care competencies (Ries, McManis, & Daniels, 2005) inclusive of all fields of mental health.

c. *Know the local, state, and federal laws that relate to clinical practice.* Laws regarding mental health as well as specific licensing or certification statutes should be well known to the therapist.

d. *Keep up with the research.* Know the research as it applies to ethical situations, but also to evidence-based practice and outcome research. McCabe (2006) provides an excellent article with practical strategies for accessing, appraising, and adopting clinical and research findings to clinical practice. He details how to use studies, syntheses, synopses, and systems, all replete with online Web sites to access this information.

e. *Be aware of ethical or legal land mines.* There are several areas within couple and family therapy treatment that should increase therapist attention to potential ethical or legal problems. These areas have been controversial in mental health and the legal system. These include the following:
    i. Divorce and custody cases
    ii. Abuse cases that involve repressed memories (especially if the client is considering litigation against the abuser)
    iii. Dual or multiple relationships
    iv. Client abandonment
    v. Clients previously treated by an unethical therapist

3. *Define the Ethical Problem*—What issue or dilemma is currently confronting the therapist? There may be more than one ethical problem; the therapist must be able to manage ambiguity in the process in order to not foreclose on a decision prematurely.

4. *Gather Information From All Relevant Sources and Formulate and Weigh All Possible Alternatives.*
   a. *Consider all courses of action and possible ramifications of each decision.* Using Steps 1 and 2 above, what information is needed in order to make the best ethical decision in this scenario?
   b. *Decide what sources of information are needed, and assemble the sources.* Go carefully through Steps 1 and 2 of this model in order to ensure a thorough ethical decision (this includes personal values and client's values).
   c. *What input does the client or client family have in this decision?* Can this decision be ethically made *with* the client?
   d. *Consult as necessary.* The following questions are posed as a guide to help the therapist in this process. They include an evaluation of the moral principles of *autonomy, nonmaleficence, justice, fidelity, beneficence* (Beauchamp & Childress, 2001), and *veracity.*
   i. With each person's happiness being equally important, what *action* will produce the most good for the most people?
   ii. How do rules of conduct affect this decision?
      A. Have you respected each person's *autonomy* (Beauchamp & Childress, 2001)? Autonomy is the belief that people should be allowed freedom of choice and action.
      B. Have you adhered to the maxim of *nonmaleficence* (Beauchamp & Childress, 2001)? Nonmaleficence means "above all, do no harm."
      C. Have you been advocating for *justice* (Beauchamp & Childress, 2001)? Justice means that all humans should be treated fairly, and that goodness and badness should be distributed justly among them. According to Jacques Thiroux, there are three ways this can happen:
         • Good and bad can be distributed to people based on their merits.
         • There is an equal distribution of good and bad.
         • Good and bad are distributed according to the needs and abilities, or both, of the client (Thiroux, 1980, p. 125).
      D. Is there *fidelity* in your action? Fidelity refers to honoring commitments and promoting trust.
      E. Is there *veracity* (Beauchamp & Childress, 2001) in your action? Veracity refers to the importance of truth-telling.
      F. Have you promoted *beneficence* (Beauchamp & Childress, 2001)? Beneficence refers to promoting good.

iii. Are you willing to make your decision an ethical imperative for all to follow? How would you defend your course of action?

iv. In this situation, what do you believe *X* would do? (*X* may be Gandhi, Christ, Buddha, Oprah Winfrey, the President, Ganesh, the Cardinal, your mother or father, and so on.)

v. What *intuitively* do you think you should do?

vi. What does (do) the stakeholder(s) want?

5. *Together With the Stakeholders (If Possible), Choose the Best Ethical Alternative and Implement the Decision*—After careful consideration and weighing of the factors listed above, a decision should be made and executed either by the therapist or the supervisor.

6. *Monitor the Decision and the Outcome of the Decision, and Reevaluate If Necessary*—Is everyone satisfied with the outcome of the decision? Why or why not? Has there been harm done by the decision? Is there relational repair that needs to occur because of the decision? Should another decision be put in place at this juncture? Are the stakeholders satisfied with the decision? Does intuition still indicate that the decision was a good one?

7. *Carefully Document the Response to the Ethical Issue*—See Chapter 13, *Ethical Issues in Clinical Practice,* for information on documentation.

Case Scenario 1

The Johnsons attend therapy with concerns about their daughter Lucy, age 13. Mrs. Johnson is concerned that Lucy likes boys at such a young age, she wants a cell phone, and she is asking for frequent trips to the mall. Mr. Johnson is upset that Lucy only wants to wear ragged jeans or skimpy outfits and talk on the phone incessantly. They lament that Lucy would rather watch television than do her homework, unlike her more studious older brother. Lucy is also getting B's in school instead of A's, which her parents expect of her. They attend family therapy so that the therapist can help "get Lucy in line." Lucy complains that her brother does not have to help with the housework, and he gets many more privileges than she does. The therapist notices there appears to be extreme adherence to traditional gender roles in the household. During the course of a private interview with Lucy, the family therapist learns from Lucy that Mr. Johnson physically abuses Mrs. Johnson. He has never hit the children, but altercations occur with Mrs. Johnson after the children are asleep. Lucy begged the therapist not to speak of the abuse, citing that both parents will simply deny that it occurs.

Decision-Making Process

1. *Awareness of therapist and client* ᵛ*Memes*—The ᵛMemes of the involved entities are at odds. The parents appear to have a center of gravity at a Blue level, and the therapist is likely operating with a center of gravity at a Green level (as many therapists do because of their value of relationships). Lucy

may be differentiating as an adolescent, with concomitant clashes with her parents. The therapist must be careful to couch her intervention within a value framework that works for a family operating at a Blue level.

2. *Awareness of potential ethical issues*—The therapist should have a good working knowledge of the law surrounding domestic violence issues, confidentiality and minors, minors and informed consent, her code of ethics, research around domestic violence or intimate partner violence (IPV), and so on.

3. *Define the ethical problem*—The therapist runs the risk of not acting and Mrs. Johnson getting seriously injured or killed. Conversely, she runs the risk of breaking Lucy's confidentiality in order to discuss the issue with the parents, thereby damaging her relationship with Lucy. In addition, there are several other ethical and legal factors to consider:

   a. For example, the AAMFT Code of Ethics (2001) Subprinciple 2.2 states the following with regard to client confidentiality:

   Marriage and family therapists do not disclose client confidences except by written authorization or waiver, or where mandated or permitted by law. Verbal authorization will not be sufficient except in emergency situations, unless prohibited by law. When providing couple, family or group treatment, the therapist does not disclose information outside the treatment context without a written authorization from each individual competent to execute a waiver. In the context of couple, family or group treatment, the therapist may not reveal any individual's confidences to others in the client unit without the prior written permission of that individual.

   b. Depending upon state statute, Lucy may have legal rights to confidentiality. She may also have had to have given legal consent to treatment. Some states give minors as young as 12 the right to consent to treatment. If she is threatened by the therapist's actions, she may withdraw her consent to treatment.

   c. Another consideration is whether or not the abuse rises to the level of *duty to protect*. (See Chapter 3, *Legal Issues*.)

   In addition, as Lucy points out, the action may be for naught, as the parents may deny any abuse is occurring. The therapist could bring in Mrs. Johnson and discuss the abuse with her, but Lucy is against this idea. In addition, the therapist has no way of knowing if Lucy is telling the truth about the idea.

4. *Gather information from all relevant sources, and formulate and weigh all possible alternatives*—At this point, the therapist would want any legal information on IPV, shelter information, input from Lucy on what she thinks might be most helpful in protecting her mother, state protection law, and consultation with colleagues or supervisors.

   a. *What action will produce the most good for the most people?* The ideal action would be to get Lucy's permission to share her concern with her mother so her mother's safety could be assessed and the therapist could be sure that everyone is out of harm's way.

   b. *Have you respected each person's autonomy?* Yes, if Lucy agrees to let the therapist speak to her mother.

    c. *Have you adhered to the maxim of nonmaleficence?* Yes, if the therapist goes with the ideal action to promote Mrs. Johnson's safety.

    d. *Have you adhered to the principle of justice (Beauchamp & Childress, 2001)?* Yes.

    e. *Is there fidelity in your action?* Yes.

    f. *Is there veracity in your action?* Yes, the therapist has told the truth to Lucy.

5. *Together with the stakeholders (if possible), choose the best ethical alternative and implement the decision*—The therapist chooses to urge Lucy to allow her to speak to her mother in order to keep her mother from further harm. She states the many advantages of this and highlights Lucy's inherent need to protect her parents, and how helping her mother change her relationship with her father will ultimately protect her. Lucy eventually agrees, and the therapist carefully assesses the level of danger to the mother in her interview with her.

6. *Monitor the decision and the outcome of the decision, and reevaluate if necessary*—The therapist continues to work with this family and monitors the impact of this decision on Lucy and on the family. The therapist made the initial ethical decision, but it is only a preliminary ethical decision at the beginning of treatment. Further clinical work will need to be done in order to assess the level of violence and how best to intervene. Of course, the therapist runs the risk of the family not returning to therapy, thereby eradicating a chance to intervene with the IPV.

7. *Carefully document the response to the ethical issue*—For both the protection of Lucy and the liability of the therapist, the therapist carefully documents her actions. The therapist should document the reasons for taking the action she did.

Case Scenario 2

Juanita, a wealthy businesswoman, and Alex, a teacher, commenced couple therapy due to a crisis brought on by the revelation of Juanita's most recent extramarital affair. Juanita traveled frequently for her job and was extremely career focused and driven. Alex complained that Juanita worked too much, yet enjoyed the large house and other material benefits her position brought. Alex soon grew disgusted with what he perceived as Juanita's lack of investment in therapy, and dropped out, citing that Juanita was the one who needed to change, due to her frequent affairs. Juanita, worried that Alex would finally divorce her, decided that she would stay in therapy to please Alex. No amount of pleading could get Alex to rejoin her, though he had no immediate plans to divorce her either. The therapist, Ben, decided it would be a good chance to do some transgenerational work with Juanita to understand her need to have frequent affairs, and Juanita agreed. Juanita, however, stated that she could not stop having sex with other men. In the course of therapy, Juanita revealed that she had recently learned from a home testing kit that she has HIV that she apparently contracted during a recent extramarital liaison. Juanita did not want to tell Alex because she knew for sure that he would leave her. She forbid Ben from telling Alex and threatened the therapist with legal action should he tell.

Decision-Making Process

1. *Awareness of therapist and client ᵛMemes*—The therapist, Ben, is likely at a Green ᵛMeme level, is dealing with a client who is likely at an Orange ᵛMeme level who is used to being in control in her work environment, and it typically extends to his relationships outside of work as well. Her emphasis is on status and control, while Ben's is on dialogue and relationships. Their value differences will surface in this ethical dilemma.

2. *Awareness of potential ethical issues*—The therapist should be aware of the literature on HIV and duty to warn (cf. Schlossberger & Hecker, 1996), ethical issues surrounding infidelity (cf. Snyder & Doss, 2005), as well as state law on whether knowingly transmitting HIV is a criminal offense, and if a therapist can reveal a client's HIV status. In addition, the therapist needs to know her code of ethics and state privilege statutes, and exceptions therein.

3. *Define the ethical problem*—The issue at hand is that Juanita is putting Alex at risk. She is not open to the therapist's suggestions to divulge her HIV status to Alex, and she is not open to Alex attending therapy with her to discuss the issue. Ben has been threatened legally by the client should he break confidentiality. Nevertheless, Alex remains at risk for unknowingly contracting HIV.

4. *Gather information from all relevant sources and formulate and weigh all possible alternatives*—The therapist needs to help Juanita focus on her fairness of her knowing about her disease and her husband not knowing. The therapist can do the following:
   a. Be complicit with Juanita in keeping the disease from her husband.
   b. Anonymously warn her husband.
   c. Go against Juanita's wishes and warn her husband, risking a lawsuit.
   d. Work with Juanita regarding ways to disclose to her husband.
   e. Threaten to terminate therapy if Juanita does not tell her husband.
   f. Terminate therapy immediately.

   Given the options, the most fair seems to be that the therapist would work with Juanita to find ways to tell her husband about the test results. The therapist may first recommend testing by a physician to confirm the home test results. If she refuses, then the therapist would need to decide the next step of action. Starting with the option that the therapist would work with Juanita to tell her husband, the follow-up questions are answered below.
   a. *What action would produce the most good for the most people?* This solution produces the most good for the most people.
   b. *Have you respected each person's autonomy?* Yes, both people have choice of freedom and action; a remedy to the problem at hand.
   c. *Have you adhered to the maxim of nonmaleficence?* Yes, the solution creates nonmaleficence.
   d. *Have you been advocating justice?* Yes, both parties are treated fairly.
   e. *Is there fidelity in your action?* Yes, trust has been promoted in the therapeutic relationship.
   f. *Is there veracity in your action?* Yes, Juanita is now telling the truth to Alex.

g. *Are you willing to make your decision an ethical imperative for all to follow?* Yes, this is a situation that would be recommended to all in a similar situation.

5. *Together with the stakeholders (if possible), choose the best ethical alternative and implement the decision*—The therapist worked with Juanita to tell Alex, who was devastated. However, because he had previous knowledge of her affair, he was not as devastated as Juanita had predicted. He tested negative for HIV and did not divorce Juanita. He decided to reengage in therapy, and the couple decided to do some things together that they had been putting off due to Juanita's busy business schedule. When Juanita was officially tested by a physican for HIV, she did not test seropositive.

6. *Monitor the decision and the outcome of the decision and reevaluate if necessary*—If Juanita had refused to disclose her HIV status, the therapist would have had to make a decision on disclosure and duty to warn, based on state statutes, consultations, legal advice, and various other components of ethical decision making. More specific advice regarding HIV and duty to warn is given in Chapter 14.

7. *Carefully document the response to the ethical issue*—The therapist should document any consultations he had while wrestling with the ethical decision, conversations he had with Juanita around the decision and her response to his voicing his concerns, how decisions were made, and actions that were taken by both the client and the therapist.

Ethical Decision Making Summarized

1. Be aware of therapist and client ᵛMemes.
2. Be aware of potential ethical issues.
   a. Know the professional codes of ethics.
   b. Know and practice core competencies.
   c. Know the local, state, and federal laws that relate to clinical practice.
   d. Keep up with the research.
   e. Be aware of ethical or legal land mines.
3. Define the ethical problem.
4. Gather information from all relevant sources, and formulate and weigh all possible alternatives.
5. Together with the stakeholders (if possible), choose the best ethical alternative and implement the decision.
6. Monitor the decision and the outcome of the decision and reevaluate if necessary.
7. Carefully *document* the response to the ethical issue.

Summary

Ethical decision making rests on therapists knowing themselves as individuals, what their own values are, as well as those of the couples and families that are seen in therapy. Spiral dynamics (Beck & Cowan, 1996) is offered as a theory of values from which to gain a basic schema to understand the evolution of values. This is presented as a conceptual tool only, not a categorization tool. Therapists must be able to tolerate ambiguity while making ethical decisions. An ambiguous situation is one where there is information that is novel, complex (with competing solutions), or seems insolvable (Budner, 1962). Ethical dilemmas typically are ambiguous, and therapists must be able to tolerate some ambiguity as the factors to a complex situation are examined and evaluated. The ethical decision-making model presented is a guide to aid the family therapist by providing a framework to navigate the ambiguities presented in ethical dilemmas. The complexities of ethical situations, which often present with clinical, ethical, and often legal issues intertwined, lend themselves to need a structure from which the therapist can work to make well-reasoned decisions using all of the resources of the therapist—cognitive, affective, and intuitive.

References

American Association for Marriage and Family Therapy (AAMFT). (2001). *Code of ethics.* Alexandria, VA: Author.

American Association for Marriage and Family Therapy (AAMFT). (2004). *Marriage and family therapy core competencies.* Alexandria, VA: Author.

Beauchamp, T. L., & Childress, J. F. (2001). *Principles of biomedical ethics* (5th ed.). New York: Oxford University Press.

Beck, D., & Cowan, C. (1996). *Spiral dynamics: Managing values, leadership, and change.* London: Blackwell.

Budner, S. (1962). Intolerance of ambiguity as a personality variable. *Journal of Personality, 30*(1), 29–50.

Forester-Miller, H., & Davis, T. (1996). A practitioner's guide to making ethical decisions. American Counseling Association. Retrieved June 18, 2007, from: www.counseling.org/Resources/CodeOfEthics/TP/Home/CT2.aspx.

Haas, L. J., & Malouf, J. L. (1989). *Keeping up the good work: A practioner's guide to mental health ethics.* Sarasota, FL: Professional Resource Exchange.

Hill, M., Glaser, K., & Harden, J. (1995). A feminist model of ethical decision-making. In E. J. Rave & C. C. Larsen (Eds.), *Ethical decision-making in therapy: Feminist perspectives* (pp. 18–37). New York: Guilford Press.

Kitchener, K. S. (1984). Intuition, critical evaluation and ethical principles: The foundation for ethical decisions in counseling psychology. *Counseling Psychologist, 12*(3), 43–55.

Mailloux, N. (1977). Ethical issues in the psychologist-client relationship. *International Journal of Psychology, 16,* 115–119.

McCabe, O. L. (2006). Evidence based practice in mental health: Accessing, appraising and adopting research data. *International Journal of Mental Health, 35*(2), 50–69.

Ries, S. A., McManis, A. M., & Daniels, A. S. (2005). The Annapolis coalition: A review of the behavioral health workforce competencies. *Family Therapy Magazine, 4* (July/August), 14–18.

Schlossberger, E., & Hecker, L. (1996). HIV and duty to warn: A legal and ethical analysis. *Journal of Marital and Family Therapy, 22*(1), 27–40.

Seymour, W. R. (1982). Values in conflict: Therapist/client values, III. *Journal of Family Therapy Collections, 1,* 41–60.

Snyder, D. K., & Doss, D. B. (2005). Treating infidelity: Clinical directions. *Journal of Clinical Psychology, 61*(11), 1453–1465.

Spiral Dynamics. (2006). About Spiral Dynamics: The theory. Retrieved October 30, 2008, from: www.spiraldynamics.org/aboutsd_theory.htm.

Stadler, H. A. (1986). Making hard choices: Clarifying controversial ethical issues. *Counseling and Human Development, 19* (September), 1–10.

Taggart, M. (1982). Linear versus systemic values: Implications for family therapy. In J. C. Hansen & L. L. L'Abate (Eds.), *Values, ethics and legalities and the family therapist* (pp. 23–39). Rockville, MD: Aspen.

Thiroux, J. (1980). *Ethics: Theory and practice.* New York: Collier Macmillan.

Wilber, K. (2000). *A theory of everything: An integral vision for business, politics, science, and spirituality.* Boston, MA: Shambala Publications.

Woody, J. D. (1990). Resolving ethical concerns in clinical practice: Toward a pragmatic model. *Journal of Marital & Family Therapy, 16*(2), 133–150.

3

Legal Issues

*Rebecca A. Nestor, Ursula Tina Steiner,
and Jeffrey M. Stewart*

Janet and her 3-year-old daughter Monique began attending sessions with Dr. Royce due to concerns with adjusting to the separation of Janet and Rudolph. After Janet and Rudolph separated, a preliminary decision was made by the court stating that Janet and Rudolph had joint legal custody of Monique. It was also decided that the child was to live with Janet, staying with Rudolph each weekend.

Janet described concerns of depression, anger, and inability to communicate with Rudolph about Monique. She believed that Monique's behavior had declined over the past 6 months and was worried about her adjustment. She had witnessed behavior problems in Monique after returning from Rudolph's home. The behavior ranged from Monique throwing fits when she did not get her way to her getting physically violent with Janet at multiple times throughout the week.

Over several sessions, Janet and Monique addressed concerns regarding adjustment to the family dynamics; however, Dr. Royce believed that Monique would benefit from her parents attending sessions together to work on parenting concerns. Janet agreed with the therapist that it could be useful. Dr. Royce set up an appointment with the parents. Janet and Rudolph discussed concerns each had about Monique and their parenting styles. Janet and Rudolph met with Dr. Royce several times. The sessions seemed to go fairly well considering the status of the couple, but they continued to have problems agreeing on the parenting of their daughter.

After Janet and Rudolph had attempted to work on their concerns regarding Monique, Dr. Royce received a subpoena from Rudolph's attorney to appear and testify about the case. Specifically, Rudolph's attorney had hoped to reveal that Janet was not capable of parenting Monique, demonstrated by her attending sessions with Dr. Royce, and was petitioning for a change in custody arrangements.

With the example above, it can be demonstrated how law, ethics, and clinical practice are intertwined. For example, when Janet and Monique began attending sessions, the legal question arose as to who signs the informed consent to therapy for treatment of a minor in the case of joint legal custody. What if a parent refuses to give consent and a minor could benefit from therapy or it is clear it is in his or her best interest? What are the clinical and ethical implications of not including the other parent in therapy? Couple and family therapists then encounter an ethical and legal dilemma of whether to suspend treatment until permission from both parents is obtained or to treat the child with permission of only one parent.

When two separated parents begin attending sessions together, after one had been seeing the therapist already individually, confidentiality may become an ethical issue. What information from individual sessions should be shared in joint sessions? When a client's attorney subpoenas a therapist to testify about the case and the therapist must comply, what information is permitted to be shared, what information must be shared, and who is the client?

This chapter consists of discussion surrounding the legal and ethical issues in couple and family therapy and illuminates how law, ethics, and clinical practice are interconnected.

Confidentiality and Privileged Communication

Confidentiality is an *ethical* obligation of the therapist and is at the core of any therapeutic relationship. It has also become a legal obligation of the therapist through common law. Common law occurs when law is established through case law instead of state statute.

A confidential relationship is defined as a relationship in which the therapist refrains from disclosing information obtained in the course of treatment (Houston-Vega, Nuehring, & Daguio, 1997). Confidentiality is the foundation on which the therapeutic relationship is built; its importance cannot be overstated. Trust is fundamental to the therapeutic relationship. The importance of confidential communication between the therapist and the client is recognized by mental health professional organizations and sanctioned in their codes of ethics. If therapists break confidentiality (outside of *permissible* situations stipulated by one's professional organization *or the law*), that may result in actions taken by the organization and may make therapists vulnerable to legal action.

Privilege is the right to *legal protection* of a client's confidentiality, governed by state statute, and applies only to court proceedings. Not all clients are protected by privilege; it depends on whether or not one's state statute is written to cover the therapist's profession (usually designated by the professional's license). "Since the client holds the privilege he or she can choose to waive privilege or not. If privilege is waived then the therapist may testify. If the client does not waive privilege, the therapist is barred from testifying" (Boyan & Termini, 2005, p. 79).

The legal protection of confidentiality (privileged communication) is limited. A therapist may be forced to break his or her ethical obligation of keeping confidentiality in order to fulfill his or her legal duty to comply with a subpoena. In contrast, for example, the privilege the attorney–client relationship enjoys is not limited. The attorney–client relationship, for example, is privileged—an attorney has the right to refuse to disclose information even if he or she is subpoenaed to do so, whereas if a subpoenaed therapist refuses to disclose information, he or she may be held in contempt of court.

Issues dealing with confidentially and privileged communication have been disputed in court for years (DeBell & Jones, 1997). In the federal case of *Jaffee v. Redmond* (1996) the U.S. Supreme Court supported therapist–client privileged communication (Mosher & Swire, 2002). In this case, Mary Lu Redmond was the first police officer to respond to a fight in progress at an apartment complex. Upon arriving at the scene, two men came running out of the building. When the second man raised a knife to stab the first man, Redmond shouted "Stop! Police!" The man did not stop. When the man, later identified as Ricky Allen, did not stop, Redmond shot him to prevent a homicide. Allen's relatives, who had called police to stop a fight between Allen and the other man, now watched him die. Redmond later sought counseling with a licensed clinical social worker, Karen Beyer, in order to help her through the traumatic experience (Beyer, 2000).

The administrator for the decedent Allen's estate, Carrie Jaffee, filed a civil lawsuit against Redmond and the apartment complex, which employed Redmond, stating that Allen's constitutional rights were violated. During the pretrial, Jaffee learned of Redmond's counseling sessions with Beyer. Jaffee sought out Beyer's notes from her sessions with Redmond to use during cross-examination. Beyer and Redmond resisted, but the court still ordered the notes be disclosed. Beyer and Redmond refused to comply, so the court ordered the jury to assume the notes would be unfavorable to Redmond. Jaffee was awarded just over half a million dollars from Redmond. The case was appealed several times over until it came to the U.S. Supreme Court.

The decision by the Supreme Court read as follows: "Confidential communications between patient and psychotherapist, including licensed social worker in course of psychotherapy, held privileged from compelled disclosure under FRE 501" (*Jaffee v. Redmond,* 1996). Thus, the Supreme

Court perceived in this case evidentiary needs for disclosure secondary to the right of privacy (DeBell & Jones, 1997).

In the *Jaffee v. Redmond* (1996) ruling, the Supreme Court paralleled the psychotherapist–patient with the attorney–client relationship and therewith laid the foundation of the legal protection of the confidential nature of the psychotherapist–patient relationship (The Federal Psychotherapist–Patient Privilege, n.d.). Although the ruling *Jaffee v. Redmond* (1996) and later court decisions provided support for the protection of therapist–client communication and the establishment of a psychotherapist–patient privilege, they did not result in uniform jurisdiction. "Although *Jaffee's* full impact remains uncertain, those who have followed its brief history agree that its impact on future state and federal court decisions and laws will undoubtedly expand beyond where it has reached so far" (Daly, 2006, p. 13).

Exceptions to Confidentiality and Privileged Communication

Confidentiality is of the utmost importance in the therapeutic relationship, but there are exceptions to which the therapist and the client must be educated. These infringements include the following:

- When there are reporting duties such as abuse, neglect (Glosoff, Herlihy, Herlihy, & Spence, 1997), elder abuse, and domestic violence (Fritchman, 2007).
- When the therapist has a duty to warn because there is danger to others (Fritchman, 2007; Glosoff et al., 1997).
- When the therapist believes there is a risk of suicide (Fritchman, 2007; Glosoff et al., 1997).
- When the therapist is in a court-appointed role such as when doing a psychological assessment (Glosoff et al., 1997). Clients may also lose some rights to confidentiality when ordered into treatment by employee assistance programs and the Department of Transportation (Fritchman, 2007).
- When investigated by the Department of Homeland Security, clients lose confidentiality rights (Fritchman, 2007).
- When the client files a malpractice claim or other lawsuit against the therapist (Glosoff et al., 1997).
- When a mental condition is used as a claim or defense in a lawsuit (Glosoff et al., 1997).
- When issues of competency and hospitalization are at hand (Glosoff et al., 1997).

Clients may waive their rights to confidentiality at any time through a written release. Additionally, state statute will specify exceptions to legal privilege.

Duty to Protect

The duty to protect a third party from peril from a client arose from the landmark case of *Tarasoff v. Regents of the University of California* in 1976. In this case, Prosenjit Poddar was attending therapy voluntarily at the University Counseling Center in August 1969. Poddar expressed that he was going to kill his girlfriend but did not provide her name, though the therapist was able to readily identify of whom Poddar spoke. The police were informed, took Poddar into custody for questioning, and found him to be rational. They released him. Two months later, he killed Tatiana Tarasoff upon her return to campus. The Tarasoff family filed a lawsuit against the Board of Regents of the university. The case was dismissed by the lower courts, and eventually it was tried by the California Supreme Court. The California Supreme Court found that the university personnel involved failed to warn the intended victim. The court ruled that "The protective privilege ends where the public peril begins."

The final ruling of the *Tarasoff v. Regents of the University of California* (1976) gave therapists *three factors to consider* in regard to the duty to warn an intended victim and provide protective mechanisms:

1. *A "Special Relationship Exists"*—They found that one person cannot control the actions of others; however, when a person is in a "special relationship" with either the person threatening harm or the potential victim, then that person has a duty to inform the potential victim. A therapeutic relationship was found to be a "special relationship."
2. *There Is a Foreseeable Risk*—This is not an easily definable factor, so a therapist must rely on his or her own judgment on whether or not his or her client is a real threat to someone else's safety. This criterion can itself be a legal bind. If a therapist does not warn the potential victim, and the client does harm to him or her, the therapist could face a lawsuit. However, if the therapist does warn, he or she is still taking the risk of having a lawsuit brought against him or her for breaching confidentiality.
3. *There Is an Anticipated Victim*—If the victim can be readily identified by the therapist, then this criterion is met. It is central to note that the potential victim does not have to be named directly. For instance, in the *Tarasoff v. Regents of the University of California* (1976) case, although

Poddar did not explicitly name Tatiana Tarasoff, she could have been easily identified with the information Poddar presented to the therapist.

By being aware of and using these three criteria, a therapist can greatly reduce the chance of experiencing litigation. State laws *must* be checked regarding duty to warn as each varies with respect to specific criteria. What triggers a duty to protect may differ from state to state. For example, the duty to warn does not require an explicit threat in some states. In addition, there are a few states that do not have duty to protect statutes and disallow duty to warn.

Mandated Reporting

Child Abuse and Neglect

Child abuse and neglect is an important aspect of the duty to report for therapists. Child abuse and neglect is defined by the Child Abuse Prevention and Treatment Act as (GPO Access, n.d.):

> Physical or mental injury, sexual abuse or exploitation, negligent treatment, or maltreatment of a child under the age of 18 or the age specified by the child protection law of the state in question, by a person who is responsible for the child's welfare, under circumstances which indicate that the child's health or welfare is harmed or threatened thereby.

No federal laws are in place making child abuse and neglect illegal; however, they do make money available to the states to put laws, guidelines, and other qualifications in place. State laws provide the guidelines therapists should follow when dealing with the issue of child abuse and neglect. All states require the reporting of child abuse and neglect by therapists as well as by those in many other professions.

It is important for all mental health practitioners to be aware of their state's laws regarding this matter. For example, some states require that abuse or neglect be reported even if it is only *suspected* abuse. Mental health practitioners should be conscious of the liability that exists for the failure to report child abuse and neglect, which is variable per state statute.

There is a safeguard in place for mental health practitioners when it comes to reporting. All states are required to provide immunity to mandated reporters by the Child Abuse Prevention and Treatment Act (GPO Access, n.d.). This immunity protects all mandated reporters from civil and criminal liability when reporting. This statute keeps therapists from being sued for damages that arise from a report. In order to protect oneself from litigation dealing with child abuse and neglect reporting, the therapist must follow the details of the statute within his or her state. Note that immunity does not apply to self-reporters (Small, Lyons, & Guy, 2002). There are times that it is a positive therapeutic event for a client to take responsibility and self-report abuse as part of therapy. However, therapists should be cautioned that by doing this, clients give up their right to due process should they choose this reporting venue. What is therapeutically useful may be legally harmful.

Elder Abuse/Dependent Adult Abuse

With 3% of all adults over age 60 being victims of elder abuse or neglect (Welfel, Danzinger, & Santoro, 2000), couple and family therapists need to be aware of this highly camouflaged problem. By 1985, all states had instituted some form of adult protection program, and by 1993, all states had enacted laws regarding elder abuse in domestic and institutional settings (Jogerst et al., 2003). State laws covering elder or dependent adult abuse may include physical, psychological, fiduciary, neglect, sexual abuse, abandonment, abduction, and isolation. Self-neglect may also be included in the state law. To be cognizant of the definitions of an "elder" and "dependent adult" as well as what constitutes "abuse" and "neglect" is crucial. Certain types of abuse are subject to criminal prosecution, depending upon the conduct of the perpetrator and the consequences for the victim. Mandated reporters are immune from criminal or civil liability except in the case of self-reporters.

Typically, elder abuse reporting falls under Adult Protective Services. There are three ways that elder abuse laws can differ:

> First, some states require mandatory versus voluntary reporting, meaning that the reporter is obligated by law to file suspicions of elder abuse. The second major difference refers to the targeted elder population served by the law. For example, some states, in an effort to restrict intrusion into the private lives of citizens, limit their laws to vulnerable and incapacitated elders...Third, laws differ in the authority granted to the EAP [Elder Abuse Protection] practitioner to conduct investigations of alleged abuse and neglect and to intervene in cases that are substantiated. (Bergeron & Gray, 2003, p. 98)

Victims have various levels of say in the process, depending upon the state. Seventy-six percent of states have a criminal penalty for failure to report (Welfel et al., 2000).

Subpoenas and Court Orders

A subpoena is a *summons* to appear in court or at a deposition; it may also include a command to produce specific documents (a subpoena duces tecum). A court order is a *ruling* by the judge. A summons may ask that you appear or provide documents. A judge's order *commands* you to do something in particular or face contempt of court charges and potential jail time.

A subpoena may be issued by an attorney or a court. A subpoena may not necessarily be signed by a judge, but it always requires a timely response (American Psychological Association [APA], 2006). The therapist can contact his or her client and ask what avenue the client would like the therapist to pursue. For example, in child custody cases, it is typically in the client's best interests to comply with the court order. If the client does not, he or she runs the risk of appearing as if he or she is hiding something about his or her mental health. For a client who does not want his or her therapeutic information revealed, the client may ask his or her attorney to have the subpoena quashed (i.e., made void or invalid) or modified (APA, 2006). If attempts to quash or modify a subpoena have been unsuccessful, the therapist will have to appear in court and possibly testify if ordered to do so by the judge. The therapist should be very clear that the client has either waived his or her right to privilege or that the judge has ordered the therapist to testify. The therapist's job is to uphold the confidentiality; the client's legal privilege should be respected until it is clear that *the judge has ordered it.* A subpoena requires a response, but only a court order dictates a disclosure of information (APA, 2006).

In the event the therapist is unavailable for the court date due to an unavoidable situation, all parties (the judge, representing attorneys, and the client) should be written, with the reason for the inability to attend the proceeding. The attorney issuing the subpoena will typically request a change in court date; if not, the therapist will need to hire an attorney to file a motion to quash the subpoena (Boyan & Termini, 2005, pp. 80–81).

The client's right of confidentiality is crucial to psychotherapy practice as explained above. When a therapist is ordered to testify, this clearly infringes upon the client's right of confidentiality. This is due to the truth finding in a legal process being valued higher than the client's right of confidentiality. It is a general principle of law that all citizens are required to provide information necessary for deciding issues before a court when subpoenaed (APA, 2006). There are statutes, rules of civil and criminal procedure, and rules of evidence regulating the collection of such information. One way to collect relevant information is through subpoenas. Therapists, however, must exercise due care to uphold client confidentiality or privilege whenever feasibly possible, and to divulge information only when a judge so orders.

Strategies for Dealing With Subpoenas and Court Orders

The APA recommends the following strategies to deal with a subpoena. First, it has to be determined if the subpoena is a legally valid demand for the disclosure of confidential information. The subpoena has to be issued by the court, or an attorney receiving his or her subpoena power from the court, which has jurisdiction over the therapist or the guardian of the records. For example, if a therapist practicing in Indiana is subpoenaed by a district court in Illinois, the subpoena is not legally binding because the Illinois court does not have jurisdiction in Indiana. Also, a subpoena has to be served properly according to the procedure law, which may vary from state to state. The therapist may want to seek legal advice to determine the validity of a subpoena (APA, 2006).

As a second step, the therapist has to contact and notify the client about the subpoena of their information as well as who is requesting the information (APA, 2006). It is also important that the therapist informs the client how testifying might affect the client and the therapeutic relationship (Gottlieb, 2000). The client usually has the following possibilities: (a) The client may sign the consent to release the requested information; (b) if the information is requested by the client's attorney, the therapist may consult with the client's legal counselor with the client's written consent. If the client gives written consent, the therapist may discuss the relevant issues and explain how testifying may affect the therapeutic relationship negatively. A conversation with the client's attorney may also reveal that the legal strategy is not congruent with the information the therapist will have to reveal (Gottlieb, 2000); (c) the client or the client's attorney files a motion to quash or modify the subpoena, or files a protective order. A motion to quash a subpoena is a formal application made to the court requesting that the subpoena be declared invalid (APA, 2006). A motion for a protective order seeks an order or decree from the court that protects the client from the discovery of confidential information. The therapist or the therapist's attorney can also file such a motion. The therapist has a legal obligation but not a legal right to keep client's information confidential; (d) the client could also choose not to waive his or her right to release the information. In this situation, the therapist or the therapist's attorney may try to negotiate with the requester of the information to prevent disclosure (APA, 2006).

Preparation for Testimony

Preparing the Client

The therapist should inform the client about the content of the testimony so that the client does not hear the testimony for the first time when sitting in the courtroom. This is information the client would never have heard otherwise (Gottlieb, 2000). Even if the testimony is not going to reveal any new information for the client, it is still important to discuss the testimony with the client. It is likely that the language the therapist will be using in the testimony will be very different from the language used in the therapy room. The therapist will want the client to hear what may be said about him or her prior to the courtroom testimony in order to decrease feelings of vulnerability the client may have, as well as to minimize potential damage to the therapeutic relationship.

Preparing the Therapist

Many witnesses are plagued with the anxiety of having to testify. Brodsky (2004) suggests the use of imagery to reduce anxiety when put in the unfamiliar setting of a courtroom. The opposing attorney may try everything to discredit the witness. Bullying attorneys look for vulnerabilities and count on the intimidation of the witness. A strategy to deal with bullying attorneys is to behave in the opposite way. For instance, if the attorney asks loud and aggressive questions, the witness should try to respond in a quiet, assured, and measured way (Brodsky, 2004). Attorneys sometimes push witnesses to reply with a "yes" or "no" answer. Brodsky (2004) proposes for these situations the following:

> There is no "yes" or "no" answer to that question.
> It would be professionally irresponsible for me to give a "yes" or "no" answer to that question.

Offering an admit–deny reply to complex questions, so that the part of the question that is true is acknowledged and the part that is untrue is vigorously denied. (p. 190)

However, Brodsky (2004) warned that such a reply carries the hazard that the court may think the witness is engaging in game playing. This, in turn, could undermine the credibility of the whole testimony. It is possible that the attorney may tap into private or embarrassing issues of the witness in a court hearing to try and discredit the witness. A way to handle situations like this may be for a witness to say, "These false suggestions are insulting and offensive to me. I do not know what the law and the bar allow, but that kind of accusation is profoundly offensive" (Brodsky, 2004, p. 124).

An essential part of preparing for testimony is the anticipation of the adversarial attorney's tactics and strategy. Being aware of tactics the adversarial attorney may use, as well as understanding their tasks and demands, is helpful in order to be an effective witness (Brodsky, 2004). If possible, it is useful to know what questions the attorney who is representing the therapist's client is going to ask in a cross-examination (Gottlieb, 2000). It is critical to remember that witnessing is not about winning. Any testimony should be to the best knowledge of the therapist. Witnesses should not let themselves be contaminated by the adversarial atmosphere. The witness has to be clear about the boundaries of the testimony. For therapists who have never been a witness before, it is helpful to role-play the testimony in advance. It might also be advisable to have a fake trial and videotape it. This allows the witness to observe body gestures as well as the whole appearance of himself or herself (Brodsky, 2004).

There are two kinds of witnesses: fact witnesses and expert witnesses. The fact witness and the expert witness have different roles in the process (Gottlieb, 2000). Persons who testify their direct observations are fact witnesses. Anybody can be a fact witness. In contrast, expert witnesses testify about a specialized knowledge they have (Brodsky & Anderer, 2000). Therapists are usually called as fact witnesses. However, it is possible that a therapist may be called as an expert witness regarding a diagnosis, prognosis, or treatment of the client (Gottlieb, 2000). Expert witnesses are those who give opinions to the court. Witnesses are deemed "expert" by the judge, based on their qualifications. Although expert witnesses have traditionally been psychologists, marriage and family therapists are entering the courtroom as experts with more frequency. Marriage and family therapists can aid the court as expert witnesses specifically because of their ability to see complex relational dynamics (Cobb & Roberson, in press).

Preparing the Therapist as a Witness

When a therapist is a fact witness, it is absolutely necessary that the therapist carefully prepares his or her testimony and has good knowledge of the case. It is advisable for the therapist to contact the client's attorney and get to know the legal strategy (Gottlieb, 2000).

The following suggestions when testifying as an expert witness are based on Brodsky (2004):

- It is vital that the therapist has very good knowledge about the field of expertise.
- A good preparation does not take place immediately before the trial but is an ongoing process of learning.
- It may help to know that most of the time, expert witnesses do not have to testify.
- The expert witness generally knows more than what the other people involved do.
- Brodsky points out that the expert witness does not have to have an answer for everything.
- Just because a therapist is called onto the stand as an expert witness does not imply that the therapist knows everything.
- The expert witness retains a sense of ordinariness from being on the witness stand.
- Appropriate appearance is certainly of importance, but a good testimony is not dependent on the witness's clothing.
- Being too self-conscious about appearance may interfere with the effectiveness of the witness.
- The expert witness should try to find a good middle ground between being human but not needy, and objective but not cold.
- Expert witnesses are asked to testify about their expertise, which requires clear thinking and expressing themselves clearly without using technical words.

Attorneys may approach experts to fulfill their agenda. In spite of this, the agenda is often only implicitly stated. In cases where a therapist is approached as an expert witness, it is useful to think through the request.

This prevents the therapist from agreeing to testify beyond a boundary that is professional (Brodsky, 2004).

A few tips for the therapist when testifying as a fact witness are as follows (C. Miller, personal communication, November 3, 2004; T. Rucinski, personal communication, October 13, 2004):

- Never answer a question immediately. Take a few seconds to think before answering a question.
- Have a question repeated if it is not understood.
- Try to keep the answers as brief as possible.
- Answer the question to the best of your knowledge. Only say things known, do not express speculations and assumptions.
- Be honest if you do not remember something.
- Try to avoid defensiveness.
- After testimony, it is advisable to debrief with the client and the attorney. However, this might not be possible right after the testimony (Gottlieb, 2000).

Deposition

A deposition is a testimony that is made in advance of the trial (Committee on Professional Practice and Standards, 2003) in front of a court reporter. Court reporters are notaries and are qualified to swear witnesses in so that testimony can be given under oath, under penalty of perjury. The reporter takes down everything that is said during the deposition and creates a transcript. The witness is then asked to sign the transcript in front of the notary. Depositions are usually made in an attorney's office. Other than the differences explained above, the procedure of depositions is very much the same as it would be in front of the court. Hence, the preparation for a deposition should be identical to the preparation for witnessing in a trial.

Malpractice

It is important for a therapist to be aware of malpractice possibilities due to the increase in the number of malpractice claims brought against clinicians in recent years (Jobes & Berman, 1993). Although malpractice claims occur, it seems as if clinicians feel "immune" to the possibility of a claim or lawsuit against them. Montgomery, Cupit, and Wimberley (1999) asked 284 participants to complete an eight-page survey exploring professional awareness, personal experiences, and practice activities related to complaints, malpractice, and risk management. The researchers demonstrated with the data collected that most respondents (78.5%) felt little concern regarding a complaint being filed against them and even less concern regarding a malpractice lawsuit being filed against them during their career. In contrast, this research indicated that 72% of the respondents knew colleagues who had a complaint filed against them with the state licensing board, and almost 40% knew a colleague who had been sued for malpractice (Montgomery et al., 1999). The data from this survey reveal an incentive for clinicians to be aware of types of malpractice claims and strategies useful in order to avoid them.

Definition of Malpractice

There are three criteria for malpractice to occur:

1. The therapist's actions must fall below the "appropriate standard of care."
2. The therapist's actions must result in an injury to the client.
3. The injury is a direct result of the therapist's action (also known as "proximate cause").

Standard of care as viewed by the judicial system is how the average therapist would have conducted himself or herself in a similar situation. In most cases, expert witnesses will be hired by both the defense and the plaintiff to define the standard of care. This definition of standard of care is most often defined by the various experts provided (Jobes & Berman, 1993). The way this definition is created is by the expert witnesses offering their specialized knowledge that pertains to the specific case at hand (Gottlieb, 2000).

Injury is defined in legal terms as "damage or wrong done to another's person, property, reputation, or rights. Not synonymous with 'damages,' since a right may be infringed without causing any monetary loss. No action at law is maintainable without a legal injury" (American Bar Association, 1997). This definition is important to the therapist as it may be different from any ethical obligation they have toward a client. An essential aspect of this definition is that the injury does not have to cause monetary loss. Although this type of loss is possible, the therapist should be careful to not restrict his or her definition of injury by monetary loss. The various types of damage that can be done to another's person, property, or reputation also make this definition extremely complicated. By following this definition, the therapist must be aware of the multitude of possible damages done to a client and attempt to limit the possibility of these occurring.

Another essential part to the definition of malpractice is the causal connection between the failure to provide the appropriate standard of care and the injury to the client. This causality may be difficult to prove in many cases; however, the therapist should not believe he or she is "immune" to such a connection. It is important for therapists to be aware of the fact that "any attorney, on receiving negative comments about a couples and family therapist from a disgruntled consumer, could locate numerous causes of action that would potentially apply to the consumer's expressed problem" (Woody, 2000, p. 466).

Common Malpractice Claims

According to research, common malpractice claims include misdiagnosis, practicing outside one's area of competence, failure to obtain informed consent for treatment, negligent or improper treatment, physical contact or sexual relations with clients, failure to prevent clients from harming themselves or others, improper release of a hospitalized client, failure to consult another practitioner or refer a client, failure to supervise students or assistants, abandonment of a client, and breach of confidentiality (Stromberg & Dellinger, 1993). Although these are the common malpractice claims, the therapist is not limited to these and should continue to educate himself or herself on common malpractice claims due to financial and psychological consequences of a complaint or malpractice claim.

Consequences of a Complaint or Malpractice Claim

When a complaint or malpractice claim is filed, there may be various financial and psychological consequences for the clinician. To begin, insurance companies often choose the attorney to defend the clinician. This attorney may be ordered to settle a case by the insurance company regardless of the therapist's innocence and the impact this decision may have on the therapist's career. "Some therapists have stated that when they have faced complaints, their professional associations have abandoned them in favor of catering to consumers' interests" (Woody, 2000, p. 463).

A settlement can also damage the therapist's reputation, as many believe that settlement admits guilt, negatively affecting their career. Many therapists are not aware of the fact that after a settlement is made, insurance companies often do not pay for the settlement in full, requiring the therapist to pay a portion of the amount agreed to out of his or her own pocket. Additionally, when a complaint or malpractice claim is made, therapists may have to self-report to a variety of agencies, bringing about added financial consequences, including increases in malpractice insurance rates (Woody, 2000).

If the complaint is brought about before the licensing board, the therapist may often feel he or she has to "prove" the case in order to keep his or her license. This becomes a predicament because very few boards use the "beyond reasonable doubt" standard (Van Horne, 2004). Van Horne (2004) also claimed that it may cause a therapist to be extremely anxious to know that the board's evidence may only need to be slightly greater for the decision to be made in opposition to the therapist.

Not only does a complaint or malpractice claim have financial consequences, but there may also be psychological costs for the therapist. "A complaint about a therapist's professional conduct is an assault on the inner core of the therapist's self-esteem" (Woody, 2000, p. 467). The types of psychological consequences the therapist may experience include depression, tension, anger, and symptoms of physical illness (Woody, 2000). It could also be argued that the therapist may experience a great amount of anxiety while going through this process, which is extremely stressful.

As noted earlier in the discussion of financial consequences, the therapist's reputation can be damaged when a complaint or malpractice claim is made. This damage to one's reputation can have significant psychological consequences. Woody (2000) also noted that there could be adverse effects on marital and familial relations, career motivation, and general satisfaction with life. There appears to be a "snowball" effect when it comes to these consequences. As the therapist goes through the experience of having a complaint or claim made against him or her, this may cause overwhelming damage to his or her relationships or marriage.

Malpractice Prevention

Although there is the possibility a therapist will never have a complaint or malpractice claim brought against him or her, it is important that the therapist carries out risk management strategies. This includes measures taken to reduce a risk of liability regarding ethical charges from a state licensing board and a malpractice suit (Knapp, 1997).

Kennedy, Vandehey, Norman, and Diekhoff (2003) gave several reasons why mental health professionals should be concerned about risk-management behaviors. These include the amount of stress that comes with a complaint or a malpractice suit; the amount of time and money consumed by being involved in a malpractice complaint or suit; the restrictions possibly placed on a therapist per an ethics committee or state board in the form of supervision or monitoring of cases; increased costs or loss of malpractice insurance; possible loss of income or possible damage to the therapist's reputation.

In addition to these, Bennett, Bryant, VandenBos, and Greenwood (1990) stated that malpractice claims do not only arise against dishonorable practitioners but also against those who are quite honorable. The honorable practitioner is at risk of having a claim brought against him or her when a window of vulnerability to malpractice is opened as a consequence of either his or her actions or inactions. There are many things a therapist can do to reduce his or her chances of becoming involved in a malpractice suit.

Jobes and Berman (1993) propose that risk management that would decrease the possibility of a malpractice claim involves the awareness of central issues related to foreseeability and reasonable care. Montgomery et al. (1999) stated that one of the most important components to risk management is insurance coverage. They reported that almost three-fourths of their entire sample currently obtains insurance. Although this is a majority of the sample, it seems that more therapists would purchase insurance in response to the various consequences they can face when having a complaint or malpractice claim against them.

Kennedy et al. (2003) also provided recommendations for risk-management practices. They believe that it is useful to do the following:

- Attend risk-management workshops regularly to remain up to date.
- Use treatment contracts with clients explaining standards of practice, fees, confidentiality, and so forth.

- Develop policies and procedures for suicide assessment, and incorporate these into each intake session.
- Assign a diagnosis, and make note of it in the client's file as well as on the insurance billing form, as approximately 7% of complaints being processed by the American Psychological Association (APA) are insurance and fee problems.
- Keep detailed and thorough notes regarding diagnosis, content of sessions, assessments, reason for treatment, and any changes in prognosis.
- Review every client's file often.
- Contact a client who has failed to appear for an appointment or who suddenly terminates therapy and document attempts to contact the client.
- Document reasons for terminations.
- Identify potential multiple relationships.
- Consult when one has a difficult client.

It would also be imperative for the therapist to obtain an informed consent when necessary, to use release-of-information forms, and to know one's ethical codes (Hecker, 2003).

Summary

The interplay of clinical work with the legal arena occurs in many facets of couple and family therapy. In addition, couple and family therapists are typically regulated by state statutes of which they should have good working knowledge. Confidentiality is the foundation on which therapy is built; privilege is a legal right owned by the client. There are numerous legal exceptions to confidentiality that should be explained to clients prior to treatment. Duty to warn is an important exception to confidentiality; child and elder abuse reporting are also limitations. Therapists must know how to respond to subpoenas in order to protect their clients' privilege and their practice. Being a fact or expert witness may be part of one's professional duty. Additionally, in this litigious era, therapists must be aware of potential legal pitfalls in order to decrease their risks of liability and claims of malpractice. Therapists must not have their practice governed by fears of litigation, but they should have knowledge that informs their couple and family therapy by acting wisely from a legal perspective.

References

American Association for Marriage and Family Therapy (AAMFT). (2001). *AAMFT Code of ethics.* Alexandria, VA: Author.

American Bar Association. (1997). *Gilbert law dictionary.* Orlando, FL: Harcourt Brace and Company.

American Psychological Association. (2006). Strategies for private practitioners coping with subpoenas or compelled testimony for client records or test data. *Professional Psychology: Research and Practice, 37,* 215–222.

Bennett, B. E., Bryant, B. K., VandenBos, G. R., & Greenwood, A. (1990). *Professional liability and risk management.* Washington, DC: American Psychological Association.

Bergeron, L. R., & Gray, B. (2003). Ethical dilemmas of reporting suspected elder abuse. *Social Work, 48*(1), 96–104.

Beyer, K. (2000). First Person: *Jaffee v. Redmond* therapist speaks. *The American Psychoanalyst, 34*(3), 1–4. Retrieved July 4, 2007, from: http://jaffee-redmond.org/articles/beyer.htm.

Boyan, S. M., & Termini, A. M. (2005). *The psychotherapist as parent coordinator in high conflict divorce: Strategies and techniques.* New York: Haworth Press.

Brodsky, S. L. (2004). *Coping with cross-examination and other pathways to effective testimony.* Washington, DC: American Psychological Association.

Brodsky, S. L., & Anderer, S. J. (2000). Serving as an expert witness: Evaluations, subpoenas, and testimony. In F. W. Kaslow (Ed.), *Handbook of couple and family forensics: A sourcebook for mental health and legal professionals* (pp. 491–506). New York: Wiley.

Cobb, R., & Roberson, P. (in press). Ethical considerations for marriage and family therapists and expert testimony. *American Journal of Family Therapy.*

Committee on Professional Practice and Standards. (2003). Legal issues in the professional practice of psychology. *Professional Psychology: Research and Practice, 34,* 595–600.

Daly, R. (2006). Too early to judge impact of precedent-setting ruling. *Psychiatric News, 41*(12), 13.

DeBell, C., & Jones, R. D. (1997). Privileged communication at last? An overview of *Jaffee v. Redmond. Professional Psychology: Research and Practice, 28,* 559–566.

Fritchman, S. C. K. (2007). Ethics: Essential knowledge for today's counseling, mental health, and healthcare professionals. Workshop conducted by CMI Education Institute, Indianapolis, IN.

Glosoff, H. L., Herlihy, S., Herlihy, B., & Spence, B. (1997). Privileged communication in the psychologist–client relationship. *Professional Psychology: Research and Practice, 28*(6), 573–581.

Gottlieb, M. C. (2000). Consulting and collaborating with attorneys. In F. W. Kaslow (Ed.), *Handbook of couple and family forensics: A sourcebook for mental health and legal professionals* (pp. 491–506). New York: Wiley.

GPO Access (n.d.) Electronic code of federal regulations: Child Abuse Prevention and Treatment Act. Retrieved October 20, 2008, from: http://ecfr.gpoaccess.gov/cgi/t/text/text-idx?c=ecfr&sid=a17fed40d7054b262a214ed6dfc3a673&rgn=div5&view=text&node=45:4.1.2.5.15&idno=45.

Hecker, L. L. (2003). Ethical, legal, and professional issues in marriage and family therapy. In L. L. Hecker & J. L. Wetchler (Eds.), *An introduction to marriage and family therapy,* (pp. 493–537). Binghamton, NY: Hawthorne Press.

Houston-Vega, Mary Kay, Nuehring, Elane, M. & Daguio, Elisabeth, R. (1997). *Prudent practice: A guide for managing malpractice risk.* Washington, DC: National Association of Social Workers.

Jobes, D. A., & Berman, A. L. (1993). Suicide and malpractice liability: Assessing and revising policies, procedures, and practice in outpatient settings. *Professional Psychology: Research and Practice, 24,* 91–99.

Jogerst, G. J., Daly, J. M., Brinig, M. F., Dawson, J. D., Schmuch, G. A., & Ingram, J. G. (2003). Domestic elder abuse and the law. *American Journal of Public Health, 93*(12), 2131–2136.

Kennedy, P. F., Vandehey, M., Norman, W. B., & Diekhoff, G. M. (2003). Recommendations for risk-management practices. *Professional Psychology: Research and Practice, 34,* 309–311.

Knapp, S. (1997). Professional liability and risk management in an era of managed care. In D. T. Marsh & R. D. Magee (Eds.), *Ethical and legal issues in professional practice with families* (pp. 271–288). New York: Wiley.

Montgomery, L. M., Cupit, B. E., & Wimberley, T. K. (1999). Complaints, malpractice, and risk management: Professional issues and personal experiences. *Professional Psychology: Research and Practice, 30,* 402–410.

Mosher, P. W., & Swire, P. P. (2002). The ethical and legal implications of *Jaffee v. Redmond* and the HIPAA Medical Privacy Rule for Psychotherapy and General Psychiatry. *Psychiatric Clinics of North America, 25,* 575–584. Retrieved October 10, 2008, from: http://jaffee-redmond.org/articles/mosherswire.pdf.

Small, M. A., Lyons, P. M. Jr., & Guy, L. S. (2002). Liability issues in child abuse and neglect reporting statutes. *Professional Psychology: Research and Practice, 33,* 13–18.

Stromberg, C., & Dellinger, A. (1993). A legal update on malpractice and other professional liability. *The Psychologist's Legal Update, 3,* 3–15.

Tarasoff v. Regents of the University of California, 17 Cal. 3d 425 (1976).

The Federal Psychotherapist–Patient Privilege (nd). Retrieved October 18, 2008, from: http://jaffee-redmond.org/.

Van Horne, B. A. (2004). Psychology licensing board disciplinary actions: The realities. *Professional Psychology: Research and Practice, 35,* 170–178.

Welfel, E. R., Danzinger, P. R., & Santoro, S. (2000). Mandated reporting of abuse/maltreatment of older adults: A primer for counselors. *Journal of Counseling and Development, 78,* 284–292.

Woody, R. H. (2000). Professional ethics, regulatory licensing, and malpractice complaints. In F. W. Kaslow (Ed.), *Handbook of couple and family forensics: A sourcebook for mental health and legal professionals* (pp. 461–474). New York: Wiley.

4

Ethics in Therapy With Children in Families

Lorna L. Hecker and Catherine Ford Sori

Elisa Madison and her children, David, age 13, Matt, age 8, and Mitzy, age 5, attend an intake session with Ms. Tuttle, a licensed marriage and family therapist. The family appears to be underorganized and arrives late to session. At the intake, Ms. Madison discusses that the reason they are there is that Matt was diagnosed with attention deficit disorder (ADD). Matt interrupts to say it is actually attention deficit/hyperactivity disorder (ADHD). The school referred them because of Matt's continued disruptions at school. Ms. Madison is refusing to medicate Matt for the ADHD, and the school is at a loss of how to deal with Matt. Matt is failing several of his subjects, but the school also appears not to be following his IEP (Individualized Education Plan). Ms. Madison appears unsure of how to navigate the school system and get the help she needs on Matt's behalf. David appears sullen and withdrawn during the session. Mitzy often tries to capture the therapist's attention by dancing throughout the session.

Who is the client in this scenario? Is it Matt, all the children, or the family unit? What impact will Matt's diagnosis have on him? How was he diagnosed? How does the therapist work successfully with the parent, the child, and the school system? What does the therapist do regarding the issue of empirical evidence in the treatment of ADHD, conflicting values, and medication and the treatment of Matt's ADHD? If the therapist focuses on Matt, what happens to the needs of the other children or of the family unit?

In family therapy, it is often difficult to balance the needs of individuals with those of the family (see discussion in Bailey & Sori, 2000; Sori, Dermer, & Wesolowski, 2006). That is even more difficult when some voices are those of minors. What is distinct in family therapy and child therapy is that children are seldom voluntary clients (Berg & Steiner, 2003). A child is brought for therapy at the request of the parents, school, clergy, the courts, or other sources involved in the child's life. Children do not have the same cognitive capacities as adults, so treatment types and agendas differ from adult clients. Diagnostic labels can affect how the child is treated and can even shape how the child is viewed into adulthood.

There are potentially conflicting guidelines regarding various laws and regulations, ethical guidelines and professional standards, and the ethical conundrum of balancing family versus individual needs (Keller, 1999, p. 119). Therapists who must make decisions about child welfare inevitably rely on a web of views, values, and morality. The question is *whose* values and morality should guide decisions regarding children's best interests? This decision making must take into account the values, beliefs, and socio-cultural context of all the stakeholders in the treatment dilemma (Hill, Glaser, & Harden, 1995; Keller, 1999), though it is ultimately the parents who make the majority of the choices for the child based on those values (Buchanan & Brock, 1989).

Who Is the client?

Therapists who work with children can encounter challenges in determin-ing the identity of the client (Koocher & Keith-Spiegel, 1990). When par-ents bring a child to therapy, the therapist must evaluate the extent of a child's individual problem versus the problem arising from issues within the family system. The treatment unit must then be identified. What deci-sion rules are made and for who is involved in therapy? Families can be part of a child's problem and will likely be part of the solution to the prob-lem. Yet a child may need to have the sanctuary of individual therapy in order to find relief from symptoms. See Sori, Dermer, and Wesolowski (2006) for a more in-depth discussion of this decision-making process.

The choice of therapeutic goals can reflect the conflict therapists have in identifying who the client is. Is the therapist guided by his or her own goals, the child's goals, or the parents' goals for the child (Koocher & Keith-Spiegel, 1990)? If the child has no stated goals, does treatment con-tinue? When and how are the parents and family integrated into treat-ment? How does the therapist avoid labeling the child, or aiding a family in scapegoating the child as an "identified patient?" There is a struggle to maintain integrity in the treatment of the family as well as in the treat-ment of a child who may be at risk (Keller, 1999). Split loyalties may occur when the therapist faces the need to balance the interests of the family and manage the risk of harm to the child or children (Keller, 1999, p. 118).

When external agencies are involved, such as the courts or child protection services, the loyalty concerns may be even more exaggerated.

Likewise, the exclusion of children from therapy can be problematic. One study that explored children's views of family sessions found that although often excluded, children overwhelmingly wanted to participate in family sessions, *even when they were not the focus of treatment* (Stith, Rosen, McCollum, Coleman, & Herman, 1996). Another study found that even when children were physically present in therapy, they were not actively engaged in therapy, and they spoke only 3.5% of the total words spoken (Cederborg, 1997). Unfortunately, children are largely excluded from family therapy sessions due to a large degree to the therapist's lack of comfort with children, and the therapist's inadequate training in child-focused family therapy (Johnson & Thomas, 1999; Korner & Brown, 1990). Therapists have an ethical responsibility to obtain the necessary training to successfully engage and treat children in a family context (Sori, 2006; Sori & Hecker, 2006; Sori & Sprenkle, 2004).

Determining the client treatment unit has ripple effects throughout treatment and case management. Assessments must include whether to treat from an individual child perspective or from a family perspective. Assessment instruments, treatment modality, treatment interventions, and diagnostic labeling vary depending upon your perspective with regard to whom to treat; the child, the family system, the parental executive system, and various iterations all change the course of treatment and record keeping. Some recommend a multimodal approach that assesses and may treat several or all of these components of the family (including individuals), based on the needs of the clients (see Bailey & Sori, 2000; Sori, Dermer, & Wesolowski, 2006). Labeling a child can have lifelong consequences, and therapist competency and conceptualization of the case can have long-term consequences.

Conversely, family systems therapists often advocate seeing the entire family and may even believe that seeing a child or adolescent alone, depending upon their theoretical orientation, is countertherapeutic. Many child problems can be alleviated by family therapy, given that symptoms may arise as a function of family system dynamics. However, children can remain symptomatic even after family therapy has been a success (Sori, Dermer, & Wesolowski, 2006; Wachtel, 1991). Even one's treatment modality can bring unique ethical and clinical concerns. For example, in the 1996 Fort Bragg Evaluation Project (Helfinger, Nixon, & Hamner,

1999), the majority of disclosures of suicide ideation were revealed only when therapists saw children individually without their parents. In the Fort Bragg project, 84% of suicidal intent by children or adolescents was disclosed by the child or adolescent with the interviewer *when the parent was not present.*

Consent to Treatment

When working with minors, depending upon state law, parental consent is typically needed in order to commence treatment. Generally, either parent has the right to obtain mental health treatment for their child. However, it is strongly recommended to get consent to treat from both parents (Koocher & Keith-Spiegel, 1990) in order to avoid any potential pitfalls. There are several drawbacks to not including both parents in the treatment of a minor. First, generally when both parents are helping to institute modifications in the child's life, change is more likely to occur. Second, if the therapist fears the parents may disagree about consent, he or she can quickly detriangle from potential conflict by requiring both parents to sign the treatment consent.

In the event of divorce or custody issues, the (legal) custodial parent may bring the child to therapy without the other parent's consent. If a couple is not yet divorced, joint custody is assumed, and unless stated otherwise in the provisional divorce decree, either parent may present the child for therapy. It is recommended that the therapist ask the parent to bring a copy of the most recent divorce or custody decree, or a provisional order if the couple is not yet divorced. A call to the client's attorney can confirm that the copy presented to the therapist is the most recent order. However, therapists must first obtain a signed, written release before contacting the client's attorney. A therapist is wise to include the alternate parent in treatment; it makes sense clinically, and inevitably if one does not, in short order the therapist may risk receiving an angry phone call demanding to know why the parent was not contacted regarding his or her child receiving services.

Minors in many states can consent for contraceptive services, prenatal care, as well as testing and treatment for sexually transmitted diseases (American Civil Liberties Union [ACLU], 2003). Minors' access to mental health outpatient treatment varies from state to state (for a summary, see *The Guttmacher Report on Public Policy*, 2000). In terms of outpatient mental health treatment, children may be seen without parental consent when the child presents with an emergency (e.g., suicide, homicide) or when it would be in the minor's best interest, such as in cases of abuse, neglect, or endangerment. When minors receive treatment for these legally obtained exceptions to parental consent, the records are kept confidential from parents. However, if a child is not seen under one of these exceptions, parents are generally privy to the records.

An exception to parental consent is when the minor is emancipated. *Emancipated minors* are those who are at least 14 and under 18. Children who voluntarily live apart from parents or guardians and support themselves can give consent to their own therapy treatment. Being on active duty in the armed forces or married also constitutes an emancipated minor (Arroyo, 2001, p. 14). An unemancipated minor is a person who has not reached the age of majority, which in all states but four, is 18. In Alabama and Nebraska, the age of majority is 19. In Pennsylvania and Mississippi, the age of majority is 21 (though in Mississippi the age of consent for health care is 18) (ACLU, 2003).

Mature minors are children who are believed to be capable of giving informed consent for therapy treatment and to be able to authorize the release of confidential information (Bartlett, 1996; Morrissey, Hofman, & Thrope, 1986). The term *mature minor* is generally applied to children over the age of 16 (Lawrence & Kurpius, 2000), but the age can vary as it is defined by state statute (Sori & Hecker, 2006, p. 168).

Although some states regulate who can give consent to treatment, children's rights to consent to treatment are largely ignored. However, research indicates that minors may be capable of providing it (Hall & Lin, 1995). A child's lack of consent can seriously impair the therapeutic relationship and inhibit therapy's effectiveness (Levine, Anderson, Ferretti, & Steinberg, 1993). The child's development of self-determination is largely nonexistent. Therapists must mediate between the best interests of the child and the intention of the parents, which is sometimes played out in the courtroom (Keith-Spiegel & Koocher, 1985).

A child should be provided with the option to have some decisional influence in therapy, whenever possible. This gives the child some control in therapy and can therapeutically increase the child's capacity for self-determination (Levine et al., 1993). Minors may be able to give *assent* to treatment (Lawrence & Kurpius, 2000). DeKraai and Sales (1991) defined assent as "affirmative agreement by a youth to participate even though the youth lacks the legal capacity to consent, and is generally required when youths are determined incapable of providing consent" (p. 855). Generally, the social science literature states that the decision-making process of children over the age of 13 is virtually indistinguishable from adults with regard to medical procedures (Tremper & Kelly, 1987). Yet even young children can make decisions to contribute to their own welfare and treatment. Margolin (1982) suggests a child over the age of 7 provide assent. The therapist's language in explaining assent should be appropriate to the client's level of understanding.

Despite the virtuous intentions of assent, none of the literature reviewed provided suggestions for placating a child who refuses to provide assent. In such a case, the clinician may be deemed untrustworthy by the client, as she or he will be required to continue in therapy despite dissent. This dilemma in itself raises ethical questions. The therapist must balance the needs of the child, the wishes and needs of the parents, and the law. The courts have largely placed responsibility upon the mental health professionals to mediate between the best interest of the child and the intentions of the parents (Keith-Spiegel & Koocher, 1985). In these cases where treatment is mandatory, therapists may work collaboratively with young clients to identify what has to happen for them to not have to attend therapy.

Minors and Confidentiality and Privilege

As covered in Chapter 2, *confidentiality* is the ethical obligation to keep a client's personal information in therapy private. State statutes establish *privilege*, which is a client's legal right not to have the information he or she reveals in therapy disclosed in legal proceedings. Not every state grants client privilege. When privilege is established by state statute, minors are often not covered by privilege statutes. Reid (1999) noted that some states grant privilege for particular issues to minors who are 16 or older. Roberts and Dyer (2004) noted that "Even when a state statute allows for minors to consent to alcohol, drug, or outpatient mental health treatment, minors may not possess the right to authorize the release of information to third parties other than their guardians" (p. 123).

When a minor is seen in therapy, parents typically have the right to be informed of the child's treatment, depending upon state law. In keeping with good treatment, it is recommended that, whenever possible, parents be integrated into the treatment in order to transfer changes made in therapy into the child's home. Therapists enhance decisional rights of all clients when they allow the clients to make decisions about privacy in treatment when seeing families. If a child is to be seen alone, apart from his or her family, it is best to engage all members in a discussion of how to preserve confidentiality when seeing the child or adolescent individually.

There are six possible ways that confidentiality can be defined. It is recommended that this process be defined and agreed upon in writing before the commencement of therapy. Hendrix (1991) made four recommendations, and Sori and Hecker (2006) offer two additional recommendations. These include: *complete confidentiality, limited confidentiality, informed forced consent, no guarantee of confidentiality* (Hendrix, 1991), *mutual agreement regarding confidentiality, and a "best interests" agreement* (Sori & Hecker, 2006). See Table 4.1 for a description of each of these agreements along with their advantages and disadvantages. Complete confidentiality affords the minor privacy about everything besides that which is prohibited by law. In limited confidentiality, the minor knows ahead of time what the topics are that will be discussed with parents. In informed forced consent, the child has no voice in what is told to his or her parents, but is told ahead of time what will be told, and when parents will be told. When there is no guarantee of confidentiality, this must be explained to the minor at the outset of therapy. In mutually agreed upon confidentiality, the therapist and parents mutually agree on what topics will be shared with parents and what topics are off limit. In the "best interests" agreement, parents place faith in the therapist to share with them what the therapist deems to be in the best interest of the child. Information should be shared with parents when it is determined that it is in the best interests of the child to do so (Roberts & Dyer, 2004). However, "best interests" is open to interpretation. It is agreed upon that confidentiality will be maintained unless the therapist believes that the child is being harmed in some way if the information shared in therapy is not revealed to his or her parents.

Mrs. Smith brought her 9-year-old son, Tommy, to Dr. Ray because she and Tommy's father were going through a divorce, and she was concerned about the effects of the divorce on Tommy. Mrs. Smith wanted Dr. Ray to see Tommy so Tommy would have a "neutral place" to discuss the divorce, and wanted to make sure Tommy was coping adequately with the family changes. Dr. Ray explained to Tommy that what would be said in their sessions together would be shared just between them, unless there was an emergency or something very important about which his mother or father needed to know. Tommy agreed and several sessions were held where Tommy expressed both positive and negative feelings about both of his parents and the difficulties of the divorce. A few months later, Mrs. Smith called Dr. Ray requesting a copy of Tommy's records for the custody hearing. Dr. Ray was in a difficult spot, because legally in their state, Mrs. Smith had access to Tommy's records, but ethically, he had promised Tommy confidentiality.

TABLE 4.1   Types of Confidentiality Agreements Between Therapist, Children, and the Children's Parent(s)

Type of Confidentiality	What Is Shared With Parents	Advantages	Disadvantages
Complete confidentiality[a]	Only information mandated by law is shared	Child may divulge more personal information in therapy without fear of reprisal	Therapist may learn information that he or she believes is important for parents to know (e.g., pregnancy, substance abuse) but loses maneuverability
Limited confidentiality[a]	Any information *may* be shared with parents, and the child waives his or her right to know what will be revealed to parents at the onset of counseling	The therapist has enhanced maneuverability in therapy and can aid the parents in helping the child with risky or potentially harmful situations	The child may feel forced into this agreement and will be less likely to divulge important information to the therapist
Informed forced consent[a]	Child is informed before therapist discloses information to parents; child has no voice in decisions regarding disclosure	Therapist has complete maneuverability and a chance to explain the importance of divulging the information to the child; parents can assist the child with risky or potentially harmful situation	The child has no sense of agency in this situation; the child will be less likely to divulge important information to the therapist
No guarantee of confidentiality[a]	Any information or all information may be shared	Therapist has complete maneuverability to handle information as he or she sees fit	The child has no sense of agency in this situation and may be much less likely to divulge important information to the therapist

TABLE 4.1   Types of Confidentiality Agreements Between Therapist, Children, and the Children's Parent(s) (continued)

Type of Confidentiality	What Is Shared With Parents	Advantages	Disadvantages
Mutually agreed upon confidentiality	Only information the therapist, parents, and child agree upon at the onset of therapy is shared (information mandated by law is automatically included)	Both parents and child have a sense of agency in this agreement; child knows ahead of time what will be shared with parents	There may be information divulged outside of the scope of what is agreed upon that the therapist may be uncomfortable keeping from the parents
"Best Interests" confidentiality	The therapist shares only what he or she considers to be in the "best interests" of the child to be shared with regard to health, welfare, or significant relationships	The parents and child may be unclear about what will be held confidential and what will be shared	The child may not trust that the therapist has his or her best interests in mind, or may be unclear what "best interests" may include, so divulging private information may be slowed or halted

[a]Adapted from Hendrix, D. H. (1991). Ethics and intrafamily confidentiality in counseling with children. *Journal of Mental Health Counseling, 13*(3), 323–333.

According to Health Insurance Portability and Accountability Act of 1996 (HIPAA) regulations, parents have access to children's health information, unless state law is more rigorous in protecting the child's information (Chaikind et al., 2003). If the information is not protected, there may be cases where, ethically, a therapist may wish to advocate for a child's right to privacy of some therapy information, depending upon the nature of the information disclosed. This example is not uncommon and brings ethical issues to the forefront when a parent indicates to a therapist that he or she wants his or her child to be able to discuss feelings about a divorce in therapy on neutral ground. It is often therapeutic to allow a child to disengage from parental conflict or to have a forum to discuss issues that he or she feels may burden a parent. It would not be unusual in such a situation for a child to unburden any negative feelings about the divorce or the behavior of one or both parents.

Therapists have a responsibility, in conjunction with the child's needs and wishes, to inform the parents of ways in which they may be helpful with the child's transition with respect to the divorce. Parents may, however, subsequently ask for access to the child's therapy records. Intentions for this action vary: A parent may genuinely want to know all he or she can about the child to help the child, or the parent may be excessively intrusive in the child's life, or the parent may request copies of the records to "prove" in a custody evaluation or court proceeding that he or she has been a good parent to the child and has accessed professional services to alleviate distress. In more difficult situations, the parent may be requesting records to "show" the court how the other parent has negatively affected the child. The therapist is now in the crux of a legal and ethical conundrum. Legally, the parent has access to the child's therapy records, but ethically both the parent and the therapist have indicated to the child that therapy is to be a neutral environment, free from reprisals and conflict. It would be unethical to make this promise and subsequently release records for others to review. The therapist needs to advocate for child privacy in these and other similar situations. Just because a client is a minor, it does not mean that he or she loses the right to privacy, especially when adults have promised this privacy. In some cases, parents who request records are satisfied with a written statement from the therapist that therapy has been sought for the child, and the statement may include dates of service. In other cases, parents may wish the records to be released to the court, despite the therapist's objections. It should not be assumed that a child can freely give assent to release records in this type of pressured situation. If need be, therapists can petition the judge not to release the records, and explain to the court or custody evaluator the need to protect the child's privacy in situations such as these. Mainly, however, the courts are more interested in the discovery process and do not side with the therapist's view in these cases.

One potential way to alleviate this situation is to add a statement to one's informed consent form, such as the following: "It is important that you agree not to call me as a witness or to attempt to subpoena records in the event you choose to pursue a divorce. Although a judge may overrule this agreement and issue a court order for information, your signature below reflects your agreement not to call me as a witness or attempt to subpoena therapeutic records." This type of statement is controversial because at times therapists are needed in the legal arena in order to protect children. An alternative is to have a separate informed consent for clients who are intending to utilize the therapist in legal proceedings, so that expectations, confidentiality issues, and payment for services can be clearly detailed. (It is recommended that all forms be reviewed by the therapist's attorney prior to use.)

Custody Issues

Presently, the terms *custody* and *visitation* are being replaced with more amicable terms such as *parenting agreements* and *parenting time*. The outdated legal terms *physical custody* and *legal custody* hopefully will follow. According to Hecker and Sori (2006), "*physical custody* refers to the residence and daily care of the child. *Legal custody* refers to who makes decisions for the child such as education, health care and religious training" (p. 181). Noncustodial parents are granted *visitation*, though many courts now use the preferable term *parenting time*.

The following is a list of custody configurations that may occur (Hecker & Sori, 2006, p. 181):

1. Sole legal custody with one parent; sole physical custody with the same parent
2. Joint legal custody with both parents; sole physical custody with one parent
3. Joint legal and joint physical custody
4. Sole legal custody with one parent; joint physical custody with both parents
5. Sole legal custody with one parent; sole physical custody with the other parent

The most common parenting arrangement is joint legal and sole physical custody. One unconventional arrangement is referred to as *split custody*, which occurs when the children are split up between two homes. Each parent has custody of one or more children. According to Hodges (1991), approximately 5% of parents use a split custody arrangement.

Issues Related to Custody Evaluations and Custody Decisions

Custody evaluations aid judges in deciding which parent should gain custody. They are typically conducted by psychologists or other mental health professionals (Hecker & Sori, 2006). Custody evaluation guidelines have been prepared by the American Psychological Association (APA, 1994), and they "include a focus on parenting capacity, the psychological and developmental needs of the child, and the resulting fit between the parent and child" (Hecker & Sori, 2006, p. 182). Those who wish to provide custody evaluations must receive specialized training. Most judges incorporate custody evaluations as one criterion in determining custody. However, some use the custody evaluation as the principal criteria in making decisions regarding child custody issues. If a therapist is providing therapy to a family, or a family member, it is considered unethical to provide the family with the custody evaluation (Sori & Hecker, 2006).

Sometimes a therapist may be contacted by a custody evaluator or be subpoenaed to testify as a witness in a custody hearing (Sori & Hecker, 2006). This puts therapists who work with children and their parents in a different type of working relationship than what was originally contracted. Because therapy is to aid the family in increasing their functioning and is concerned with the child's best interests, how is the therapy process changed when parents think they may influence the therapist's testimony? If a therapist does not want to go to court (or one of the parents forbids it based on invoking privilege), is the therapist denying the court relevant information that may have a direct bearing on the case at hand? Might a child be done a disservice if his or her therapist does not want to be involved in the custody considerations? If the therapist has promised the child confidentiality, but then a judge orders the therapist to court, what does one then tell the child? In addition, what if one parent wishes for the therapist to release information to the court, but the other parent prohibits the therapist from releasing information? Therapists are advised to have the consultation services of a reputable attorney available in the event any such issues arise.

Because of the reliance on psychological testing, family therapists have tended not to perform custody evaluations. Others use a team approach that includes either having a psychologist as part of the team or contracting with a psychologist for the testing and interpretation used as part of the evaluation. Yet, family therapists may be missing the opportunity to provide a service that they are uniquely qualified to offer.

A child or family therapist should remember the limitations of what they can attest to as a *fact witness*. A fact witness (as opposed to expert witnesses) can only testify to what he or she has witnessed in therapy sessions. It is important to remember that the treating therapist has not done a custody evaluation and should *never give a recommendation for custody based on having been a therapist in the case*. This is up to the custody evaluator, who has gathered information from multiple sources. To form a custody decision based simply on therapy sessions would result in the therapist's conduct falling significantly below "the appropriate standard of care," thus opening up the therapist to a lawsuit. One of the most litigious areas in therapy practice involves issues emanating from child custody conflicts.

In addition, when therapists have been seeing parents prior to their decision to divorce, the therapist may be of great help in aiding the couple in establishing a cooperative parenting relationship with each other. Yet, therapists must be careful not to give legal advice, because this is clearly outside of the therapist's "scope of practice." Therapists need to know when to refer a client to his or her attorney. Although many states are moving toward providing families with *parenting arrangements* instead of *custody,* it is naïve to think that the legal system has strayed far from the adversarial system on which it was built. This system may give the therapist quite a challenge to keep the couple in a collegial stance with regard to parenting arrangements. Chapter 12, *Ethics, Legal, and Professional Issues in Mediation and Parent Coordination,* explores options such as mediation and parent coordination, which are promising alternatives.

If a child's interests diverge significantly from that of the parents' interests, a *guardian ad litem* may be appointed by the court. A guardian ad litem may be an attorney, therapist, or another mental health professional, who is, at times, defined by state law. Guardians ad litem are not always necessary, even when there are conflictual divorces. They are appointed only if one or both parents do not have the child's best interest in mind. If couples are conflictual but keep the majority of their conflict from the child, and both have the child's best interests in mind, a guardian ad litem is typically not needed.

Child Maltreatment

All 50 states have some sort of reporting requirement following the 1974 creation of the Child Abuse Prevention and Treatment Act. Reporting laws have been adopted under the authority of *parent's patriae.* Parent's patriae is the state's right to assume the role of a parent when a child is abused or neglected. Therapists must consult state statutes regarding reporting abuse or neglect, as they differ in terms, who is a mandatory reporter, as well as how and under what conditions reports must be filed (Wagner, 2003). Parents generally may care for their children without interference from the state, as long as their parenting behavior falls within social norms and is not outside of state law. What is considered abuse and neglect varies from state to state (Stein, 1998). Therapists working with children are only to *report* suspected abuse, not investigate it. Child protection agencies and law enforcement are required to investigate reported allegations or suspicions. In a 1993 federally funded study entitled the *National Incidence Study by the Department of Health and Human Services* (n.d.), it was found that only about one-third of the cases known to professionals were reported to child protective agencies. There is no statute of limitations on reporting child sexual abuse; physical abuse must be reported within 2 years (Berman, 1997).

Definitions of child abuse include physical abuse, sexual abuse, and neglect, but what become ethical quagmires for some therapists include the less obvious forms of abuse. These include the following less obvious forms of abuse listed by the *National Incidence Study of the Department of Health and Human Services* (n.d.):

- Extreme or habitual verbal abuse or other overtly hostile, rejecting, or punitive treatment.
- Abandonment or other refusal to maintain custody, such as desertion, expulsion from home, or refusal to accept custody of a returned runaway.
- Permitting of or encouragement of chronic maladaptive behavior, such as truancy, delinquency, serious drug or alcohol abuse, and so on; "permitted" means that the child's caregiver had reason to be aware of the existence and seriousness of the problem (such as by having been informed of previous incidents), but made no reasonable attempt to prevent further occurrences.
- Refusal to allow needed treatment for a professionally diagnosed physical, educational, emotional, or behavioral problem, or failure to follow the advice of a competent professional who recommended that the caregiver obtain or provide the child with such treatment, if the child's primary caregiver was physically and financially able to do so.
- Failure to seek or unwarranted delay in seeking competent medical care for a serious injury, illness, or impairment, if the need for professional care should have been apparent to a responsible caregiver without special medical training.
- Consistent or extreme inattention to the child's physical or emotional needs, including needs for food, clothing, supervision, safety, affection, and reasonably hygienic living conditions, if the child's primary caregivers were physically and financially able to provide the needed care.
- Failure to register or enroll the child in school (or homeschool), as required by state law.

Some states also require that abuse of emancipated minors be reported, but others do not. In addition, there are legal and ethical issues around whether or not a fetus is considered a person with regard to reporting abuse or neglect (Leslie, 2003). Some states require written reports; others require a telephone report, or both. In spite of mandatory reporting laws, some therapists hesitate to report (Beck and Ogloff, 1995), presumably for fear of losing the therapeutic alliance with clients.

Use of Touch in Therapy

It is natural to embrace children; hugs can be therapeutic and rewarding in and of themselves. In fact, it is difficult to counsel children without using some form of touch, even if it only involves helping or restraining a child (see McNeil-Haber, 2004). Using touch with children in therapy, however, can be fraught with ethical issues. Does the parent approve of the touch? Has the child had any negative experiences with touch from an adult? Ethical and professional issues that emanate from touch include the following:

- *Boundaries*—How does the therapist know when he or she is broaching improper boundaries, compared to increasing intimacy by providing therapeutic touch?
- *Gender*—Cross-gender touch may be viewed more as a boundary violation than same-gender touch.
- *Client Background*—Children who have been abused may interpret touch much differently than those who have not been abused. The therapist certainly does not want to create further damage to a child who may see touch as threatening.
- *Consent*—The therapist should respect children's boundaries as they do adult boundaries, and ask if he or she may hug or touch a child. In addition, it is wise to ask the parent's position on therapeutic touch.
- *Therapist Self-Protection*—In this litigious era, there are times when the therapist must think about how the touch would be interpreted in a legal arena.
- *Power Differentials*—The therapist must be cognizant of the power differentials with children and be sure to guard against exploitation of any sort.

Although therapist-initiated touch appears to be widespread, therapists should carefully consider the following before initiating any touch with children (see McNeil-Haber, 2004):

- How might the child benefit from being touched? For example, might touch help to calm the child, serve as reinforcement, or be an expression of acceptance?
- How might this particular child interpret being touched? Would this child be empowered enough to comment?
- Has this child experienced any abuse or safety issues that might make touch feel inappropriate or alarming?

Before touching a child, therapists should always check themselves to determine whose needs are being served—those of the child or the needs of the therapist (Holub & Lee, 1990). The needs of the child should always be foremost, and therapists should be alert to any countertransference issues that might impair their judgment. It is also important to consider the cultural and ethnic background of the child and family, as there are cultural differences in how touch can be used with children, or as a means of emotional expression (McNeil-Haber, 2004).

Because of the power differential between adults and children, and because we live in a litigious society, touch should be used sparingly with children. A child could have an undisclosed history of abuse that could lead him or her to sexualize or misinterpret any therapist-initiated touch. In working with sexually abused children, therapists must be gentle but firm in setting boundaries regarding inappropriate child-initiated touch (Gil, 2006).

Therapists should discuss the potential use of touch with parents at the outset of therapy, explain when it might occur (e.g., returning a child-initiated hug or to keep a child from harm), and ask permission to use appropriate touch (Sori & Hecker, 2006).

Emergent Issues in Child-Focused Therapy

Just as children grow and develop, so does our knowledge about them. Change is inevitable, and the following section focuses on changes in the context of the child's home environment and changes in the environment of child research.

Summary

Children are almost never voluntary clients in therapy and bring unique ethical issues to the forefront for family therapists to consider. First, the therapist must decide who the client is—the child, or the family unit, or subsystems within the family unit. The family therapist ultimately must decide if family needs are emphasized, or if the individual needs of the child are paramount. Confidentiality concerns are unique when a minor is involved in therapy; minors may be mentally capable of giving consent but not legally capacitated to do so. Children who are unable to give consent may be able to give assent, and the therapist must take special consideration to use language that is accessible to this client population. Because of the power and privilege held by adults over children, the therapist must be ever aware of how children can be hurt by abuse of power by adults, with special attention paid to issues such as child maltreatment and potential issues of oppression. These issues may surface in the therapy room with the simple issue of the use of touch in therapy. Boundaries, a child's history with abuse, consent, and power are all issues to consider in the use of touch in therapy. Children in alternate family forms may also experience discrimination and oppression.

Of special consideration in working with children are custody considerations. Family therapists will want to consider issues of who can give consent to the child's therapy, who has access to records, and making therapy a respite for a child from parental conflict while working with the parents and legal system. These can be difficult issues for family therapists to navigate, but the children placed in these sometimes acrimonious situations have the most to benefit from the services of a child-focused family therapist who can decrease the conflict and increase the functioning of the family system that nurtures the child's development.

The family therapist is well advised to gain specialized training in working with children and to stay current on legal and ethical issues emanating from working with children and their families. Therapists should know their state statutes and have ready access to a knowledgeable attorney.

References

American Civil Liberties Union (ACLU). (2003). Protecting minors' heath information under the federal medical privacy regulations. New York: Author.

American Psychological Association. (1994). Guidelines for child custody evaluations in divorce proceedings. *American Psychologist, 49*(7), 677–680.

Arroyo, W. (2001). Children, adolescents and families. *Ethics primer of the American Psychiatric Association* (pp. 11–22). Washington, DC: American Psychiatric Association. Retrieved September 5, 2008, from: www.psych.org/Departments/EDU/residentmit/ethicsprimer.aspx.

Bailey, C. E., & Sori, C. E. F. (2000). Involving parents in children's therapy. In C. E. Bailey (Ed.), *Children in therapy: Using the family as a resource* (pp. 475–502). New York: W. W. Norton & Company.

Bartlett, E. E. (1996). Protecting the confidentiality of children and adolescents. In J. Lonsdale, S. Powell, & L. Soloman (Eds.), *The Hatherleigh guide to child and adolescent therapy* (pp. 275–290). New York: Hatherleigh Press.

Beck, K. A., & Ogloff, R. P. (1995). Child abuse reporting in British Columbia: Psychologists' knowledge of and compliance with the reporting law. *Professional Psychology: Research and Practice, 26,* 245–251.

Berg, I. K., & Steiner, T. (2003). *Children's solution work.* New York: W. W. Norton & Company.

Berman, P. S. (1997). Ethical issues in child maltreatment. In D. T. Marsh & R. D. Magee (Eds.), *Ethical and legal issues in professional practice with families* (pp. 183–196). New York: John Wiley & Sons.

Buchanan, A. E., & Brock, D. W. (1989). *Deciding for others: The ethics of surrogate decision making.* New York: Cambridge University Press.

Cederborg, A. D. (1997). Young children's participation in family therapy talk. *American Journal of Family Therapy, 25*(1), 28–38.

Chaikind, H. R., Hearne, J., Luke, B., Redhead, S., Stone, J., France, C., et al. (2003). *Health insurance portability and accountability act (HIPAA): Overview and analysis.* Hauppauge, NY: Novinka Books.

DeKraai, M., & Sales, B. (1991). Legal issues in the conduct of child therapy. In T. R. Kratochwill, & R. J. Morris (Eds.), *The practice of child therapy* (2nd ed.), (pp. 441–458). Elmsford, NY: Pergamon.

English, A., & Ford, C. A. (2004). The HIPAA privacy rule and adolescents: Legal questions and clinical challenges. *Perspectives on Sexual and Reproductive Health, 36*(2) (March/April). Retrieved September 5, 2008, from: www.guttmacher.org/pubs/journals/3608004.html.

Gil, E. (2006). *Sand therapy integrated with play therapy: Theory and application.* Training provided by Starbright Training Institute for Child and Family Play Therapy, Fairfax, VA.

Hall, A. S., & Lin, M. -J. (1995). Theory and practice of children's rights: Implications for mental health counselors. *Journal of Mental Health Counseling, 17*(1), 63–80.

Hecker, L. L., & Sori, C. F. (2006). Divorce and stepfamily issues. In C. F. Sori (Ed.), *Engaging children in family therapy: Creative approaches to integrating theory and research in clinical practice* (pp. 177–204). New York: Routledge.

Heflinger, C. A., Nixon, C. T., & Hamner, K. (1999). Handling confidentiality and disclosure in the evaluation of client outcomes in managed mental health services for children and adolescents. *Education and Program Planning, 19*(2), 175–182.

Hendrix, D. H. (1991). Ethics and intrafamily confidentiality in counseling with children. *Journal of Mental Health Counseling, 13*(3), 323–333.

Hill, M., Glaser, K., & Harden, J. (1995). A feminist model for ethical decision making. In E. J. Rave & C. C. Larsen (Eds.), *Ethical decision-making in therapy* (pp. 18–37). New York: The Guilford Press.

Hodges, W. (1991). *Interventions for children of divorce: Custody, access and psychotherapy.* New York: Wiley & Sons.

Holub, E. A., & Lee, S. S. (1990). Therapists' use of nonerotic physical contact: Ethical concerns. *Professional Psychology, Research, and Practice, 21*(2), 115–117.

Johnson, L., & Thomas, V. (1999). Influences on the inclusion of children in family therapy. *Journal of Marital and Family Therapy, 25*(1), 117–123.

Keith-Spiegel, P., & Koocher, G. P. (1985). *Ethics in psychology: Professional standards and cases.* Hillsdale, NJ: Lawrence Erlbaum Associates.

Keller, S. A. (1999). Split loyalties: The conflicting demands of individual treatment goals and parental responsibility. *Women and Therapy, 22*(2), 117–133.

Koocher, G. P., & Keith-Spiegel, P. C. (1990). *Children, ethics, and the law: Professional issues and cases.* Lincoln: University of Nebraska Press.

Korner, S., & Brown, G. (1990). Exclusion of children from family psychotherapy: Family therapists' beliefs and practices. *Journal of Family Psychology, 3*(4), 420–430.

Lawrence, G., & Kurpius, S. E. R. (2000). Legal and ethical issues involved when counseling minors in nonschool settings. *Journal of Counseling and Development, 78,* 130–136.

Leslie, R. S. (2003). Duty to report child abuse. *Family Therapy Magazine, 2*(2), 44–45.

Levine, M., Anderson, E., Ferretti, L., & Steinberg, K. (1993). Legal and ethical issues affecting clinical child psychology. In T. H. Ollendick, & R. J. Prinz (Eds.), *Advances in clinical child psychology: Volume 15* (pp. 81–117). New York: Springer.

Margolin, G. (1982). Ethical and legal considerations in marital and family therapy. *American Psychologist, 37*(7), 788–801.

McNeil-Haber, F. M. (2004) Ethical considerations in the use of nonerotic touch in psychotherapy with children. *Ethics and Behavior, 14*(2), 123–140.

Morrissey, J. M., Hofman, A. D., & Thrope, J. C. (1986). *Consent and confidentiality in the health care of children and adolescents.* New York: The Free Press.

National Incidence Study of the Department of Health and Human Services (n.d.). Definitions of qualifying abuse or neglect. Retrieved September 9, 2008, from: https://www.nis4.org/DefAbuse.asp.

Reid, W. H. (1999). *A clinician's guide to legal issues in psychotherapy: Or proceed with caution.* Phoenix, AZ: Zeig, Tucker & Co.

Roberts, L. W., & Dyer, A. R. (2004). *Ethics in mental health care.* Washington, DC: American Psychiatric.

Sori, C. F. (2006). On counseling children and families: Recommendations from the experts. In C. F. Sori (Ed.), *Engaging children in family therapy: Creative approaches to integrating theory and research in clinical practice* (pp. 3–20). New York: Routledge.

Sori, C. F., Dermer, S., & Wesolowski, G. (2006). Involving children in family counseling and involving parents in children's counseling: Theoretical and practical guidelines. In C. F. Sori (Ed.), *Engaging children in family therapy: Creative approaches to integrating theory and research in clinical practice* (pp. 139–158). New York: Routledge.

Sori, C. F., & Hecker, L. L. (2006). Ethical and legal considerations when counseling children and families. In C. F. Sori (Ed.), *Engaging children in family therapy: Creative approaches to integrating theory and research in clinical practice* (pp. 159–176). New York: Routledge.

Sori, C. F., & Sprenkle, D. H. (2004). Training family therapists to work with children and families: A modified Delphi study. *Journal of Marital and Family Therapy, 30*(4), 479–495.

Stein, T. J. (1998). *Child welfare and the law* (rev. ed.). Washington, DC: CWLA Press.

Stith, S. M., Rosen, K. H., McCollum, E. E., Coleman, J. U., & Herman, S. A. (1996). The voices of children: Preadolescent children's experiences in family therapy. *Journal of Marital and Family Therapy, 22*(1), 69–86.

The Guttmacher Report on Public Policy (2000). Minors and the right to consent to health care, *3*(4), 4–7. Retrieved September 5, 2008, from: www.guttmacher. org/pubs/tgr/03/4/gr030404.html.

Tremper, C. R., & Kelly, M. P. (1987). Mental health rationale for policies fostering minor's autonomy. *International Journal of Law and Psychiatry, 10*, 111–123.

Wachtel, E. F. (1991). How to listen to kids. *Networker, 15*(4), 46–47.

Wagner, W. G. (2003). *Counseling, psychology and children: A multidimensional approach to intervention.* Upper Saddle River, NJ: Pearson Education.

5

Power, Privilege, and Ethics

Jonathyn Piper and Sophia Treyger

Power is a critical concept in making sense of how relationships work (Adams, 2008, p. 105), with the definition of power traditionally emphasizing relational influence and control (Lyness, Haddock, & Zimmerman, 2003). Within the realm of couple and family therapy, the guiding theoretical orientations that have focused on power have been feminist family therapy (Goodrich, Rampage, Ellman, & Halstead, 1988; Luepnitz, 1988; McGoldrick, Anderson, & Walsh, 1989; Walters, Carter, Papp, & Silverstein, 1988) and narrative family therapy (Freedman & Combs, 1996; Freedman, Epston, & Lobovits, 1997; White & Epston, 1990). Feminist family therapy advocates strongly critiqued the field of marriage and family therapy for not taking into account the influence and impact of power within systems, and specifically its impact on women (e.g., Goodrich et al., 1988; Luepnitz, 1988; McGoldrick et al., 1989; Walters et al., 1988). Narrative family therapists have taken a different route, one that offers a theoretical model to incorporate the exploration of power and the influence that such power has had on an individual or system (Freedman & Combs, 1996).

Privilege is defined as situations in which a person of societal advantage or a person who holds power, gains from the disadvantaged persons of the same society.

Power and privilege play complementary roles with one another. Without power differentials in relationships, one would not have the privilege of benefiting from the power. If privilege did not exist in such relationships, then power would be dismantled by the inability to gain advantage. Because of this pattern of interconnectedness, it is often difficult to delineate between the two.

The Pervasiveness of Power and Privilege

Power and privilege imbalances pervade most relationships, if not all of them (DeLozier, 1994; Dolan-Del Vecchio, 1998; Peterson, 1994). According to Peterson (1994), it is futile to dispute the existence of such imbalances within particular relationships. However, it is relevant and necessary to discuss these imbalances within a therapeutic framework in order to discover just how these imbalances impede (DeLozier, 1994; Knox, Burkard, Johnson, Suzuki, & Ponterotto, 2003; Werner-Wilson, Price, Zimmerman, & Murphy, 1997; Willbach, 1989) or, in some cases, foster growth of clients (Ryder & Hepworth, 1990), and how they guide the therapeutic process and outcome (Cardemil & Battle, 2003; de Shazer, 1988; Goldberg & Perry-Jenkins, 2004; Leslie, 1995; Lorion & Parron, 1987; Peterson, 1994).

Furthermore, it is insufficient to discuss power and privilege imbalances only within the confines of a therapist–client relationship (Dolan-Del Vecchio, 1998). It is relevant, therefore, to explore the wider implications of power and privilege imbalances within families (Graham-Bermann & Brescoll, 2000) and society (Dolan-Del Vecchio, 1998) and how broader issues influence the therapeutic process and outcome (Leslie, 1995; Lorion & Parron, 1987).

If the therapist is Caucasian and the clients are African American, power differentials exist at some level. Peggy McIntosh (1998) pointed out, "Whites are taught to think of their lives as morally neutral, normative, and average, and also ideal, so that when we work to benefit others, this is seen as work which will allow 'them' to be more like 'us'" (p. 148).

Power is not just limited to that of white persons. Another type is male power and is defined as when a man influences and controls the existence of a woman, and male privilege is defined as advantages that men gain from women's disadvantages. It is also important to note that men not only perpetuate male power but also fall victim to the limitations that male power and privilege set for them. An aspect that lies inside of the discourses from which male power and privilege emanate is that of men being strong, stoic, and nonemotional. This discourse limits how men are free to relate to their partners, children, and other men.

Power and privilege are not only attributed to physical characteristics that can be viewed externally, such as gender and race. Sexual orientation, an attribute that has nonvisible characteristics, also has power and privilege ramifications. Sexual orientation has recently been brought to the forefront of political and social controversy. Heterosexual power encompasses heterosexual persons having dominance in sociopolitical decisions that affect the quality of life of homosexual persons on many levels. An example of heterosexual power that has been brought to people's attention is the recent creation of laws that ban homosexuals from the same rights that heterosexuals hold. The persons creating such laws— predominately heterosexuals—are exploiting their power to deny others and therefore affecting the quality of homosexuals' lives. "Whereas many groups suffer from prejudice, lesbians, gay men, and bisexuals are particularly disadvantaged because discrimination and intolerance are often openly supported by governmental, religious, and social institutions" (Purcell, Swann, & Herbert, 2003, p. 325).

Another potential example of heterosexual power and privilege is the mere name of *Marriage* and Family Therapy. It is worth exploring the nomenclature of the field with regard to power and privilege. Do couples need to be married to be seen as legitimate? Is there a message transmitted by the dominant majority by the choice of the word *marriage* and family therapy? What does this convey to couples who are not married by choice or cannot be married because of constraints of the law?

Power and privilege are inherent in all interactions, including the therapeutic relationship. The ability to ignore power differentials typically reflects privilege. "The power differential is a given in the therapeutic relationship. It reflects the difference of roles" (Peterson, 1994, p. 65). According to Peterson (1994), there are certain roles ascribed to the therapist, such as caregiver, and to the client, such as care-receiver. As far as codes of ethics are concerned, "… [they] regulate the power differential between therapist and client: that is, they protect clients' vulnerability by prescribing and limiting how we can use our greater power in the relationship" (Peterson, 1994, p. 51).

Ethical Implications of Power and Privilege

In evaluating the theory and practice of family therapy, there is a body of therapists who historically have believed that therapy is inherently a political act, and that it is the responsibility of the therapist to use his or her power position to highlight and eradicate inequalities evident in the relationships presented in therapy (Dolan-Del Vechhio, 1998; Hare-Mustin, 1987; Luepnitz, 1988). If you do nothing to eliminate the status quo, you, in effect, support it (Lyness et al., 2003). In Dolan-Del Vecchio's (1998) critique of white male privilege within family therapy, he urges, "White men need to acknowledge both our responsibility for transforming our own predicaments and, because we are the dominating class, our responsibility for working toward liberation of women, children, and racial and sexual minorities" (p. 167). Dolan-Del Vecchio (1998) believed that only through this awareness can the power hierarchy be dismantled. McIntosh (1998) also believed that power can be relinquished only when groups who have unearned advantage and conferred dominance, such as white male privilege, willingly relinquish their privilege in society. It is not enough to become aware of our privilege; it is necessary for therapists to broach topics of power and privilege, challenge the bestowment of unearned privileges, and take steps to aid in the relinquishment of unearned power *inside* and *outside* of therapy. Power differentials inside therapy include challenging power imbalances in couple and family therapy. In the American Association for Marriage and Family Therapy (AAMFT) *Code of Ethics* (2001), Principle 1.8 states that "marriage and family therapists respect the rights of clients to make decisions and help them understand the consequences of these decisions." Although therapists may challenge client positions, they still must respect the rights of clients to make decisions about their own lives. Clients may choose to remain in the status quo position, even with recognition of the position.

Outside of therapy, activity may include political action on the part of the therapist. In a Delphi study examining family therapists' views of strengths and weaknesses of U.S. families, it was recommended that

> Family therapy can strengthen the context that impinges upon a family's internal life by becoming politically active. Poverty and all of its ramifications is the major threat to family life in decades to come.... Political activity includes challenging the U.S. government to make families a budgetary priority...it includes lobbying for educational, medical, and mental health reforms and for reproductive rights for women. (Stone Fish & Osborn, 1992, p. 414)

Although there is a plethora of power and privilege imbalances that influence ethical dilemmas for therapists, the authors have limited the discussion to imbalances within the therapeutic relationship in reference to gender inequities, gender role ideology and partner abuse, cultural diversity (including race and ethnicity), therapist expertise, and definition of the family. It is insufficient to describe such imbalances as distinct from one another as in, for example, race or gender for an African American woman. Particular imbalances cannot be separated, and they interact to influence the therapeutic relationship (Dolan-Del Vecchio,

1998; Fitzpatrick, Salgado, Suvak, King, & King, 2004; Graham-Bermann & Brescoll, 2000; Leslie, 1995). Though this interaction is recognized, for simplicity's sake, we will divide each power and privilege imbalance individually for analysis.

Gender Inequities

> Marissa and Joe are cofacilitating an anger management group. The participants of the group are predominantly mandated clients who are on probation for domestic violence or violence in general. The therapists are finding over time that the men are tending to blame their arrests on their significant other. They often exclaim that if it wasn't for something she did, they would not have had to hit her or defend themselves against her. Marissa is finding herself more sensitive to the derogatory and generalized remarks (such as "you know how women get") that perpetuate gender stereotyping than her male colleague, Joe. Even though Marissa is attempting to utilize the comments therapeutically, they bother her. Furthermore, she notices that Joe corroborates with the men when they are making generalizations about women.

A belief that needs to be demystified is that of heterosexual partners holding equal power and privilege in a relationship and in society. Both female and male therapists tend to perpetuate the myth by ignoring the wider sociocultural influences on the dynamics between heterosexual partners and between individuals of different ethnic and racial backgrounds. For example, "men and women use different conversation strategies and receive different treatment in cross-gender dialogue" (Werner-Wilson, et al., 1997). Werner-Wilson et al. (1997) investigated the association between the number of interruptions during a therapy session and therapist and client gender. According to the authors, gender influences power, which in turn influences the number of interruptions. In fact, they found that "overall, marriage and family therapy doctoral students interrupted women clients three times more than men clients" (p. 375) during therapy, regardless of the therapist's gender and, as a result, perpetuated gender inequality.

Therapists also tend to perpetuate gender stereotyping. The cultural expectations of how men and women are to fill their roles and the economic resources of family members have been largely ignored by therapists as factors contributing to conflict between family members. Leslie (1995) stated that

> Failure to fully recognize the importance of gendered role expectations and economic resources and incorporate them into treatment has led to

misunderstandings of couple dynamics and inadequate, if not potentially harmful, treatment for both White and racial-ethnic minority couples. (p. 360)

Couple and family therapists need to be aware of such gender-role ideologies and the power differential inherent within them, and they need to be aware of how these roles affect the family. Why do women traditionally do a disproportionate amount of housework compared with their spouses (two to three times as much more than men), and see this as fair (Coltrane, 2000)? Do therapists uphold the status quo by not challenging this dynamic? Is the status quo of unequal power and privilege acceptable? Goldberg and Perry-Jenkins (2004) investigated the relationship between the division of household labor and child care and working-class women's well-being across the transition to parenthood and, in fact, found that few relationships emerged between actual division of labor and women's well-being. However, "violated expectations regarding child care were associated with increased symptomatology.... Women who ended up performing less child care than they anticipated were the most distressed" (Goldberg and Perry-Jenkins, 2004, p. 233). That is, women who held more traditional gender ideologies experienced more distress when their husbands contributed to more of the child care. They believed that their competence was being challenged by their husbands, and they felt guilty for not meeting up to societal expectations for them to be competent mothers. Another result showed that women's perceptions of unfairness in terms of division of labor were unrelated to their well-being. It was the expectations that women held for themselves that influenced their well-being. Expectations, however, are shaped by the family-of-origin and society. Although power differentials played a part in forming such expectations and women did not express psychological distress, is it ethical for therapists to challenge such beliefs, or to uphold the status quo by not addressing the issue? Grote, Clark, and Naylor (2002) also found that women's perceptions of unfairness regarding disproportional division of labor were associated more with their own expectations and beliefs than the actual division of labor. They surmised that women tend to not make comparisons with their partner or spouse regarding disproportional division of labor unless they already feel distress.

Therapists need to be aware of the discrepancy between expectations and psychological well-being for women, and in addition to influencing women's partners to contribute to child care, therapists need to validate and praise women's efforts for taking on the important responsibility of child care. Many pioneering experts in feminist family therapy, such as Walters, Carter, Papp, and Silverstein (Simon, 1992; Walters et al., 1988), believe that blaming women for being overprotective or overinvolved in their children's lives detracts from their contribution in the family as loving and nurturing individuals. Therapists tend to both minimize women's contributions and perpetuate the power hierarchy of father as provider and mother as caregiver.

Some therapists clearly acknowledge their role in challenging such inequities. With the added role of being a parent and employee, there is a particular regression toward traditional gender roles. This is especially salient for couples who, prior to becoming parents, more or less had an egalitarian relationship regarding housework.

> In addition to money, the issues of time, isolation, sexual dissatisfaction, and problems with distribution of chores arise out of the power shift that pushes couples back toward traditional roles. These are often the complaints that resound endlessly in therapy sessions, tempting the therapist to work on practical solutions to specific issues instead of on the power imbalance itself, which, when righted, will enable the couple to negotiate fair resolutions of their own. (Carter, 1999, p. 254)

Cultural Diversity

> Mrs. Gonzalez attends therapy with her daughter Ana due to sleeping problems. The therapist, Dr. Amagadzie, conducts therapy with the mother and daughter without progress. Dr. Amagadzie asks the father to attend therapy. The therapist speaks with Mr. and Mrs. Gonzalez about working together as a team to help their child. All of the therapist's suggestions are ignored, and each week therapy is thwarted. Dr. Amagadzie, in an attempt to break the stalemate of therapy, begins to ask questions regarding each partner's family. The therapist learns to his surprise that each partner is of a different culture—Mr. Gonzalez is Mexican and Mrs. Gonzalez is Puerto Rican. The therapist assumed that they were of the same ethnicity. He treated the family as if they were simply Latino, and he conceptualized all Latinos to be alike.

"Just as in dealing with gender, to ignore multicultural influences is to legitimize only one reality—that of the dominant culture" (Lyness et al., 2003, p. 426). Therapists need to consider many things when working with families from a multicultural perspective. Therapists need to view families through a cultural lens in order to be able to assess problems and provide interventions for different families. Using culture as a metaphor or speaking a family's "language" for therapy implies understanding people within their own context (Lyness et al., 2003). For example, "one core metaphor for Native Americans is harmony with nature" (Lyness et al., 2003, p. 430). Speaking a client's or a family's "language" helps them by empowering them to change within their context.

Another example of therapists upholding power imbalances is in the quality and amount of discussion raised regarding cultural issues, including race and ethnicity, during therapy. It has been noted that therapists who hold negative or stereotypical attitudes toward minority clients impede client progress and even deter such populations from seeking therapy (Lorion & Parron, 1987). Regardless of the client's socioeconomic status, race influences the therapist's attitude toward the client. Lorion and Parron (1987) found that therapists would attribute certain behaviors (such as tardiness or insistence on immediate symptom change) as an immutable characteristic of a particular population and thereby attribute attrition, resistance, and poor prognosis to the client's racial status. The authors, however, showed that therapist's knowledge and awareness of such attitudes improved minority clients' view of therapy and prognosis. It is the therapist's responsibility to learn about the client's problem context and to keep abreast of the client's reality within their context as stated by Principle 3.3 of the AAMFT (AAMFT, 2001) ethical standards: "marriage and family therapists pursue knowledge of new developments and maintain competence in marriage and family therapy through education, training or supervised experience."

Similarly, Knox et al. (2003) found that therapists in their study acknowledged that broaching topics of race had a positive impact on therapy, and that avoiding topics of race or addressing topics of race inaccurately in certain situations had a negative impact on therapy. The researchers also found a deficit in cultural awareness and training within graduate school training programs. European American therapists, especially, acknowledged a lack in training and knowledge regarding how to work with clients from various cultural backgrounds. African American therapists, however, exhibited a propensity for seeking supervision during sessions in which cultural issues were indicated and attending workshops addressing culture in therapy. It seemed that due to their position as a disadvantaged group, they showed more sensitivity to power and privilege issues, and they were more comfortable discussing cultural differences within therapy.

Therapist Expertise

> Dr. Johnson has been seeing Nancy and John who complain about a continual lack of intimacy in their relationship. During the course of therapy, it is revealed that the couple's first baby, who is now 13 months old, shares the couple's bed. John is very frustrated with this and turns to the therapist and says "Don't you think that the baby should sleep in her own bed by now?"

The form of power and privilege that is consistently present within the therapist–client relationship is the power and privilege of expertise. Under the circumstances that a therapist is being sought out for services, there is the assumption that the therapist rendering a service is capable of something that the client receiving the service is incapable of doing. The power of expertise is the assumption that an individual in the relationship has the ability to control another based upon the assumption that such a person has an immense amount of knowledge (Hill, Glaser, & Harden, 1995).

The manner in which the power of expertise is present within the field's influence in general is that which constitutes normalcy and dictates if a person is considered mentally healthy or not. In the above scenario, the therapist is put in the role of expert by the husband. He has turned to the therapist to seek the "correct" answer as a mental health professional. Oftentimes, clients will look to a therapist for answers to problems that rely on the therapist taking a position of expertise to answer. When a therapist embodies the role of an expert, the client's expertise on his or her own life is disregarded. In order for a therapist to stray from becoming the expert in the room, it is useful to acknowledge that clients have more knowledge and expertise about their own life. At the same time, however, this needs to be balanced with the expertise the therapist does hold in his or her field of study. At times, the therapist may ethically want or need to give a professional opinion in order to increase client functioning or decrease harm to the client. It is important to be mindful of the power imbalance in the therapist–client relationship when extolling expertise so as not to exploit one's status in relation to the client.

Multiple Relationships

> A therapist is assigned a family case involving a mother, Janet, and her 11-year-old son, Jared, who is having behavioral issues at home. Therapy lasts four sessions, and after many attempts at scheduling an appointment with Janet, the therapist closes the case. Several months later, the therapist receives an intake from a depressed

man. In the first session, the man, Walter, speaks at length about difficulties in his relationship with his fiancé, Janet. He says that Janet needs help and in fact has been to the agency before. The facts surrounding the fiancé sound familiar to the therapist. After the session, the therapist reads over the assessments Walter has completed and sees that her former client, Janet, is in fact Walter's fiancé.

There are instances when multiple relationships are strictly prohibited, such as in engaging in sexual relationships with current and past clients (DeLozier, 1994). However, there is less clarity when it comes to nonsexual multiple relationships. At times, multiple relationships are simply unavoidable. For example, in small rural communities, a therapist may encounter clients outside of therapy quite frequently. Conversely, therapists have a choice of whether to engage in some forms of multiple relationships. It is of paramount importance that therapists know their boundaries and communicate those boundaries to their clients because clients are not as aware of ethical standards as therapists would like to believe. Claiborn, Berberoglu, Nerison, and Somberg (1994) surveyed individuals who had been clients and ones who had never been clients about what constitutes ethical and unethical practices and with what frequency these practices had occurred. They found that clients and nonclients had a fairly good idea of what is ethical in practice. However, participants expressed uncertainty about several practices in reference to multiple relationships. It is unequivocally the therapist's responsibility to specify what constitutes appropriate boundaries and under what circumstances the boundaries can be crossed because of the presumed power differential inherent in the therapeutic relationship (Smith & Fitzpatrick, 1995).

> First, the therapeutic relationship is characteristically a one-way relationship in which the therapist learns much about the client's most private thoughts and feelings, whereas the client learns very little about the therapist. Second, clients are presumed to be more emotionally needy than therapists and, consequently, more vulnerable to psychological injury.... Finally, there is the power traditionally ascribed to healers in our society. (Smith & Fitzpatrick, 1995, p. 501)

It is incumbent upon the couple and family therapist to manage boundaries professionally. In Section 1.3 of the AAMFT *Code of Ethics* (2001), it is stated that "Therapists, therefore, make every effort to avoid conditions and multiple relationships with clients that could impair professional judgment or increase the risk of exploitation." There are instances when engaging in multiple relationships is not harmful to the client and not engaging in such relationships may actually offend or harm the client such as in minor gift acceptance. Engaging in multiple relationships per se is not the issue; the differences in status and power facilitate exploitation. A therapist's decision to either cross a boundary or refuse to cross it depends on whether the client will be harmed by the engagement or refusal to cross the boundary. Minor boundary crossings, especially those initiated by the client, can provide a platform for exploring client issues. For example, how will a client benefit from the acceptance or refusal of a gift received from the client, the exchange of services between a therapist and a client, or occasional compliments from the therapist? In the example above, will Janet, Walter, or Janet's son be harmed if the therapist continues treatment with Walter? The therapist will want to do a reasoned analysis of the situation. Janet's confidentiality is an issue at hand. In addition, what if Janet would like to return to therapy at some point? What if Walter would like Janet to attend couples therapy? What if Walter wants to attend couples therapy, but Janet wants to maintain her anonymity about her individual therapy, thus engaging the therapist in a secret with the client?

There are some situations that are very clear boundary violations, such as sexual relations with clients. However, there is no clear distinction between crossing and violating a boundary. The danger of boundary crossing is that it may lead to boundary violations.

Therapists inherently hold more power within a therapeutic relationship due to the following factors (Claiborn et al., 1994; Smith & Fitzpatrick, 1995):

- It is a one-way relationship. Therapists learn much more private information from clients than clients do from therapists.
- Clients are more emotionally needy and therefore more vulnerable to psychological injury.
- Clients consider the therapist an authority and will follow directives even if they feel uncomfortable or they deem the behavior inappropriate.
- Clients believe that therapists have their best interests at heart and so will not question directives.
- Clients fear abandonment by the therapist if they do not follow the therapist's directives.

Peterson (1994) provided an elaborate model on how to detect boundary violations when the code of ethics falls short. Therapists are responsible for avoiding boundary violations, and when therapists stray from making certain changes within therapy, clients have the increased risk of being exploited. Therapists need to take care not to engage in *role reversal with clients* (client becomes caregiver when therapist self-discloses inappropriately), not to *harbor secrets with or from clients* (such as avoiding certain topics in therapy), not to *place the client in a double bind* (displeasure with therapy versus fear of displeasing therapist), and not to *indulge one's professional privilege* (exploiting client's vulnerabilities in order to advance career). Peterson's model is useful when specific ethical guidelines fail to address more elaborate situations.

Defining the Family

> Mary, a Caucasian therapist, is performing a genogram of an African American family. She is frustrated with them when she finds she cannot seem to find who is related to whom in the family, and who is "in" and who is "out" of the family system; her drawing is met with a lot of erasing and redrawing. The family has two female matriarchs, Alma and Ruth, who live in a lesbian relationship. Alma is attempting to get custody of her recently deceased niece's children, who live with her and Ruth. Ruth's niece, Chantrelle, and her two children also live with the family. Chantrelle takes primary responsibility for parenting her children as well as Alma's niece's children. There is tension between Chantrelle and Alma. There are no males in the home, though Chantrelle has a boyfriend who visits, and Alma's deceased niece's husband visits his children.

A main quandary that has been posed to the field of marriage and family therapy is the implications that the name holds. Society has created certain images that arise when one hears the words *marriage* and *family*. The current political state of marriage discounts many families that do not fit into the idea of a heterosexual male and heterosexual female making a ceremonial commitment to one another. The term *family* also brings up ideas that refer to the idea of heterosexual parents with children. In today's society, most people do not fit into the traditional ideals of marriage and family. This ideal is always influenced by the norms of the person who is judging the situation. In the case scenario above, the therapist may be prone to see the African American family as not fitting into the "norm" for a number of reasons. The family may not fit her idea of a normal family if the therapist came from a middle-class, white, heterosexual background. This sociopolitical background of the therapist may lead her to ignore or discredit families that are not composed of a nuclear family headed by two heterosexual parents.

What is "normal?" In many circumstances, therapists use their power and privilege to formulate those definitions. McGoldrick and Hardy (2008) noted that "Family therapy has organized our theory and practice to replicate the dominant value systems of society with employed fathers and homemakers who devote themselves to care of the husbands and children" (p. 5). They went on to note that this is less than 6% of the U.S. population. Some forms of family systems are denied recognition, even though they operate as families in their daily lives. The following forms of systems are often not recognized as a "family": homosexual couples, single-parent families, families of affiliation, blended families or stepfamilies, homosexual parental dyad families, mixed-orientation families, or grandparents raising grandchildren.

There are both overt forms of oppression and covert forms of oppression in lieu of what is considered "normal." An example of an overt form is not recognizing families of affiliation, and a more covert form is seeing some forms of family as "less than." The therapist's frustration within the case scenario is an example of covert oppression. The frustration of mapping a family of affiliation could be translated into the client feeling that his or her family is not legitimate or recognized by the therapist.

Implications for Couple and Family Therapists

In a study by Keeling and Piercy (2007) examining how marriage and family therapists from diverse cultural backgrounds addressed the issues of gender, power, and culture, it was found that participants recommended a respectful, nonthreatening approach in addressing gender and power issues with clients. In this study, participants utilized nonthreatening approaches, client-centered work, culture-centered work, the therapist's use of self, and deconstruction and reconstruction of meaning.

The client is competent, an expert on his or her life, and an equal partner in identifying solutions. Therapists are responsible for helping to *empower* clients; understanding the multicultural context of the clients can help enable this process.

Summary

The first step in decreasing the harmful effects of power and privilege within a therapeutic relationship is to become aware of and accept the power differential that exists between a client and a therapist. (Reflection questions are provided in Appendix 5.1 for further self-exploration.) This chapter provides only a primer to ethical issues that exist and may arise during a therapeutic relationship. Each therapist needs to wrestle with the question: Are we agents of social change? This question is integral to feminist and narrative family therapies. Therapists are in a unique position to challenge societal norms that many times are harmful to clients. Many macrosystemic variables are at play, such as gender inequities, racism, and diverse cultural views, within families and between therapists and families, which prevent progress.

Perhaps the most important issue is the lack of and hesitancy of communication between therapists and their clients. Because therapists hold a position of power, they are responsible for using that power to broach pertinent topics that usually serve as a barrier within the relationship. Clients are keenly aware when certain topics are taboo to discuss or broach in therapy, and clients very often follow the therapist's lead. If a client senses that a therapist does not want to discuss a topic, the client will not attempt to address it. Because of the negative effects power and privilege structures can have on clients and their families, it is the responsibility of therapists to educate clients on macrosystemic variables affecting their lives. This translates into therapists becoming comfortable with broaching these important topics.

Traditional family therapies often overlook environmental and cultural factors; symptoms are seen as originating within the couple or family system. Feminist family therapy or narrative therapy can be solutions to these theoretical constraints. They may be seen as stand-alone theories or paradigms or as being integrated into existing theories. The goal of both theories is to expand client choices. In both theories, contextual factors such as culture and values within the family's context are acknowledged. Oppression is contextualized as an expression of power relationships. This can have the effect of liberating clients from inappropriate internalizations of self-blame or other character defects. Therapists and clients develop a more egalitarian and collaborative relationship that focuses on empowerment. Couple and family therapists have the ability to promote change both inside and outside of the therapeutic relationship.

Appendix 5.1

1. How does privilege influence your work with clients?
2. What types of privilege do you experience (in relation to gender, race, sexual identity, class, able-ism, culture, etc.)?
3. How might this affect your clinical work?

4. Do you believe you are an agent of social change? Why or why not? Should your agency of social change extend both inside and outside the therapy room? Why or why not?

5. What might make it difficult for you to discuss issues of privilege?

6. Are there issues of oppression that influence your work with clients? What are they?

7. How do you know if you are using your power or privilege in therapy? What type of feedback might you get from clients?

8. If you see another person acting in a powerful or privileged way, what would your response be? What could or should your response be?

9. When one party in therapy is being suppressed based on unequal power allotted to him or her by society, what should the therapist's response be?

10. What types of "isms" are relevant to your life (e.g., racism, classism, sexism, etc.)? How do you respond to these?

11. How would you respond to a client using a racial slur in session?

12. Do you consider yourself to be a feminist? Why or why not?

References

Adams, P. J. (2008). *Fragmented intimacy: Addiction in a social world.* New York: Springer.

American Association for Marriage and Family Therapy (AAMFT). (2001). *Code of ethics.* Alexandria, VA: Author.

American Psychological Association. (2007). Lesbian, gay, bisexual, and transgender concerns. Retrieved September 11, 2008, from: www.apa.org/pi/lgbc/publications/justthefacts.html#2.

Cardemil, E., & Battle, C. L. (2003). Guess who's coming to therapy? Getting comfortable with conversations about race and ethnicity in psychotherapy. *Professional Psychology: Research and Practice, 34,* 278–286.

Carter, B. (1999). Becoming parents: The family with young children. In B. Carter & M. McGoldrick (Eds.), *The expanded family life cycle: Individual, family, and social perspectives* (pp. 249–273). Columbus, OH: Allyn & Bacon.

Claiborn, C. D., Berberoglu, L. S., Nerison, R. M., & Somberg, D. R. (1994). The client's perspective: Ethical judgments and perceptions of therapist practices. *Professional Psychology: Research and Practice, 25,* 268–274.

Coltrane, S. (2000). Research on household labor: Modeling and measuring the social embeddings of routine family work. *Journal of Marriage and the Family, 62,* 1208–1233.

DeLozier, P. P. (1994). Therapist sexual misconduct. *Women and Therapy, 15,* 55–67.

De Shazer, S. (1988). A requiem for power. *Contemporary Family Therapy, 10,* 69–76.

Dolan-Del Vecchio, K. (1998). Dismantling white male privilege within family therapy. In M. McGoldrick (Ed.), *Re-visioning family therapy: Race, culture, and gender in clinical practice* (pp. 159–176). New York: Guilford Press.

Fitzpatrick, M. K., Salgado, D. M., Suvak, M. K., King, L. A., & King, D. W. (2004). Associations of gender and gender-role ideology with behavioral and attitudinal features of intimate partner aggression. *Psychology of Men and Masculinity, 5,* 91–102.

Freedman, J., & Combs, G. (1996). *Narrative therapy: The social construction of preferred realities.* New York: W. W. Norton.

Freedman, J., Epston, D., & Lobovits, D. (1997). *Playful approaches to serious problems: Narrative therapy with children and their families.* New York: W. W. Norton.

Goldberg, A. E., & Perry-Jenkins, M. (2004). Division of labor and working-class women's well-being across the transition to parenthood. *Journal of Family Psychology, 18,* 225–236.

Goodrich, T. J., Rampage, C., Ellman, B., & Halstead, K. (1988). *Feminist family therapy, a case book.* New York: W. W. Norton.

Graham-Bermann, S. A., & Brescoll, V. (2000). Gender, power, and violence: Assessing the family stereotypes of the children of batterers. *Journal of Family Psychology, 14,* 600–612.

Grote, N. K., Clark, M. S., & Naylor, K. E. (2002). Perceiving the division of family work to be unfair: Do social comparisons enjoyment, and competence matter? *Journal of Family Psychology, 16,* 510–522.

Hare-Mustin, R. (1987). The problem of gender in family therapy. *Family Process, 26,* 15–27.

Hill, M., Glaser, K., & Harden, J. (1995). A feminist model for ethical decision making. In J. Rave & C. Larsen (Eds.), *Ethical decision making in therapy: Feminist perspectives* (pp. 18–37). New York: Guilford Press.

Keeling, M. L., & Piercy, F. P. (2007). A careful balance: Multinational perspectives on culture, gender and power in marriage and family therapy practice. *Journal of Marital and Family Therapy, 33*(4), 443–463.

Knox, S., Burkand, A. W., Johnson, A. J., Suzuki, L. A., & Ponterotto, J. G. (2003). African American and European American therapists' experiences of addressing race in cross-racial psychotherapy dyads. *Journal of Counseling Psychology, 50,* 466–481.

Leslie, L. A. (1995). The evolving treatment of gender, ethnicity, and sexual orientation in marital and family therapy. *Family Relations, 44,* 359–367.

Lorion, R. P., & Parron, D. L. (1987). Countering the counter transference: A strategy for treating the untreatable. In P. Pederson (Ed.), *Handbook of cross-cultural counseling and therapy* (pp. 79–86). New York: Greenwood Press.

Luepnitz, D. (1988). *The family interpreted: Feminist theory in clinical practice.* New York: Basic Books.

Lyness, K. P., Haddock, S. A., & Zimmerman, T. S. (2003). Contextual issues in marital and family therapy: Gender, culture, and spirituality. In L. L. Hecker & J. L. Wetchler (Eds.), *An introduction to marriage and family therapy* (pp. 409–448). Binghamton, NY: Haworth Press.

McGoldrick, M., Anderson, C. A., & Walsh, F. (1989). Women in families: A framework for family therapy. New York: W. W. Norton.

McGoldrick, M., & Hardy, K. (2008). Introduction: Revisioning family therapy from a multicultural perspective. In M. McGoldrick & K. Harding (Eds.), *Re-visioning family therapy: Race, culture and gender in clinical practice* (2nd ed.) (pp. 3–24). New York: Guilford Press.

McIntosh, P. (1998). White privilege: Unpacking the invisible knapsack. In M. McGoldrick (Ed.), *Re-visioning family therapy: Race, culture, and gender in clinical practice* (pp. 147–152). New York: Guilford Press.

Peterson, M. (1994). Client harm and professional accountability: A feminist model. In M. Snyder (Ed.), *Ethical issues in feminist family therapy* (pp. 49–67). New York: Haworth.

Purcell, D. W., Swann, S., & Herbert, S. E. (2003). Sexual orientation and professional ethics. In W. O'Donahue & K. Ferguson (Eds.), *Handbook of professional ethics: Issues, questions, and controversies* (pp. 319–342). Thousand Oaks, CA: Sage.

Ryder, R., & Hepworth, J. (1990). AAMFT ethical code: "Dual relationships." *Journal of Marital and Family Therapy, 2,* 127–132.

Simon, R. (1992). *One on one: Conversations with the shapers of family therapy.* New York: Guilford Press.

Smith, D., & Fitzpatrick, M. (1995). Patient–therapist boundary issues: An integrative review of theory and research. *Professional Psychology: Research and Practice, 26,* 499–506.

Stone Fish, L., & Osborn, J. L. (1992). Therapists' views of family life: A Delphi study. *Family Relations, 41,* 409–415.

Walters, M., Carter, B., Papp, P., & Silverstein, O. (1988). *The invisible web: Gender patterns in family relationships.* New York: Guilford Press.

Werner-Wilson, R. J., Price, S. J., Zimmerman, T. S., & Murphy, M. J. (1997). Client gender as a process variable in marriage and family therapy: Are women clients interrupted more than men clients? *Journal of Family Psychology, 11,* 373–377.

White, M., & Epston, D. (1990). *Narrative means to therapeutic ends.* New York: W. W. Norton.

Willbach, D. (1989). Ethics and family therapy: The case management of family violence. *Journal of Marital and Family Therapy, 15,* 43–52.

6

Sexuality, Boundaries, and Ethics

Teresa L. Young

It is well documented that sexual intimacy between therapist and client is both unethical and potentially harmful (Bates & Brodsky, 1989; Bouhoutsos, Holroyd, Lerman, Forer, & Greenberg, 1983; Edelwich & Brodsky, 1991; Gabbard, 1989; Pope, 1988; Rutter, 1989: Strean, 1993). The American Association for Marriage and Family Therapy (AAMFT) *Code of Ethics* (2001) clearly prohibits sexual intimacy between couple and family therapists and clients in Subprinciples 1.4 and 1.5:

> Subprinciple 1.4: Sexual intimacy with clients is prohibited.
> Subprinciple 1.5: Sexual intimacy with former clients is likely to be harmful and is therefore prohibited for two years following the termination of therapy or last professional contact.

However, the topic of sexual ethics in the field of couple and family therapy (as well as other helping professions) is much more complex than the issue of whether or not one engages in sexual relations with clients. The actual incidence of sexual relations with clients may be on the decline, but sexual abuse perpetrators account for about 4.4% of all therapists (7% males; 1.5% females) when data from national studies are pooled (Pope, 2001).

Bohmer (2000) noted that therapists who have sex with their clients are taking advantage of the natural transference process of therapy noted by Freud; feelings from the patient's past are transferred onto the therapist. Thus, feelings on the part of the therapist and of the client are connected to the therapy process. Rutter (1989) warned that all professionals have this "latent potential" to sexually exploit clients. In the late 1960s and early 1970s, some therapists actively "prescribe[ed] sexual gratification as a legitimate form of psychotherapy" (Strean, 1993, p. 23). Notably, McCartney (1966) asserted that clients "need" to fondle, caress, and engage in sexual intercourse with him as part of treatment. Still, it may be argued that the focus of sexual ethics should not be so narrowly defined as the black-and-white issue of whether or not to engage in sexual relations with clients. In other words, it is no longer sufficient to treat the matter of sexual ethics in couple and family therapy as a topic adequately covered by the ethical mandate, "Don't have sex with your clients." Couple and family therapists are likely to face a *broad* range of sexual ethical dilemmas, as comes with the territory of the intimate nature of their work. The need for a wider lens regarding sexual ethics is highlighted by findings that a majority of couple and family therapists who have never engaged in sexual relations with clients experience feelings of sexual attraction toward clients (Nickell, Hecker, Ray, & Bercik, 1995).

Consequences for the Client

Several researchers documented the negative effects for clients of sexual exploitation in therapy (Bouhoutsos et al., 1983; Bates & Brodsky, 1989; Coleman & Schaefer, 1986; Disch & Avery, 2001; Pope, 1988). These effects are sometimes compared to the consequences commonly suffered by victims of incest (Barnhouse, 1978; Bates & Brodsky, 1989; Gabbard, 1989). The boundary crossed when engaging in sexual relations with a client is "symbolically incestuous" (Barnhouse, 1978) in that the therapeutic relationship is inherently intimate with a power differential that mirrors a parent–child relationship. The symptoms of clients sexually exploited by professionals may include confusion, loss, emotional turmoil, shame, fear, self-blame, loss of trust, isolation, and rage (Disch & Avery, 2001). Shame, intense guilt, poor self-esteem, and suicidal or self-destructive behavior are also potential symptoms (Gabbard, 1989). Leupker (1999) surveyed 55 women who had been sexually exploited by mental health practitioners and found the clients suffered from posttraumatic stress disorder, major depressive disorder, suicidality, increased use of prescription drugs, disrupted relationships, and disruptions in their work or earning potential. In an earlier study by Bouhoutsos et al. (1983), 11% of clients who engaged in sex with a former therapist were hospitalized, and 1% committed suicide.

Consequences for the Therapist

Clients are not the only individuals at risk of suffering often dire consequences stemming from the breach of sexual ethics in couple and family therapy. Edelwich and Brodsky (1991) outlined some of the possible consequences for the therapist if ethical sexual issues are not dealt with properly (p. xiv):

- Diversion of time and energy from the professional relationship to the fulfillment of personal needs and desires.
- Loss of therapeutic effectiveness and of therapeutic benefits for the client.
- Self-doubt, frustration, and reduced job satisfaction.
- Personally or professionally compromising situations ... resulting in some cases in loss of job, livelihood, and career; civil liability; and/or criminal prosecution.
- Additional civil liability for supervisors, consultants, and employing agencies.

Although most would agree that the harm inflicted upon one's client should be the greatest distracter from one engaging in behaviors that violate sexual ethics, it should also be taken into consideration that sexual misconduct is the most common allegation in malpractice suits (Eddington & Shuman, 2004). Thus, even the majority of professionals who feel strongly opposed to engaging in sexual relations with clients (and who say with confidence that they would never cross such a line) may benefit from further and continued education on the topic, such that they may garner the knowledge to protect themselves both legally and professionally.

Areas of Ethical Consideration

Sexual Attraction to Clients

Iris is a couple and family therapist who is currently seeing a 30-year-old named Samuel. The first time she saw Samuel, Iris instantly noticed that he was quite an attractive man. Iris tried to ignore her feelings and proceeded as usual. Weeks passed and Iris could not shake her feelings of attraction. When talking to Samuel, she felt shy and nervous and worried that he could sense her attraction to him. Every time she laughed at something funny Samuel said, she stopped herself so as to not let him catch on that she was having feelings that crossed a therapeutic boundary. As therapy continued, it became so problematic that Iris felt she had to avert Samuel's eye contact such that she did not have to acknowledge her growing feelings of sexual attraction. Iris was overwhelmed with questions. Should she be transparent with her feelings and have a conversation with Samuel? Should she refer Samuel to another therapist, or would the referral do more damage than good?

Iris is not alone in her experience (and her confusion) regarding the ethical dilemma of sexual attraction to clients. In a study of 189 clinical members of AAMFT, Nickell et al. (1995) found that a majority of family therapists experience feelings of attraction to clients. In fact, 100% of male respondents and 73% of female respondents indicated at least rare to occasional feelings of sexual attraction (Nickell et al., 1995). The researchers also found that 62% of males and 36% of females reported engaging in sexual fantasy about clients within the past 2 years. Additionally, 28% of respondents believed that feeling sexual attraction is "definitely unethical" or "ethical under rare circumstances" (Nickell et al., 1995, p. 323).

As many believe feelings of sexual attraction to be unethical, it is no wonder that Iris feels ill prepared to manage the situation (let alone divulge her feelings to a colleague or supervisor). As Harris (1998) explained, thoughts such as, "this shouldn't be happening, I could never tell anyone about this, or my supervisor will think I wanted it to happen" are typical for therapists in this uncomfortable (albeit common) position (p. 7). In a study of 575 psychotherapists, Pope, Keith-Speigel, and Tabachnick (1986) reported that half the respondents reported no training regarding sexual attraction to clients.

Just why are feelings of sexual attraction so common in the therapeutic setting? Strean (1993) explained that the therapy setting is an "ideal milieu for extraordinary intimacy" (p. 14). Consider the following observations about a therapeutic exchange as related by Edelwich and Brodsky (1991): Therapist and client(s) meet alone, sitting close to one another. They often meet frequently and regularly, during which time the client often shares intimate details regarding his or her life. He or she may share hopes, memories, disappointments, and fears, while the therapist carefully listens and empathizes. These are the stories and feelings that one typically only shares with close intimates (if with anyone else at all). It follows, then, that there is a fine line between the intimate nature of the joining process described above and sexual attraction (Harris, 1998).

Harris (1998) believes that the greatest problem regarding sexual attraction in therapy is that few acknowledge the potential for sexual feelings to develop during the process of "good" therapy. Not many would argue against the notion that "good" therapy involves joining, and yet joining is part of the process that leads to the intimate nature of therapy that may be confused with feelings of sexual attraction as described above. Scheflen (1965) stated:

> The fact is that the patient and the therapist do have certain feelings for each other. These feelings...provide an environment for the learning experience which psychotherapy must be if it is to be successful. (p. 257)

Thus, the therapist is left with the ultimate conundrum—the very intimate environment for which he or she strives is the same environment that may lead him or her to cross the fine line that is the ethical boundary of sexual attraction toward clients.

So what is a professional like Iris to do? It is the position of this author and the position of others (Edelwich & Brodsky, 1991; Harris, 1998; Strean, 1993) that one must first accept that as sexual human beings, therapists are not exempt from experiencing feelings of sexual attraction—even if the attraction is toward a client. In fact, experiencing sexual attraction to a client is not itself unethical, nor is having a sexual fantasy. It is making the *choice* to act on the attraction or fantasy or to deny the attraction or fantasy to a point at which it impedes therapy that is unethical. Edelwich and Brodsky (1991) explained that helping professionals must be able to distinguish between "normal human feelings" such as sexual attraction and "unethical acts" (p. xx). They also state that "whereas the feeling [such as the feeling of sexual attraction or fantasy] may be spontaneous...the act is a choice" (p. xx). Edelwich and Brodsky (1991) outline the following guidelines for responding ethically to feelings of attraction:

- Do acknowledge your own feelings (Edelwich & Brodsky, 1991):
  - "What frees the clinician to act with clear ethical purpose is an acceptance of and comfort with the normal human feelings that are incidental to the clinical interaction" (p. 120). Thus, in the case of the clinical vignette, Iris must first recognize that her sexual attraction to Samuel does not make her a "bad" or "unethical" therapist. It may be helpful for her to consider that if she were to have met Samuel in another context, she would have likely experienced a similar sexual response. As Harris (1998) stated, "we are humans first and therapists, second or third" (p. 8).
- Do not give your problems to the client (Edelwich & Brodsky, 1991):
  - The general professional consensus is that it is inappropriate to tell clients of sexual attraction, as this can run the risk of harming clients (Fisher, 2004). Edelwich and Brodsky (1991) discussed how some therapists object to this sentiment, arguing that withholding such information leads them to act unnaturally with clients. This may explain Nickell et al.'s (1995) finding that 10% of males and 4% of females discussed sexual attraction issues with clients. Edelwich and Brodsky (1991) maintained that it is the therapist's job to act

responsibly. In their view, acting responsibly means refraining from discussing sexual attraction issues with clients. The therapist must actively exhibit appropriateness with the client in his or her overt behavior while seeking help elsewhere to deal with feelings that may be unintentionally communicated in session. Fisher (2004) also noted there is potential danger that revealing sexual attraction may put the therapist at increased risk for engaging in activities in therapy that could be defined as sexual harassment, especially for male therapists.

- Thus, in the clinical vignette, Iris should not "give" her problem to Samuel by confiding in him about her sexual attraction. To do so would be to burden Samuel with the pressure to respond to a situation that he did not ask for when entering the therapeutic relationship. It may also jeopardize Samuel's trust in a professional's capability to maintain appropriate boundaries. If Iris feels that she cannot control her behavior that "gives away" her attraction to Samuel, it is her ethical responsibility to follow the next guideline.

- Do confide in your supervisor, peers, and professional consultant, and use personal therapy (Edelwich & Brodsky, 1991):
  - Harris (1998) asserted that "when we don't discuss attraction we implicitly underscore, and maybe even reinforce, the idea that experiencing sexual feelings in therapy is unethical" (p. 7). Discussing feelings of sexual attraction with a supervisor or colleague, although initially daunting, often has the effect of normalizing the situation such that the "mystery" or "fantasy" of the situation diminishes, restoring a "degree of grounding" to the therapist (Harris, 1998, p. 8). Upon speaking with a supervisor or colleague, Iris will likely notice that she is not as nervous about Samuel "catching on" to her attraction, as her feelings are already "out on the table" with someone else. This should calm her worries and refocus her energies on the therapeutic process. Keep in mind that it is common to experience feelings of guilt, anxiety, and confusion related to feelings of sexual attraction to clients (Nickell et al., 1995). Be sure to discuss these feelings with your supervisor or peers. Personal therapy can also be used simultaneously as self-care and part of risk management (Fisher, 2004).

- Do not "refer out" (Edelwich & Brodsky, 1991):
  - Should the client suffer on account of the clinician's problem? Edelwich and Brodsky (1991) discussed how referring a client due to feelings of sexual attraction may lead to the consequences of "discontinuity of care, including uncertainty, loss of time, and possible feelings of rejection" and thus recommend that a therapist not refer his or her client (p. 136). The authors felt that under the rare circumstances when

supervisory or peer support is not sufficient in achieving satisfactory results that the clinician should refer. They caution, however, that the therapist must be extremely careful not to imply rejection or abandonment and should allot time to discuss what the referral means to the client. The therapist must take complete blame and explain that he or she is "unable to support the client's needs" (p. 137).

Responding to Sexual Advances of Clients

Case Scenario 1

Lupe, age 24, is a first-year student in a couple and family therapy master's program. Lupe had been seeing a couple, George and Sarah, for several weeks when suddenly George came to therapy alone. When Lupe asked why Sarah was not present, George confided that he was attracted to Lupe. He explained that he had told Sarah that he would benefit from individual therapy before he was ready to work on couple problems. In reality, George explained that he wanted individual time to see if there was a romantic connection with Lupe. He stated that he had never "excelled" in relationships, and thought that therapy was a good place to "practice" his skills. George also made comments such as, "I'm such a lucky man to have a therapist as beautiful as you." and "We should go on a date sometime." Lupe became extremely uncomfortable and nervous. What should she say to George?

Case Scenario 2

Anton is a couple and family therapist who specializes in working with victims of sexual abuse. He is currently seeing a client named Grace who has a long history of sexual abuse both by family members and intimate partners. Anton noticed early on that Grace tended to dress provocatively. She also exhibited body language that made Anton uncomfortable, such as stroking her leg suggestively when she talked. Sometimes Anton wondered if he was reading too far into Grace's behavior. Other times, however, he felt fairly confident that Grace was coming on to him. She often made suggestive comments and told jokes that were sexual in nature. Anton did not know how to react to these comments or these jokes. He worried that he might revictimize Grace by talking with her about his perceptions that she was making covert sexual advances. At the same time, the sexualized interactions with Grace were jeopardizing the therapeutic relationship. Anton felt paralyzed.

Although the spotlight in research, literature, and media coverage tends to shine on the unethical sexual advances of therapists toward clients, one must also acknowledge that the reverse scenario exists—clients do at times covertly or overtly make sexual advances toward their therapists. Thus, it is imperative that therapists gain awareness as to how to ethically respond to such situations.

To be clear, no matter what a client says or does in terms of sexual advances, the burden to act ethically *always* falls on the professional (the only exception being a forced sexual assault by a client on a therapist). In other words, should sexual relations or sexual mistreatment of a client ensue in a scenario that involves a client's sexual advances, the professional must claim responsibility and accountability for his or her actions. Accordingly, the information provided in this section will aid the professional in ethically responding to sexual advances in a manner that does not place blame or burden on the client. Furthermore, statements made to describe manners in which clients may attempt to make sexual advances should not be misconstrued as "victim-blaming." *Nothing a client says or does justifies a professional's decision to cross a sexual boundary.*

As the two clinical scenarios demonstrate, sexual advances of clients may fall along a continuum that includes extremely obvious, overt advances, and more covert, subtle actions that a therapist may or may not perceive as sexual advances. Overt advances may include a client verbally stating that he or she would like to date/kiss/"sleep with" his or her therapist, or a client making physical advances such as sitting on the therapist's lap or attempting to kiss the therapist. Covert advances may include a client's incessant interest in the therapist's personal life, frequent contacts in the form of phone calls and office visits, flattery in the form of compliments, and body language and physical cues that may include sitting in revealing postures, touching one's body, and wearing provocative clothing.

Although there are clear differences between these two types of ethical dilemmas, there are certain guidelines provided by Edelwich and Brodsky (1991) that one may reference for both types of situations:

- Do set limits while giving the client a safe space for self-expression (Edelwich & Brodsky, 1991, p. 128):
  - "Clients who act seductively are testing limits.... It is when a boundary is clearly drawn that the client can most thoroughly explore the space within the boundary." What exactly does this type of limit setting entail? Clearly delineating appropriate boundaries may look differently depending on the situation. In Anton's position, setting a boundary may involve having a discussion about the limitations of his role as a therapist (e.g., demonstrating with tact that he will not cross a physical boundary with Grace or any other client—*see "Do confront the issue straightforwardly"*). Leaving "safe space for self-expression" may involve choosing not to comment on Grace's provocative clothing or behavior of stroking her leg. Setting the boundary by discussing Anton's personal ethical limitations is

more appropriate than setting a limit by asking Grace to change her behavior for two reasons: It demonstrates to the client that the therapist will take it upon himself or herself to maintain safe boundaries and that the burden to create the safe space is not on the client, and it lessens the chance that the client will feel embarrassed or personally attacked. Furthermore, once a client understands that his or her environment is safe (in that his or her therapist will not respond to his or her advances with sexual exploitation), the client's covert seductive behaviors and limit testing are likely to decrease.

- Do not be rejecting (Edelwich & Brodsky, 1991):
  - It is not unusual to feel bothered or even disgusted by the overt sexual advances of a client. However, therapists must proceed with caution when reacting to such behavior. Edelwich and Brodsky (1991) warned, "A cold, rejecting manner on the part of the clinician may communicate to the client that his or her sexuality is not acceptable, rather than that it is simply being directed at the wrong person" (p. 130). As such, in Case Scenario 1, Lupe (although most likely very put off by George's comments) must take care to clearly set a limit regarding her role as therapist, while maintaining a sense of consideration for her client's feelings. Edelwich and Brodsky (1991) proposed the following statement: "I appreciate your interest in me—it's flattering—but if you've found our conversations helpful to you, I think I can continue to be helpful by staying away from any other role" (p. 130).
  - The authors also suggest simply stating, "That's not what therapy is" (p. 130). Note that the response is neither rejecting nor attacking.
- Do express nonsexual caring (Edelwich & Brodsky, 1991):
  - Edelwich and Brodsky (1991) advised that "it is a mistake to react to the sexual overture [of a client] by withdrawing from the nurturing role," as the client who acts out sexually is often seeking nurturance (p. 130). By setting a boundary and defining one's role as a nonsexual caregiver, the therapist is communicating to the client that he or she does not need to act out sexually to attain warmth and caring (Edelwich & Brodsky, 1991). This may be particularly important for a client who has a history of sexual abuse, such as Grace in Case Scenario 2. Thus, Anton need not worry that by having a conversation regarding the limits of his role as a therapist that he is somehow revictimizing Grace. Quite the contrary is true—actively setting such a boundary and continuing to care for Grace in a therapeutic, nonsexual manner is the appropriate, ethical manner in which to proceed.
- Do not be drawn into answering personal questions or giving the client other "double messages" (Edelwich & Brodsky, 1991):

- A therapist is at risk of sending a "double message" to a client when turning down a sexual advance if he or she acts as though he or she is setting the limit based on an external rule. In other words, by stating, "I cannot have a sexual relationship with you because it is against the rules," the therapist may inadvertently communicate, "If it weren't for the rule, I would engage in sexual relations with you." Passing off the responsibility to an external "obstacle" may be a tempting option, but it defeats the purpose of delineating a clear, ethical boundary. Edelwich and Brodsky (1991) advised that the therapist should "speak from having internalized [the] tradition, rather than appear to be chafing against an external restraint" (p. 131). Therapists must also be careful when answering personal questions, as answering a question can be like "quicksand" in that the client takes the therapist's gesture as a sign that they can probe more and more (Edelwich & Brodsky, 1991). Thus, it is often necessary to be clear that therapeutic conversations are most helpful if they stay focused on the client and his or her life and concerns.
- Do confront the issue straightforwardly (Edelwich & Brodsky, 1991):
  - It may be unnerving to confront the issue of a client's sexual advances straightforwardly, especially in a situation in which the advances are covert. However, it is ethically appropriate to confront the perceived behavior as soon as it becomes a problem, especially if it is escalating. In Edelwich and Brodsky's *Sexual Dilemmas for the Helping Professional* (1991), a family physician acknowledges that one can have a conversation with one's client "without pejorative labeling, without imputation of motive, but simply as a perception of [one's] own that [one] is willing to have corrected" (p. 133). Consider the following statement:
    - I may be wrong, but I've noticed something in our interactions together that I want to address. Sometimes it feels like you consider our relationship to be more than professional, and I want to assure you that that is a line that I will not cross with you or any other client, because I respect our therapeutic relationship too much.
- Do not "refer out" (Edelwich & Brodsky, 1991):
  - Consider that what might feel like a "therapeutic impasse" can oftentimes lead to a "therapeutic breakthrough" (Edelwich & Brodsky, 1991, p. 137). Thus, overt or covert sexual advances made by clients are not always roadblocks to therapeutic progress, but sometimes are opportunities for deeper therapeutic exploration. Also consider the possibility that a client who is referred due to perceived or overt sexual behavior may suffer from feelings of confusion and rejection. This is especially likely considering that sexual acting out in therapy

may indicate a need for nonsexual nurturance on the part of the therapist (Edelwich & Brodsky, 1991). Thus, it is ethically appropriate for a therapist to attempt to delineate boundaries rather than automatically refer the client. Of course, there are always exceptions and instances in which a client is insistent on violating sexual boundaries. In such cases, a therapist may need to take action to protect himself or herself both physically and professionally by referring the client.

- In a study of marriage and family therapists by Harris and Hays (2008), comfort level in having sexuality-related discussions increased when the therapist had both sexual education and adequate supervision in the topic. This should be addressed in the training of therapists for both the well-being of the therapist and his or her clients.

- Do not assume the relationship is a two-way relationship:
  - One mistake that therapists may make is to assume the therapeutic relationship is a mutual, two-way relationship. However, there is a power differential that does not allow this to be true. In addition, transference and countertransference occur on an unconscious or subconscious level, not allowing either the client or the therapist to have a level playing field in terms of a mutual relationship. It is a *therapeutic* relationship. Another mistake therapists may make is to think love can heal previous harm (Gabbard, 1997), thus taking on a role of rescuer, while still in a position of power. The therapist needs to stay in a professional role to maintain therapeutic maneuverability and objectivity so as to not harm the client and to promote his or her well-being.

Engaging in Sexual Relations With Former Clients

Owen, a 35-year-old couple and family therapist, was walking his dog in the park one day when he was approached by a former client. At first he did not recognize Lucy, as it had been almost 5 years since he had seen her in therapy. Lucy said, "You don't recognize me, do you?" It was then that Owen remembered Lucy, a former client who only came to therapy for about a month to discuss the death of her mother. Owen and Lucy briefly chatted, and he learned that Lucy had recently moved into a nearby neighborhood. Weeks later Owen and Lucy ran into each other at a local market and decided to exchange telephone numbers. Their relationship progressed slowly, but several months later it was obvious that romantic feelings had developed. Owen and Lucy moved forward with their relationship and it became intimate. It was not until Owen was discussing the origins of his relationship with a friend and fellow therapist that he considered the possible ethical implications of dating a former client. His friend was adamantly against the relationship, telling Owen that sexual relationships with former clients are never okay.

Engaging in sexual relationships with former clients is another hotly controversial topic. Although there is consistent consensus in the field of helping professionals that sexual intimacy with present clients is clearly unethical, the propriety of sexual relations with former clients is less established (Herman, Gartrell, Olarte, Feldstein, & Localio, 1987; Nickell et al., 1995; Pope, Tabachnick, & Keith-Spiegel, 1987). Consistently, those professionals who maintain that sex with present clients is unethical waver on the topic of whether or not it is acceptable to form an intimate relationship with former clients. However, the AAMFT *Code of Ethics* (2001) clearly prohibits sexual intimacy with former clients within 2 years of professional contact and strongly advises against intimacy with former clients beyond 2 years.

The AAMFT also emphasizes that the burden of proof falls to the therapist to demonstrate that no harm has been inflicted on the client after the 2-year period. This is an important statement for therapists to keep in mind when considering the possibility of malpractice suits, as the AAMFT *Code of Ethics* cannot be utilized as a form of protection if a claim is filed against a therapist who engages in sexual relations with a client after the 2-year lapse.

So what about poor, love-stricken Owen in the clinical vignette? If one were to talk to Owen, he would surely provide common rationalizations for his relationship with former client, Lucy. First, he would argue that his relationship did not start until 5 years after therapy ended. He might also dispute his friend's claim that his relationship is unethical by pointing out that his meeting with Lucy was purely accidental. After all, it is not as though Owen conspired to make Lucy fall in love with him after treatment while seeing her in therapy.

It is safe to say that Owen is a well-meaning man; but his justifications for having a relationship with Lucy can be countered by various established ethical arguments. First, Owen fails to heed clear advice from the AAMFT *Code of Ethics* that engaging in sexual relations with former clients is likely harmful and possibly exploitative. Also, there is no quantitatively established length of time for a "magic cooling-off period" after which "the personal relationship [between therapist and former client] will no longer be affected by the memory of the therapeutic relationship" (Edelwich & Brodsky, 1995, p. 96). Also consider the following three grounds for concluding that engaging in sexual relations with former clients is unethical, as provided by Edelwich & Brodsky (1991):

1. Compromising of the therapeutic process: If one believes that future sexual or romantic relationships with clients are an ethical possibility, the mere prospect of such a relationship may impact the therapeutic process. For example, the therapist may avoid discussing difficult issues so as to not alienate a potential romantic partner. The therapist may also consciously or unconsciously present himself or herself in a different manner. If, on the other hand, a therapist makes a conscious decision to abide by an ethical standard that involves *never* involving himself or herself with a former client, he or she is free to act with a purely therapeutic purpose.

2. Denial of future therapeutic support: Once a therapeutic relationship becomes a romantic relationship, the availability for future therapeutic involvement is lost. Furthermore, whatever transpires in the romantic relationship may affect the former client's ability to trust other professionals in the future. In fact, even if the romantic relationship is based on love and trust, the former client may garner a general mistrust for therapists based solely on the experience of having a therapeutic relationship evolve into a romantic one.

3. Corruption of the personal relationship by the privileged knowledge and inequality of the therapeutic relationship: The therapeutic relationship between therapist and client is inherently unbalanced in terms of power. The therapist is privileged and powerful in that he or she gains access to the most vulnerable parts of a client's emotional life. This is not a reciprocal process, as the client does not have the same access to the vulnerable parts of the therapist. Also, the therapist gains privileged knowledge about the client's life including "fears and insecurities about intimate relationships" (Edelwich & Brodsky, 1991, p. 100). When a former client and therapist begin a romantic relationship "the power that resides in this inequality of knowledge remains ripe for abuse when the client and clinician attempt to make the difficult transition to a relationship of mutuality" (Edelwich & Brodsky, 1991, p. 100). Thus, the equality in the romantic relationship of former client and therapist may be severely jeopardized.

Taking into consideration these arguments and Subprinciple 1.5 of the AAMFT *Code of Ethics*, it is advised that couple and family therapists refrain from engaging in sexual or intimate personal relationships with former clients at any point in time after the termination of therapy. Adopting this ethical standard before one engages in any therapeutic conversation (and before one has the opportunity to "bump into" previous clients) gives one the advantage to avoid having to make the tricky decision of whether or not to become romantic with a former client. As for poor Owen, he will have to talk it over with Lucy.

Discussing Sex and Sexuality in Therapy

Case Scenario 1

Gina is a couple and family therapist who specializes in sex therapy. She is currently seeing a couple, Danny and Caroline, who are worried that their sex life has become dull. The problem is that when Gina asks the couple questions pertaining to their sexual relationship, Danny and Caroline go into sexual details that make Gina uncomfortable. They talk explicitly about their intimate encounters for what seems like the entire hour, and even redirect the conversation back to their sex life when Gina asks unrelated questions. Frustrated, Gina says to herself, "You are a sex therapist! You are not supposed to be ruffled when people talk about sex!" Nevertheless, Gina sometimes wonders if Danny and Caroline are there for her help or for the excitement of sharing their sexual escapades with a relative stranger.

Case Scenario 2

It has not been an easy month at the sex therapy clinic where Gina works. Gina's colleague, Henry, is seeing a couple, Emily and Zach, who are having trouble with premature ejaculation. Henry has worked with many couples with the same problem, but Emily and Zach are a particularly fun and attractive couple whom Henry enjoys working with very much. Soon Henry finds himself asking detailed questions about the couple's sex life that he is not sure he would ask other couples. Henry tries to tell himself that the purpose of his questions is to gather information, but in the back of his mind he wonders if he is more or less interested in the sexual details out of selfish curiosity. Henry cannot deny that hearing about peoples' sex lives is an exciting element of his job. The second the thought crosses his mind, however, he feels tremendous guilt. He worries that he has crossed an ethical boundary and refers Emily and Zach to another therapist right away.

These case scenarios present two different dilemmas: in Scenario 1, the therapist worries how to proceed with clients she perceives to be exhibitionistic, as the clients seem to constantly and graphically share their sexual exploits, and in Scenario 2, the therapist worries that he is a voyeur when he catches himself enjoying a client's sexual details a little too much. Although it is hard to resist the somewhat comical and obvious solution of pairing Henry, the voyeuristic therapist, with Danny and Caroline, the exhibitionistic couple, ethical matters involving the sharing of sexual information can be quite serious, uncomfortable, and possibly harmful for clients if not handled appropriately.

"Verbal exhibitionism" of clients, as demonstrated in the first vignette, can be handled in a similar matter as dealing with covert sexual advances of clients. Therapists may benefit from understanding that a client or clients who seem to excessively and graphically recount sexual details may be doing so for a number of reasons. A client may be gauging the therapist's sexual interest in the activities described or simply evading a more intimate therapeutic conversation (Edelwich & Brodsky, 1991). Moreover, the client may feel he or she gains power by sharing shocking information with the therapist. Ideally, a therapist may integrate a conversation regarding how sharing graphic details may impact the therapeutic relationship. However, if this is implausible or fails, and if the explicit conversations seem to be impeding therapy, it is appropriate for the therapist to tactfully define the limitations of his or her role as a therapist (see the ethical considerations in the section, *Responding to Sexual Advance of Clients*). In the first vignette, Gina might say:

> I'm not sure if I'm making too much of the situation, but sometimes I feel like the two of you like to gauge my reaction to your sexual stories just for the sake of pushing my buttons! You should know that I want to gather important details about your sex life, but I don't want to cross a boundary and jeopardize our therapeutic relationship. So will it be okay if I put the breaks on some of your juicy stories in the future if I think it would be helpful to move on to something else?

In the previous statement, Gina is clearly establishing a therapeutic boundary without coming across as judgmental or rejecting. She also leaves room for the possibility that her perceptions are incorrect and asks for permission to set limits in the future. Also note that Gina's statement utilizes a sense of humor and playfulness as a tool to diffuse what could be an otherwise awkward conversation (as well as to match the style of her clients, Danny and Caroline). A therapist in a similar situation should use his or her clinical judgment in determining the appropriate amount of humor that will be well received by his or her clients.

A therapist's suspicion that he or she is behaving voyeuristically in therapy can be handled in a similar manner as dealing with sexual attraction and fantasy involving clients. First, one should note that anecdotal information gathered by authors Edelwich and Brodsky (1991) in their book *Sexual Dilemmas for the Helping Professional* indicated that many helping professionals in various fields are susceptible to the impulse of eliciting sexual information from clients for one's personal gratification. That is not to say that *actively* eliciting sexual information for one's enjoyment is ethical. Rather, it comes back to the distinction between *natural human response* and the *choice to act*. As sexual beings, it is not unreasonable for a therapist to find himself or herself enjoying (or even turned on by) accounts of sexual activity. It is when a therapist *chooses* to ask questions for the purpose of sexual gratification that an ethical boundary is crossed.

Much like the therapist who recognizes that he or she is sexually attracted to a client, the therapist (like Henry in the vignette) who realizes that he or she enjoys hearing the details of a client's sex life should, (a) acknowledge that it is a natural human response and experience to enjoy and have interest in sexual information; (b) refrain from "giving" the problem to his or her client by discussing his or her feelings of enjoyment; (c) seek support from a supervisor, peer, or professional consultant; and (d) refer his or her client only should the therapist feel that the previous steps have not been successful in ensuring that his or her enjoyment in hearing the sexual details does not impede the therapeutic process or if the therapist feels that he or she cannot refrain from actively choosing to elicit sexual information for personal gratification. (See the ethical considerations in the *Sexual Attraction* section for more details.)

In the second scenario, Henry may have been too quick to refer Emily and Zach. Should he have acknowledged the normalcy of his sexual feelings and sought supervision, Henry may have noticed a reduction in his anxiety and an increase in his ability to work effectively with the couple. However, if he continued to notice that he was actively asking sexual questions of Emily and Zach that he would not ask other couples, it would be appropriate for Henry to make a referral.

Summary

Sexual ethics in couple and family therapy involves a broad range of topics and considerations. It is a disservice to therapists and clients that training involving sexual ethics is typically limited to the warning that one should not engage in sexual relations with clients, as couple and family therapists are likely to encounter many other delicate and complicated sexual ethical issues in the course of their careers. Issues pertaining to sexual attraction, sexual fantasy, sexual advances of clients, sexual relations with former clients, and sexual discussions in therapy warrant consideration and further discussion. As researchers and authors continue to increase the visibility of these important topics through literature, so too should couple and family therapists' comfort increase in discussing sexual ethical issues with supervisors, colleagues, and peers.

References

American Association for Marriage and Family Therapy (AAMFT). (2001). *Code of ethics.* Alexandria, VA: Author.

Barnhouse, R. (1978). Sex between patient and therapist. *Journal of the American Academy of Psychoanalysis, 6,* 533–546.

Bates, C., & Brodsky, A. (1989). *Sex in the therapy hour: A case of professional incest.* New York: Guilford Press.

Bohmer, C. (2000). The wages of seeking help: Sexual exploitation by professionals. Westport, CT: Praeger.

Bouhoutsos, J., Holroyd, J., Lerman, H., Forer, B. R., & Greenberg, M. (1983). Sexual intimacy between psychotherapists and patients. *Professional Psychology: Research and Practice, 14,* 185–196.

Brock, G. W., & Coufal, J. D. (1994). A national survey of the ethical practices and attitudes of marriage and family therapists. In G. Brock (Ed.), *American Association for Marriage and Family Therapy ethics casebook* (pp. 27–48). Alexandria, VA: AAMFT.

Coleman, E., & Schaefer, S. (1986). Boundaries of sex and intimacy between client and counselor. *Journal of Counseling and Development, 64,* 341–344.

Disch, E., & Avery, N. (2001). Sex in the consulting room, the examining room, and the sacristy: Survivors of sexual abuse by professionals. *American Journal of Orthopsychiatry, 71*(2), 204–217.

Eddington, N., & Shuman, R. (2004). *Ethics.* Paper presented at the meeting of Continuing Psychology Education, Austin, TX.

Edelwich, J., & Brodsky, A. (1991). *Sexual dilemmas for the helping professional.* New York: Brunner/Mazel.

Fisher, C. D. (2004). Ethical issues in therapy: Therapist self-disclosure of sexual feelings. *Ethics and Behavior, 14*(2), 105–121.

Gabbard, G. (1989). *Sexual exploitation in professional relationships.* Washington, DC: American Psychiatric Press.

Gabbard, G. O. (1997). Lessons to be learned from the study of sexual boundary violations. *Australian and New Zealand Journal of Psychiatry, 31*(3), 321–327.

Harris, S. M. (1998). Sexual attraction in therapy: Concerns and beliefs of MFTs in training. Unpublished raw data.

Harris, S. M. (1998). Sexual attraction in the therapeutic relationship. In *A marriage and family therapist's guide to ethical and legal practice: Answers to questions on current ethical topics and legal considerations in MFT practice* (pp. 4–9). Alexandria, VA: AAMFT.

Harris, S. M., & Hays, K. W. (2008). Family therapist comfort and the willingness to discuss sexuality. *Journal of Marital and Family Therapy, 34*(2), 239–250.

Herman, J. L., Gartrell, N., Olarte, S., Feldstein, M., & Localio, R. (1987). Psychiatrist–patient sexual contact: Results of a national survey, II: Psychiatrists' attitudes. *American Journal of Psychiatry, 144,* 164–169.

Luepker, E. T. (1999). Effects of practitioners' sexual misconduct: A follow-up study. *Journal of the American Academy of Psychiatry and the Law, 27*(1), 51–63.

Masters, W. H., Johnson, V. E., Kolodny, R. C., & Weems, S. M. (1980). *Ethical issues in sex therapy and research: Volume 2.* Boston: Little, Brown and Company.

Nickell, N. J., Hecker, L. L., Ray, R. E., & Bercik, J. (1995). Marriage and family therapists' sexual attraction to clients: An exploratory study. *The American Journal of Family Therapy, 23,* 315–327.

Pope, K. (1988). How clients are harmed by sexual contact with mental health professionals: The syndrome and its prevalence. *Journal of Counseling and Development, 67,* 222–226.

Pope, K. (2001). Sex between therapists and clients. In J. Worrel (Ed.), *Encyclopedia of women and gender: Sex similarities and differences and the impact of society on gender* (Vol. 2, pp. 955–962). Burlington, MA: Academic Press.

Pope, K., Tabachnick, B., & Keith-Spiegel, P. (1986). Sexual attraction to clients: The human therapist and the (sometimes) inhuman training system. *American Psychologist, 41,* 147–158.

Pope, K., Tabachnick, B., & Keith-Spiegel, P. (1987). Ethics of practice: The beliefs and behaviors of psychologists as therapists. *American Psychologist, 42,* 993–1006.

Rutter, P. (1989). *Sex in the forbidden zone.* New York: Fawcett Crest.

Scheflen, A. E. (1965). Quasi-courtship behavior in psychotherapy. *Psychiatry, 28,* 245–257.

Strean, H. S. (1993). *Therapists who have sex with their patients.* New York: Brunner/Mazel.

7

Ethical and Clinical Issues With Intimate Partner Violence

Sara Timmons, John Bryant, Rhi Anna Platt, and Denise Netko

Over 8 million couples experience intimate partner violence (IPV) annually (Stith, McCollum, Rosen, Locke, & Goldberg, 2005). Nearly two-thirds of couples experience some form of abuse prior to entering therapy (Aldarondo & Straus, 1994), yet most couples who seek treatment will not overtly present with domestic violence problems. Only about 6% of couples will specifically express violence as a problem (Stith et al., 2005). Couple and family therapists are on the front line with these clients because most victims seek help from mental health professionals rather than police, physicians, clergy, or crisis centers (Campbell, Raja, & Grining, 1999). The question of whether or not to treat violence individually or in the context of couple therapy is fraught with ethical considerations revolving around issues of power, control, and safety. Therefore, it is imperative that therapists presume there is risk for domestic violence until thorough assessment reveals otherwise.

Many clinicians are not adequately trained to work with couples where violence is present. Research exploring how extensive the training for mental health professionals in Illinois was on four forms of violence (sexual assault, domestic violence, sexual harassment, and incest) found that most (50% to 75% of sample) professionals are receiving training on incest, but not as much on sexual assault or intimate violence (Campbell, Raja, & Grining, 1999). Training in these areas is typically not mandatory in graduate school but rather most likely based in continuing education on a voluntary basis through postgraduate elective instruction.

Likewise, it appears that the field of marriage and family therapy ignores the complex issue of IPV. The prominent *Journal of Marital and*

Family Therapy failed to address the issue of intimate violence in its special issue that examined many major mental health concerns (Salts & Smith, 2003). A survey of members of the American Association of Marriage and Family Therapy (AAMFT) showed that 60% did not believe that intimate violence is a significant problem in their practice, and 40% failed to recognize the signs of partner abuse in vignettes that expressed overt indicators of abuse (Aldarondo & Straus, 1994). Furthermore, a recent qualitative study of universal screening for IPV by family therapy interns indicates that therapists vary in their common practice and attitudes of screening. Some participants believed that universal screening is unduly intrusive and may impair the therapist–client relationship; others regarded it as a core best practice that if well managed, will enhance the relationship (Todahl, Linville, Liang-Ying, and Maher-Cosenza, 2008). When faced with IPV, many clinicians may minimize its existence, or they may be ill-equipped to assess and provide treatment for couples with IPV, or both. The goal of this chapter is to outline the issues of IPV in order to ensure that family therapists are providing ethical and sound treatment.

Types of Intimate Partner Violence

The term *intimate partner violence* refers to violence between two people in a close, personal relationship. This term depicts an image of mutual violence, where both partners utilize acts of force or aggression, such as hitting, pushing, slapping, or biting, and in actuality, could hide the terror that could be occurring in the relationship. Family therapists may believe the best way to solve the problem is by changing interactions or patterns in the relationship; however, not all intimate violence is reciprocal or circular. Rather, IPV may be based in control and power. It is important to understand when IPV can be ethically treated within the relationship, and when it needs to be treated individually. Assessing for which type of violence is occurring will provide greater insight into how to treat the couple due to the distinctions between causes for the various types of violence. Johnson (2006) outlined two forms of violence: intimate terrorism (potentially with violent resistance) and situational couple violence.

Intimate terrorism consists of violent attempts to dominate a relationship. In a heterosexual relationship, it is mostly male perpetrated (Johnson, 2006). Previously referred to in the literature as patriarchal terrorism, it includes the systematic use of violence, economic subordination, threats, isolation, and other control tactics. Although there are unique tactics that may be used in same-sex dyads, such as threatening to out their partner, the patterns of control, demand, and withdrawal can be present in homosexual relationships (Johnson & Ferraro, 2000; Owen & Burke, 2005; Renzetti, 1989; Seelau & Seelau, 2005). Most clinicians and researchers agree that this type of violence is best treated individually before conjoint therapy is ever considered (Greene & Bogo, 2002; Johnson, 1995; Stith et al., 2005). *Violent resistance* may accompany intimate terrorism. It occurs when the victim of intimate terrorism decides to fight back. This can be to defend himself or herself, to attempt to stop the attack, to instill some form of justice for himself or herself (he or she should not be allowed to attack me without getting hurt himself or herself), or to escape (the only way to escape is to kill him or her) (Johnson, 2006).

Situational couple violence differs from intimate terrorism in that there is no general pattern of exerting coercive control. This form of violence is characterized by the use of bidirectional violence, in which both partners employ physical aggression that is mild to moderate in severity. It can be a one-time incident, or a chronic problem, where violence can be minor or escalate to severe (Johnson, 2006). Research suggests that common couple violence is the most common form of domestic violence seen in therapy (Greene & Bogo, 2002; Stith et al., 2005); other forms are likely seen in the legal system. Due to its relational nature, it is believed that conjoint therapy would be beneficial for mutually abusive relationships (Greene & Bogo, 2002; Stith, Locke, Rosen, & McCollum, 2003). Because situational couple violence has the potential to escalate to severe violence, it is imperative that the therapist continually assesses the level of violence in each session to consider if conjoint treatment continues to be productive, safe, and ethical.

Who Are the Batterers and Victims of Intimate Violence?

There is continued debate about whether men and women are equally abusive or if men are more abusive to women. Several studies in line with family violence experts view that an equal number of men and women abuse their partners (Abel, 2001; Chase, O'Farrell, Murphy, Fals-Stewart, & Murphy, 2003; McCarroll, Thayer, & Liu, 2000; Straus & Gelles, 1990; Stuart, 2005). Others align with the feminist view that believes women are at greatest risk when there is violence between males and females (Archer, 2000; Berns, Jacobsen, & Gottman, 1999) due to numerous studies reporting a gendered phenomenon in which women are disproportionately victims of abuse and men are inexplicably the perpetrators (Berns et al., 1999; McCloskey & Grigsby, 2005; Straus & Gelles, 1990). Research studies indicate men are responsible for 85% of marital violence, indicating that violence in families is not gender neutral or equal (Avis, 1992; Straus, 2006). Women comprise a small proportion (15%) of IPV-related arrests in the United States (Rennison, 2002), and the majority of these women report physical abuse by their male partner (Simmons, Lehman, & Collier-Tenison, 2008). This "gendered asymmetry" signifies that women suffer greater consequences of intimate violence than men (McCloskey & Grigsby, 2005, p. 265). Physical injury occurs more in violence against women by their husbands or partners than all combined incidents of car accidents, muggings, and rape reported in the United States and Canada (Avis, 1992). Furthermore, Avis (1992) reported that at least one out of six women will be physically abused by a male spouse or partner at some point in their lives, and in terms of repeated violence, one in 14 marriages will suffer from perpetual abuse with reports being filed only after an average of 35 episodes. Although mutual violence is rising for many couples (Johnson, 1995) and women are being arrested for abuse at an increasing rate (Abel, 2001), females are still disproportionately at risk of harm when it comes to IPV.

Intimate partner violence appears to have greater prevalence among same-sex couples than heterosexual couples (Tjaden, Thoennes, & Allison, 1999). Kelly and Warshafsky (1987) began shedding light onto this topic in their study of 98 gay and lesbian participants (48 women and 50 men). They used the Conflict Tactics Scale (Straus, 1979) to assess for violence and found that 100% of their sample used assertive tactics at some point in their relationship, 95% used verbal abuse tactics, 47% used physical aggression, and 3% used violence. Exploration into gender differences found that the only distinction was that the men tended to have more physically aggressive partners than the women (Kelly & Warshafsky, 1987). Using data from the National Violence Against Women (NVAW) survey, Tjaden and colleagues (1999) found that 21.5% of same-sex cohabiting men reported a history of physical assault by a male or female partner compared with 7.7% of opposite-sex cohabiting men. Similarly, 35.4% of same-sex cohabiting women reported a history of physical assault by a male or female partner, whereas 18.3% of opposite-sex cohabiting women reported incidences of physical abuse. Interestingly, the prevalence of IPV among same-sex couples was 11.4% for female partners and 13.8% for male partners (Tjaden et al., 1999).

As noted above, feminist theorists have historically believed that IPV is largely male perpetrated and has its roots in patriarchy. Conversely, family violence theorists have argued that women are as violent as men, and conflicts are rooted in everyday tensions. As it turns out, both were true, but the feminists and family violence theorists were studying different samples. Feminists were studying agency samples where the subjects were experiencing what Johnson (2006) referred to as "intimate terrorism" and a response to that terrorism termed "violent resistance." Family violence theorists were studying general survey data and were seeing what Johnson referred to as "situational couple violence" which is more gender symmetrical (Johnson, 2006). In order to provide ethical and safe treatment for IPV clients, the therapist must understand the types of violence, and when couple treatment is optimal and advisable, and when it is questionable or even dangerous.

Assessment

Family therapists need to be especially careful when assessing for violence because their systematic orientation may cause them to assign reciprocal causality when power inequities and resulting coercion tactics may be overtly or covertly in place. If the family therapist does not assess the larger societal context of oppression and power imbalances, assumes circular causality, and insists only on conjoint treatment, he or she can jeopardize client welfare and hinder maneuverability when dealing with violent couples (Jory, Anderson, & Greer, 1997). Furthermore, placing women in conjoint therapy with men who tend to minimize or deny their culpability causes harm if the men are not held accountable for their actions. Women tend to feel intimidated, disconnected, exploited, and afraid in therapy due to the lack of freedom to speak in the therapy session with the abuser (Jory et al., 1997). Given that some men do not attend therapy until their wives threaten to leave the marriage (25% of the sample in a study of males participating in marriage and family therapy) (Guillebeaux, Storm, & Demaris, 1986), conjoint therapy may only succeed in encouraging her to stay, enabling the man to possibly become a better batterer by allowing him to witness her weaknesses in therapy, and avoid accountability in the legal system by saying he is working on the problem (Jory et al., 1997).

Screening for All Couples

Bruce and Kathy met with a student therapist at a university clinic for their first session with their newborn infant in tow. They described a tumultuous relationship, with Bruce prone to fits of jealousy. Bruce seemed agitated during the session and frequently stood up during the session and walked around the room while speaking agitatedly. Kathy tearfully described how things had deteriorated since the birth of the baby just a few weeks prior, and Bruce described his frustration that Kathy had no time for him now. Midway through the session, the therapist told the couple that she was going to take a break to consult with her treatment team, and Bruce stated he was going to step outside to have a cigarette. As soon as Bruce left the room for his cigarette break, Kathy turned to the therapist and said, "I think he is going to kill me. He choked me last night, and I think he is going to try to kill me." Kathy showed the therapist the bruise marks on her neck where she alleged that Bruce had tried to strangle her. When the therapist queried if Kathy felt safe going home with Bruce, she clearly said she did not. The police were summoned, and Kathy and the baby were helped to safety and given legal and housing resources.

As evidenced above, couples clearly need to be thoroughly assessed before commencing couples therapy because to err on the side of omission may have deadly consequences. The therapist must assess the couple relationship, the manner of the referral to therapy (mandated or voluntary), the mental health of the individuals, and the commitment to couple therapy prior to making the decision to see the couple conjointly or individually. Couples may also not think abusive acts are abuse: pushing, shoving, hair-grabbing, or much worse may not be seen as abusive by some couples. Specific questions may be needed to get an accurate picture of the couple's interactions.

Individual Time in the Conjoint Interview

In the initial conjoint session, it is imperative that the therapist meet with each partner alone, regardless if there has been definite disclosure of abuse or not. This meeting will give each member of the couple an opportunity to privately divulge any IPV that he or she may feel uncomfortable disclosing in the presence of his or her partner. In the above example, Kathy likely would not have felt comfortable divulging the abuse in front of Bruce, and indeed it would likely only have served to increase her danger. However, the therapist must be cognizant that when abuse is revealed, the victim is at increased risk and must proceed cautiously (Bograd & Mederos, 1999).

Assessing the relationship in the presence of both partners is particularly risky because the true nature of the victim may be obscured by the abuser. The victim may deny abuse or appear withdrawn only because the person is alongside the abuser. In order to assess and understand the true dynamics of the relationship, the therapist will need to see them individually. The abuse may only be suggested, and not confirmed or denied, by either the victim or the abuser. It is important that clinicians follow through in the assessment with the individual session in order to verify as best as possible that the victim is safe. Implementing individual sessions to assess for violence and safety will allow the client an outlet for revealing the abuse in the present or future individual time. The individual time will also allow the victim to freely talk about the abuse without worries that the information he or she gives will result in further abuse in the therapy room and outside of the session. Mutual abuse may also be downplayed unless the therapist queries about specific acts of violence.

Assessment Questions

The majority of couples presenting for treatment do not readily disclose the extent of or the fact that any IPV is occurring in the relationship. A study conducted by Ehrensaft and Vivian (1996) found that two-thirds of couples seeking marital therapy did not disclose any incidences of domestic violence until specific questions were asked by the therapist (Bograd, 1999). Some reasons for this lack of disclosure include fear, shame, social stigma, and embarrassment. Therefore, it is important for the therapist to ask questions and carefully listen and assess the responses given by the couple both conjointly and individually. A caveat to keep in mind when asking questions is "always remember yes means yes, but no may mean many things." Denials may need to be explored.

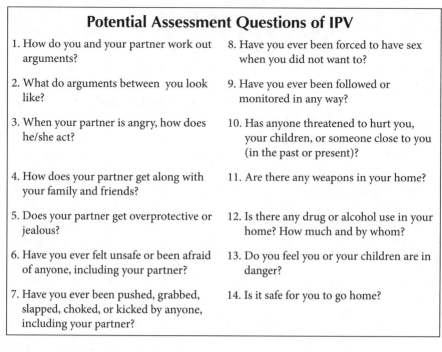

Potential Assessment Questions of IPV

1. How do you and your partner work out arguments?

2. What do arguments between you look like?

3. When your partner is angry, how does he/she act?

4. How does your partner get along with your family and friends?

5. Does your partner get overprotective or jealous?

6. Have you ever felt unsafe or been afraid of anyone, including your partner?

7. Have you ever been pushed, grabbed, slapped, choked, or kicked by anyone, including your partner?

8. Have you ever been forced to have sex when you did not want to?

9. Have you ever been followed or monitored in any way?

10. Has anyone threatened to hurt you, your children, or someone close to you (in the past or present)?

11. Are there any weapons in your home?

12. Is there any drug or alcohol use in your home? How much and by whom?

13. Do you feel you or your children are in danger?

14. Is it safe for you to go home?

Figure 7.1   Potential assessment questions of intimate partner violence.

Possible assessment questions are presented in Figure 7.1. Questioning should always start with open-ended questions, and the therapist must weigh the decision to ask further the questions with the reservations the client may seem to have in answering them; if the questions serve to frighten the client away from therapy, they have been for naught. The therapist also needs to be aware of his or her state's domestic violence reporting requirements and have communicated those to the client in the informed consent as well as verbally.

Family therapists understand that working with conflictual couples can be emotionally intense when episodes of arguing develop in session. Although observing arguments enhances assessment into the couple's interaction, IPV couples pose serious risks when this occurs. Many batterers are highly emotionally reactive and have difficulty calming down, which may induce them to strike when they perceive provocation (Gottman et al., 1995). Therefore, it is important to avoid these situations until proper coping strategies and interventions are implemented.

The most important goal in the first phase of treatment is safety for the victim during the session and insuring a secure environment for when he or she leaves.

Assessment Instruments

In addition to individual session time with each partner, if abuse is suspected or alleged, there are assessment instruments available to further screen for IPV. These range from specifically designed instruments to questions that should be asked by the therapist. These inventories can assist the clinician in creating the appropriate treatment plan for the couple. Several instruments have been developed to measure the extent of conflict and violence in relationships. Described below are some of the instruments available to therapists for assessment (Hamby, Poindexter, & Gray-Little, 1996):

> *The Revised Conflict Tactics Scales* (CTS2) (Straus, Hamby, Boney-McCoy, & Sugarman, 1996) was originally developed by Straus (the original CTS) (1979; 1990) and is the most widely used tool for detecting relationship violence. It has scales that measure victimization and perpetration (i.e., physical assault, psychological aggression, and negotiation and reasoning by the partner to reduce conflict). It also has scales to measure sexual coercion (Straus, 2007). It takes only a few minutes to administer, which allows the test to be easily incorporated within the standard intake interview questionnaire. It identifies the occurrence of violence, its severity, and its chronicity. It also targets specific behavior, thereby minimizing the amount of interpretation by clients to determine if a behavior is violent (Aldarondo & Strauss, 1994).
>
> *The Index of Spouse Abuse* (ISA) (Hudson and McIntosh, 1981) was designed to measure both physical and nonphysical abuse. The ISA consists of 30 items, three of which ask directly about physical acts of violence, one that addresses sexual coercion, and seven that pertain to physical intimidation and domination. The strength of this test is that it provides information about psychological abuse but is limited in determining actual and specific acts of violence. Furthermore, it mixes physical violence with other forms of maltreatment, which may indicate violence when no actual incident of abuse occurred (Aldarando & Straus, 1994).
>
> *The Wife Abuse Inventory* (WAI) (Lewis, 1985) was designed to identify abused women or women at risk for abuse by asking women to rate their

partners, as well as themselves, on items of family management matters. One limitation of the scale is that it focuses on the causes and whether a risk exists as opposed to if abuse is presently occurring.

The Relationship Conflict Inventory (RCI) (Arthur Bodin, 1996) as part of the efforts of the Task Force on Diagnosis and Classification of the Family Psychology Division of the American Psychological Association. The instrument consists of 114 items that measure levels of verbal and physical conflict among couples in treatment. A limitation of this measure is that it does not ask the respondent to identify the perpetrator of the violence directly. In addition, the psychometric properties of the instrument remain unknown.

Deciding If Individual or Conjoint Therapy Is Best

If the clinician has assessed there is violence present, the next step is to decide if and how to proceed in therapy with the couple. Conjoint therapy can be appropriate and helpful in some cases, yet increases danger in others. Therapists need to minimize the risks associated with couples presenting with IPV and maximize the safety of the clients. A model for decision making is presented in Figure 7.2.

Potential Risks and Benefits of Conjoint Treatment

As discussed previously, conjoint treatment can serve to send a message to the couple that the abuse is a couple problem, and may inadvertently assign blame to the victim without holding the abuser accountable for his or her actions. This is especially detrimental when the abuse does not resemble mutual situational couple violence and when relationship patterns are not influencing the violence as in the case of intimate terrorism. Another potential risk is that victims may not feel safe enough to share their true feelings and contribute to therapy for fear that their information will cause further harm and abuse after sessions (Holtzworth-Munroe, Meehan, Rehman, & Marshall, 2002). This dynamic is not conducive to successful therapy and will only serve to further isolate and intimidate the victim. Finally, a concern is that the therapeutic environment will increase the potential for violence due to the likelihood of instigating intense emotions and discussions that could lead to violence (Bograd, 1994).

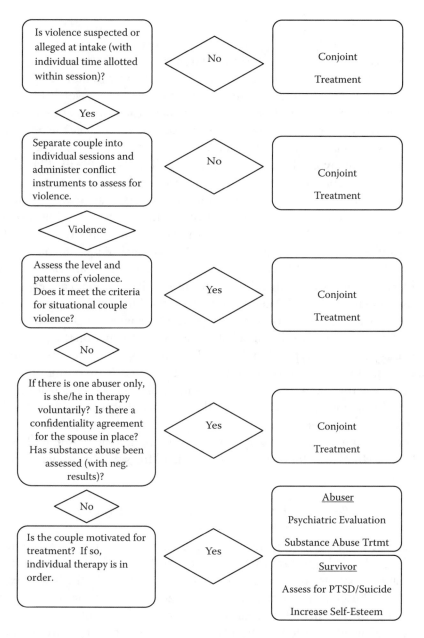

Figure 7.2   A model for deciding on conjoint or individual treatment for IPV.

Conjoint therapy has benefits if the risks are evaluated and the clinician is careful to protect against potential harm. Treating both partners allows for increased understanding and awareness of the patterns of aggression. This offers the clinician increased ways to intervene and help the clients learn skills to interrupt the cycle of violence. Holtzworth-Munroe, Meehan, Rehman, and Marshall (2002) believe that interventions can be more effective when both partners are present and can reduce the potential for abusers to use therapeutic interventions to further abuse because the victim will be involved in the process. It also diminishes the likelihood for misinterpretations of interventions and words spoken when both partners are in session. Furthermore, conjoint therapy offers a safe place to discuss heated issues that may lead to violence outside of therapy (Holtzworth-Munroe et al., 2002). The therapist can act as a mediator to diffuse the intensity while demonstrating the usefulness of techniques, such as time-outs, that can be practiced in session before attempted at home. It can offer opportunities for direct interventions into interactional patterns that may decrease violence (O'Leary, Heyman, & Neidig, 1999). As mentioned in previous sections, Greene and Bogo (2002) suggest that most violent couples treated by family therapists resemble the situational couple violence type. In this type of violence, abuse is present in the interactions, patterns, and processes of the relationship because it is commonly used by both partners and usually results from escalation of conflict (Johnson, 1995). Conjoint therapy may benefit these couples because it addresses the dysfunctional patterns of the interactions that serve to instigate the abuse. However, conjoint therapy still requires careful implementation with definite guidelines. The following sections will address this implementation.

Important Safeguards and Guidelines for Conjoint Therapy

There are no available evidence-based guidelines for conjoint treatment of violence. Some important safeguards for treatment are the protection of the abused partner's safety (or safety for both partners in the instances of conjoint abuse), confirmation that the abused wishes to remain in the relationship, the victim does not fear the abuser, and the victim feels comfortable sharing information and is not endangered by partaking in discussions of the abuse (Harris, Savage, Jones, & Brooke, 1988; Holtzworth-Munroe et al., 2002; O'Leary et al., 1999). Furthermore, most researchers agree that conjoint treatment is only appropriate if there are low to moderate levels of aggression in the relationship, and both partners believe that violence is a problem and desire to work toward a nonviolent relationship (Holtzworth-Munroe et al., 2002).

Bograd and Mederos (1999) offered three conditions that must be satisfied in order to pursue conjoint therapy: the voluntary participation of the abuser, special agreements involving confidentiality, and achievement of optimal therapeutic stance. The issue of voluntary participation is important to distinguish among abusers who are court mandated to attend therapy due to the severity of violence and those who are there to get help. The severity of the violence may prevent success in therapy due to psychological or personality problems with the batterer (Bograd & Mederos, 1999). In this case, individual treatment should be considered.

Confidentiality needs to be specially negotiated because the victim needs to be protected from the abuser; therefore, some pertinent information or secrets may be necessarily hidden from the abuser (Bograd & Mederos, 1999). This form of secrecy is usually considered inadvisable in traditional couples or family therapy because it triangulates the therapist and decreases his or her maneuverability, but in intimate violence situations it may be essential to the safety of the victim. The victim is never forced to divulge anything in couples therapy before he or she is ready to share it. Therefore, it is always important that the issues of secrets are discussed at the beginning of treatment and the therapist clearly explains the exceptions to confidentiality, such as the duty to warn, to prevent either party from feeling estranged by the process. State domestic violence statutes should also be explained and included in one's informed consent.

Bograd and Mederos (1999) also discussed achieving the optimal therapeutic stance in therapy with batterers. They suggest that therapists self-monitor their own reactions with regard to countertransference, monitor the therapy setting for safety, be compassionate without being emotionally reactive, and consistently allocate responsibility for the abuse to the abuser. They also recommend that therapists strategically frame the harmful effects of the male client's behaviors in his own self-interest, that he, in effect, is hurting his own interests by his behavior. Clear behavioral limits must also be set.

The issue of substance abuse needs to be addressed due to the high correlation between violence and the abuse of substances (Stith et al., 2005). The abuse of substances decreases impulse control and increases the unpredictability of violence (Stith et al., 2005). Therefore, it is imperative that a therapist assess for substance abuse issues in regard to working with couples that present with IPV. The therapist has an obligation to explore with the couple the relationship between substance abuse and domestic violence by asking questions, such as, "Has your partner ever been violent or threatening while under the influence?," "Is the violence worse when your partner has been drinking or doing drugs?," "Have there been violent incidents when your partner has been sober or clean?"

Treatment Tools to Decrease Risk

After deciding to do conjoint therapy, it is important for the therapist to consider using therapeutic contracts, a safety plan, negotiated time-outs, and no-violence contracts as treatment tools. These tools help ensure the safety of the clients and should be discussed early on in therapy.

Therapeutic Contracts

Due to risk of violence, a therapeutic contract needs to be provided that sets distinct limits on any type of aggression and negotiated consequences if those limits are pushed. Both partners must agree that the primary goals of therapy are the termination of the abuse, as well as a means of repairing the victim's emotional, physical, and psychological wounds (Bograd & Mederos, 1999; Holtzworth-Munroe et al., 2002). The climate of these sessions should be safe, calm, and open to both sides in order to elicit the best understanding of the patterns. There is a limited amount of safety clinicians can provide for couples, so it is advisable that the treatment plan be reviewed extensively. It is also important to explain to the couple that if the contract is broken for any reason, by any party, treatment may be terminated (Bograd & Mederos, 1999). If individual therapy or psychiatric care is recommended in addition to conjoint therapy, it should be detailed and agreed upon in the conjoint treatment contract.

A Safety Plan

In addition to the therapeutic contract, a safety plan needs to be drawn up with specific information for the abused partner. A safety plan generally includes the following components:

- Identification of the client's support network in case of an emergency, and a written list of phone numbers for those persons—a notation should be made that the client may call the police (911).
- Details of where the abused person may go temporarily if he or she senses abuse may occur, or if abuse does occur—this may be a friend's or a relative's home or a domestic violence shelter.
- A list of things the client may want to have ready to go in case of an emergency, such as:
  - Important papers (e.g., identification, immigration papers, checkbook)
  - Medications
  - Clothing
  - Children's or baby's items (baby food and formula)
- Identification of a code word with family or friends for help.
- An extra set of keys.

Another important consideration for the client is to be able to identify when and if it is safe to return to the home. It is important to review this information with the client to ensure the safety of the client and any children involved. In addition, a prevention plan can be put in place in therapy that has clear steps that the couple can take to decrease the chances of using violence. For instance, they can commit to only having heated debates in public or in therapy, and remove from their environment any potential weapons that could cause harm (Holtzworth-Munroe et al., 2002).

Negotiated Time-Outs

Initially, it is very important that the therapist discuss the use of time-outs with couples and assist them in creating and practicing a time-out plan. The first step in negotiating a time-out procedure is for both partners to be able to recognize and identify their feelings that indicate that they are beginning to escalate in their own personal cycle of anger (Rosen, Matheson, Stith, & McCollum, 2003). Once both partners are able to self-reflect and understand their escalation signals, the next step is for one or both partners to signal that a time-out is needed. It is important at this step that the partners identify a signal that will be used to indicate the need for the time-out, rather than one that can intensify their interaction (Rosen et al., 2003). In addition, important rules for use of a time-out need to be established that require both partners to respect the request made for a time-out, as well as that require both partners to collude in creating the signal, rather than one holding all the power and control in establishing and implementing a signal. Furthermore, the couple needs to separate and engage in activities that have already been identified as detours to allow them to return to a calm state. The time-out needs to last for a designated amount of time to allow each person to deescalate (Rosen et al., 2003). It is important that the therapist help the couple to identify the amount of time necessary for this cooling-off period, which is relative to the time that each partner needs to be able to deescalate and physically calm down. This will ensure that it is not used as an avoidance tactic by either person.

Finally, after deescalation, the couple reunites and decides if they are calm enough to continue the discussion or take another time-out. The therapist may also suggest that certain issues be put on hold until the next conjoint session to avoid the risk of possible violence (Stith et al., 2003). It is important that this plan be reviewed several times and even role-played in session to ensure success. If used appropriately, the negotiated time-out can be an effective tool that serves to prevent violence, as well as empower both partners by teaching skills that aid them in controlling their behaviors.

No-Violence Contracts

Finally, the therapist can create a "No-Violence" contract with the couple outlining what they will do in the event they feel that violence is about to occur in their relationship. (See Appendix 7.1 for an example of a No-Violence Contract—Level I [Hecker, 2008].) The Level I contract contains simple statements with a pledge that the person will not allow himself or herself to forcefully touch another person, and a list of alternative tactics to use instead to interrupt the cycle of violence. The therapist should also set up consequences for the violation of the no-violence contract in the event that the violence should recur. (See Appendix 7.1 for No-Violence Contract—Level II [Hecker, 2008].) Hecker (2008) developed a two-level no-violence contract system. Level I is a standard no-violence contract; Level II is a contract that is put in place if the Level I contract is violated. It is a checklist system that the therapist can personalize to the client's needs. Level II can be discussed with the client at the same time that Level I is discussed with the consequences being outlined and agreed upon at the time that the Level I contract is negotiated. This is not presented as a consequence as much as a treatment contract for keeping the couple safe. The contract will not ensure that violence will not recur, and will not necessarily decrease therapist liability, but it will make ending the violence the center of treatment. It can also tailor treatment to the couple's specific needs and serve as an outline of a treatment plan.

Summary

This chapter is presented as a guideline from which therapists can begin to formulate a framework for decision making for working with IPV clients. Intimate partner violence is a complex therapeutic issue that requires accurate assessment in order to decrease risk in treatment. The decision to treat IPV individually or within conjoint couple therapy warrants treatment considerations that ultimately affect the safety of the clients. Every couple is unique and may suffer from situational couple violence, intimate terrorism, or violent resistance, or a combination thereof; the therapist must continually assess the advisability of conjoint treatment. Clients of intimate terrorism and violent resistance are not amenable to couples therapy and need to be treated individually or in groups. As yet, there are no established criteria for physical partner abuse; however, open-ended assessment questions and assessment questionnaires can be useful tools for the therapist on an ongoing basis (Heyman et al., 2001). Staples of working with couples with IPV include treatment contracts, safety plans, and no-violence contracts. Cultural sensitivity is also needed in dealing with IPV. Further research is needed to empirically evaluate which clients will benefit most from individual versus conjoint therapy and at what point individual therapy should merge into conjoint therapy. Research is also needed to aid therapists in screening clients for conjoint versus individual therapy. Unfortunately, even when therapists are armed with an arsenal of comprehensive screening and assessment instruments, they are often left with the ethical dilemma of making reasoned speculations when engaging couples presenting with intimate partner violence in therapy.

Appendix 7.1

*No-Violence Contract, Level I**

I pledge never to allow my anger to reach the point that I forcefully touch another person, no matter how right or justified I feel I am.

I pledge to use the following tactics or procedures I have discussed with my therapist in order to avoid any potential for violence or harm to others.

In the event that I feel I may hurt someone, I promise to

1. _____

_____

or

2. _____

_____

or

3. _____

_____

If I am unable to comply with the Level I No-Violence Contract, the Level II No-Violence Contract will be put in place.

_____   _____
Client Signature   Date

_____   _____
Witness Signature   Date

---

* Developed by Lorna L. Hecker, Ph.D., 2008. (Used with permission of the author.)

*No-Violence Contract, Level II**

1. Clients will sign and follow the no-violence contract assigned by the therapists.

2. If clients fail to comply with the no-violence contract, the following things may occur:

   - The couple or perpetrator will be sent for substance abuse and/or psychiatric assessment. Clients will be required to follow treatment recommendations of the assessors.
   - The couple will not be seen in couple's treatment until the violence ceases and all parties agree that the threat has ceased for a reasonable period of time.
   - The perpetrator(s) will be referred to an anger management group for treatment and must follow through for therapy to continue.
   - _____

3. If the above measures fail, the perpetrator of the violence agrees to

   - Move out of the couple's home.
   - Receive inpatient evaluation and treatment.
   - _____

4. If the above measures fail, the victim shall agree to

   - Call the police consistently if any other *threat* of violence or actual violence occurs, and
   - File a restraining order against the perpetrator.
   - The victim shall agree not to allow the perpetrator to move back to the couple's home until substance abuse treatment and/or psychiatric treatment has been completed, and couple's therapy has recommenced.
   - _____

I agree to the above stipulations for treatment.

_____   _____
Signature   Date

_____   _____
Signature   Date

---

* Developed by Lorna L. Hecker, Ph.D., 2008 (Used with permission of the author.)

References

Abel, E. M. (2001). Comparing the social service utilization, exposure to violence, and trauma symptomatology of domestic violence female "victims" and female "batterers." *Journal of Family Violence, 4*, 401–420.

Aldarondo, E., & Straus, M. A. (1994). Screening for physical violence in couple therapy: Methodological, practical and ethical considerations. *Family Process, 33*, 425–439.

Archer, J. (2000). Sex differences in aggression between heterosexual partners: A meta-analytic review. *Psychological Bulletin, 126*, 651–680.

Avis, J. M. (1992). Where are all the family therapists?: Abuse and violence within families and family therapy's response. *Journal of Marital and Family Therapy, 18*(3), 225–232.

Berns, S. B., Jacobson, N. S., & Gottman, J. M. (1999). Demand/withdraw interaction patterns between different types of batterers and their spouses. *Journal of Marital and Family Therapy, 25*(3), 349–363.

Bodin, A. M. (1996). Relationship conflict—verbal and physical: Conceptualizing an inventory for assessing process and content. In F. W. Kaslow (Ed.), *Handbook of Relational Diagnosis and Dysfunctional Family Patterns* (pp. 371–393). New York: John Wiley.

Bograd, M. (1994). Battering, competing clinical models, and paucity of research: Notes to those in the trenches. *Counseling Psychologist, 22*(4), 593–597.

Bograd, M. (1999). Strengthening domestic violence theories: Intersections of race, class, sexual orientation, and gender. *Journal of Marital and Family Therapy, 25*(3), 275–289.

Bograd, M., & Mederos, F. (1999). Battering and couples therapy: Universal screening and selection of treatment modality. *Journal of Marital and Family Therapy, 25*(3), 291–312.

Chase, K., O'Farrell, T. J., Murphy, C. M., Fals-Stewart, W., & Murphy, M. (2003). Factors associated with partner violence among female alcoholic clients and their male partners. *Journal of Studies of Alcohol, 64*, 137–149.

Campbell, R., Raja, S., & Grining, P. L. (1999). Training mental health professionals on violence against women. *Journal of Interpersonal Violence, 14*(10), 1003–1014.

Ehrensaft, M. K., & Vivian, D. (1996). Spouse's reasons for not reporting existing marital aggression as a marital problem. *Journal of Family Violence, 14*(3), 443–453.

Gottman, J. M., Jacobson, N. S., Rushe, R. H., Shortt, J. W., Babcock, J., La Taillade, J. J., & Waltz, J. (1995). The relationship between heart rate reactivity, emotionally aggressive behavior, and general violence in batterers. *Journal of Family Psychology, 9*, 221–248.

Greene, K., & Bogo, M. (2002). The different faces of intimate violence: Implications for assessment and treatment. *Journal of Marital and Family Therapy, 28*, 455–466.

Guillebeaux, F., Storm, C. L., & Demaris, A. (1986). Luring the reluctant male: A study of males participating in marriage and family therapy. *Family Therapy, 13*(2), 215–225.

Hamby, S. L., Poindexter, V. C., Gray-Little, B. (1996). Four measures of partner violence: Construct similarity and classification differences. *Journal of Marriage and the Family, 58*(1), 127–139.

Harris, R., Savage, S., Jones, T., & Brooke, W. (1988). A comparison of treatments for abusive men and their partners within a family-service agency. *Canadian Journal of Community Mental Health, 7*, 147–155.

Hecker, L. (2008). No-Violence Contracts, Level 1 & II. Unpublished manuscript. Hammond, IN: Purdue University Calumet.

Heyman, R. E., Feldbau-Kohn, S. R., Ehrensaft, M. K., Langhinrichsen-Rohling, J., & O'Leary, K. D. (2001). Can questionnaire reports correctly classify relationship distress and partner physical abuse? *Journal of Family Psychology, 15*(2), 334–346.

Holtzworth-Munroe, A., Meehan, J. C., Rehman, U., & Marshall, A. D. (2002). Intimate partner violence: An introduction for couple therapists. In A. Gurman & N. Jacobsen (Eds.), *Clinical Handbook of Couple Therapy* (3rd ed., pp. 441–465). New York: Guilford Press.

Hudson, W. W., & McIntosh, S. R. (1981). The assessment of spouse abuse: Two quantifiable dimensions. *Journal of Marriage and the Family, 43*(4), 873–855, 888.

Johnson, M. P. (1995). Patriarchal terrorism and common couple violence: Two forms of violence against women. *Journal of Marriage and the Family, 57*, 283–294.

Johnson, M. P. (2006). Gendered communication and intimate partner violence. In Bonnie J. Dow & Julia T. Wood (Eds.), *The Sage Handbook of Gender and Communication* (pp. 71–87). Thousand Oaks, CA: Sage.

Johnson, M. P., & Ferraro, K. J. (2000). Research on domestic violence in the 1990's: Making distinctions. *Journal of Marriage and the Family, 62*, 948–963.

Jory, B., Anderson, B., & Greer, C. (1990). Intimate justice: Confronting issues of accountability, respect, freedom in treatment for abuse and violence. *Journal of Marital and Family Therapy, 23*(4), 399–419.

Kaufman, Jr., G. (1992). The mysterious disappearance of battered women in the family therapists' offices: Male privilege colluding with male violence. *Journal of Marital and Family Violence, 18*, 233–243.

Lewis, B. Y. (1985). The wife abuse inventory: A screening device for the identification of abused women. *Social Work, 30*(1), 32–35.

McCarroll, J. E., Thayer, L. E., & Liu, X. (2000). Spouse abuse recidivism in the
U.S. Army by gender and military status. *Journal of Consulting and Clinical
Psychology, 68,* 521–525.

McCloskey, K., & Grigsby, N. (2005). The ubiquitous clinical problem of adult
intimate partner violence: The need for routine assessment. *Professional
Psychology: Research and Practice, 36*(3), 264–275.

O'Leary, K. D., Heyman, R. E., & Neidig, P. H. (1999). Treatment of wife abuse: A
comparison of gender-specific and couples approaches. *Behavior Therapy,
30,* 475–505.

Owen, S., & Burke, T. (2004). An exploration of prevalence of domestic violence in
same-sex relationships. *Psychological Report, 95,* 129–132.

Rennison, C. M. (2002). Intimate partner violence, 1993–2001, *Bureau of
Justice Statistics Crime Data Brief.* Washington, DC: U.S. Department of
Justice.

Renzetti, C. M. (1989). Building a second closet: Third party responses to victims
of lesbian partner abuse. *Family Relations, 38,* 157–163.

Rosen, K. H., Matheson, J., Stith, S. M., & McCollum, E. E. (2003). Negotiated
time-out: A de-escalation tool for couples. *Journal of Marital and Family
Therapy, 29*(3), 291–298.

Salts, C. J., & Smith, A. Jr. (2003). Special topics in family therapy. In L. L. Hecker
& J. L Wetchler (Eds.), *An Introduction to Marriage and Family Therapy* (pp.
449–492). Binghamton, NY: Haworth Clinical Press.

Seelau, S., & Seelau, E. (2005). Gender-role stereotypes and perceptions of heterosexual, gay, and lesbian domestic violence. *Journal of Family Violence, 20,* 363–371.

Simmons, C. A., Lehman, P., & Collier-Tenison, S. (2008). From victim to offender:
The effects of male initiated violence on women arrested for using intimate
partner violence. *Journal of Family Violence, 23,* 463–472.

Stith, S. M., Locke, L. D., Rosen, K. H., & McCollum, E. E. (2003). Effectiveness
of couples treatment of spouse abuse. *Journal of Marital and Family Therapy,
29*(3), 407–426.

Stith, S. M., Rosen, K. H., McCollum, E. E., & Thomsen, C. J. (2004). Treating
intimate partner violence within intact couple relationships: Outcomes of
multi-couple versus individual couple therapy. *Journal of Marital and Family
Therapy, 30*(3), 305–318.

Stith, S. M., McCollum, E. E., Rosen, K. H., Locke, L., & Goldberg, P. (2005).
Domestic violence-focused couples treatment. In J. L. Lebow (Ed.), *Handbook
of Clinical Family Therapy* (pp. 406–430). New York: John Wiley & Sons.

Straus, M. A. (1979). Measuring intrafamily conflict and violence: The Conflict
Tactics (CT) scales. *Journal of Marriage and the Family, 41*(1), 75–88.

Straus, M. A. (1990). Conflict Tactics scales. In N. Fredman & R. Sherman (Eds.),
Handbook of Measurements for Marriage and Family Therapy (pp. 159–163).
New York: Brunner/Mazel.

Straus, M. A. (2006). Future research on gender symmetry in physical assaults on partners. *Violence Against Women, 12*(11), 1086–1097.

Straus, M. A. (2007). Conflict Tactic scales. In N. A. Jackson (Ed.), *Encyclopedia of Domestic Violence* (pp. 190–197). New York: Routledge: Taylor & Francis.

Straus, M. A., & Gelles, R. J. (1990). *Physical Violence in American Families: Risk Factors and Adaptations to Violence in 8,145 Families.* New Brunswick, NJ: Transaction.

Straus, M. A., Hamby, S. L., Boney-McCoy, S., & Sugarman, D. B. (1996). The revised Conflict Tactics scales (CTS2): Development and preliminary psychometric data. *Journal of Family Issues, 17,* 283–316.

Stuart, R. (2005). Treatment for partner abuse: Time for a paradigm shift. *Professional Psychology: Research and Practice, 36*(3), 254–263.

Tjaden, P., Thoennes, N., & Allison, C. J. (1999). Comparing violence over the life span in samples of same-sex and opposite-sex cohabitants. *Violence and Victims, 14,* 413–425.

Todahl, J. L., Linville, D., Liang-Ying, C., & Maher-Cosenza, P. (2008). A qualitative study of intimate partner violence universal screening by family therapy interns: Implications for practice, research, training, and supervision. *Journal of Marital and Family Therapy, 34,* 28–43.

8

Risk Factors and Suicide

*Denise Netko, Rhi Anna Platt, John
Bryant, and Lorna L. Hecker*

All mental health professionals grapple with clients who have suicidal ideation or who have attempted suicide. Even with the best treatment, it is impossible to control the actions of one's clients. Chemtob, Hamada, Bauer, Torigoe, & Kinney (1988a) found that psychologists face more than a 20% chance of losing a client to suicide, and psychiatrists face about a 50% chance of losing a patient to suicide (Chemtob, Hamada, Bauer, Torigoe, & Kinney, 1988b). Therapists are left to struggle with this complex issue, safeguarding client confidentiality while keeping clients safe, and sometimes therapists are left feeling stranded in this tenuous position. In this chapter, suicide risk factors, assessment and intervention, legal issues, and standard of care are discussed to aid therapists in keeping the client's best interests in mind while keeping their own peace of mind.

Suicide Risk

Suicide Risk Factors and Assessment of Suicide Intent

Clearly, it is of utmost importance for mental health practitioners to be familiar with the various suicidal risk factors (Rudd, Joiner, & Rajab, 2001). Understanding suicide risk factors can help to unravel myths of suicide. Some individuals may have an increased vulnerability to suicide or suicidal self-injury due to having more than one mental illness present (Henriksson et al., 1993).

Simon (2004) identified suicidal risk factors as falling into one of two categories, either acute or chronic. Those clients in the acute risk factor category have been experiencing suicidal risk factors for several days or weeks. Clients falling into the chronic risk factor category have been experiencing suicidal risk factors for at least a year prior to the assessment. Chronic suicidal clients are not an immediate risk for suicide, whereas acute suicidal clients are at great risk for suicide (Simon, 2004). The following is a summary of risk factors for suicide:

- Previous suicide attempt(s)
- A history of mental disorders, particularly depression
- A history of alcohol and substance abuse
- A family history of suicide
- A family history of child maltreatment
- Feelings of hopelessness
- Impulsive or aggressive tendencies
- Loss in the client's life (in their social or relational life, work, or financially)
- Physical illness
- Relatively easy access to lethal methods
- Cultural or religious beliefs that glorify suicide as a noble resolution to a personal dilemma
- Local epidemics of suicide
- Isolation; a feeling of being cut off from other people (Department of Health and Human Services, 2007, p. 1)

Suicide rates for gender, age, and ethnic groups have substantially changed. Men are four times more likely than women to commit suicide, whereas women are more likely to attempt. The reported rates of adolescent and young adult suicides nearly tripled between 1952 and 1996 (Centers for Disease Control and Prevention [CDC], 1995). As reported by the CDC (1995) from 1980 to 1996, the suicide rate for persons aged 10 to 14 years increased by 100% and among persons aged 15 to 19 years increased by 14%. Rates of suicide tend to increase with age due to older adult suicide victims more likely to have lived alone or been widowed or have suffered from physical illness (Carney, Rich, Burke, & Fowler, 1994).

Suicide risk is not equal across the population, as the rate of suicide varies in different ethnic groups. African Americans commit suicide less frequently than Caucasians but do so at an earlier age. Yet the rate of suicide among African American males aged 15 to 19 years increased 105% between 1980 and 1996 (CDC, 1998). The highest-to-lowest rank order of mortality from suicide by race is Caucasian, American Indians and Alaskan Natives, Non-Hispanic Blacks, Asian and Pacific Islanders, and Hispanics.

Intervention and Documentation

> Seven-year-old Tamesha presented in the emergency room with her mother after it was discovered the child's prescription medication bottle contained 20 less pills. After being questioned, the child reported she took the pills in attempt to "go to sleep and not wake up." The family had been in therapy which had been centered on alleviating Tamesha's school problems. Tamesha had no history of mental illness but had previously been sexually abused by a family friend. She also was teased relentlessly at school because of her size.

The impact of suicide risk factors can be decreased by utilizing interventions such as providing effective treatments for specific mental illnesses. According to Jacobs and Brewer (2004), once the mental health practitioner recognizes a client with suicidal risk factors, the appropriate intervention should be aimed at reducing those factors to keep the client safe. Risk factors that cannot be changed, such as a prior suicide attempt, can bring awareness to mental health practitioners when an individual has recurrence of a significant stress, mental, or substance abuse disorder (Blumenthal, 1988).

Jacobs and Brewer (2004) stated that based on the level of suicide risk within the assessment, appropriate treatment can be determined, such as inpatient hospitalization, outpatient treatment, and medication. Although every state varies in terms of its legal commitment statutes, the legal standards most often consist of severe mental illness, threat of harm to self or others, and not sufficiently caring for oneself (Jacobs & Brewer, 2004).

Interventions utilized in treatment should be focused on the safety of the client (Jacobs & Brewer, 2004). There is evidence that cognitive therapy works well for people who previously attempted suicide. In a randomized controlled study, Brown, Ten Have, Henriques, Xie, Hollander, and Beck (2005) found that cognitive therapy decreased depression in previous suicide attempters and also decreased the rate of repeated suicide attempts by 50%. Strengthening the client's support system by educating family members and involved health professionals can help to decrease suicidal risk factors (Jacobs & Brewer, 2004). In addition, Hovey (2000) stated that social support has been found to decrease suicidal ideations and improve overall mental health.

Couple and family therapists are often working within clients' relational systems in the treatment of depression. If families are involved in treatment, or the level of suicidal threat warrants intervention, families can be part of the plan to thwart suicide. Because many suicides are impulsive, families can help remove access to a method. These family interventions may include teaching suicide risks and indicators to family members, assisting family members in understanding how to effectively communicate, explaining the importance of removing or locking up medications; restricting access to alcohol or other intoxicating substances; and restricting or removing firearms from the residence. In the opening example, Tamesha was not actively suicidal, but she showed depressive symptomology. Instructions to the parents to lock up available medications would have been prudent, and more intensive depression assessment measures appear to have been warranted. The parents could have been educated that some of Tamesha's acting out behavior may also have been symptoms of depression, not just rebellious activity.

Appropriate Standard of Care

As stated previously, suicide is the most common cause of malpractice action against a mental health professional (Simpson & Stacy, 2004). When mental health professionals do not evidence a professional standard of care, claims for malpractice will likely occur. In evaluating an appropriate standard of care, the court will review whether or not the mental health professional followed similar practice as other mental health professionals would have followed under the same set of conditions (Reamer, 1995). Thus, the clinician must stay apprised of the most recent standards of care regarding suicidal clients and documenting their care of suicidal clients. These professional standards of care include performing assessments, providing appropriate treatments, and being knowledgeable in issues regarding the breaching of confidentiality (Mishna, Antle, & Regehr, 2002). Importantly, a clinician must pay special attention to documenting his or her actions in order to fend off liability. Simpson and Stacy (2004) purported that "the quality of documentation can determine whether a malpractice attorney accepts or declines a suicide case" (p. 1). They asserted that "If it isn't written down, it didn't happen" (p. 2).

The therapist should educate himself or herself about the most current standard of care regarding suicide assessment and intervention. The following is a brief compilation of suggestions to minimize liability as noted by Simpson and Stacy (2004, p. 3):

- Document carefully and thoroughly
- Document in a timely manner
- Pay attention to high-risk times (e.g., postdischarge) and document appropriately

- Document positive and negative assessment findings
- Perform historical and present assessments
- Gather information from outside sources when possible (previous treatment providers, family members)
- Document plans for intervention
- Record negative findings regarding client thoughts, intentions, and plans
- Document rationale for not choosing alternative interventions
- Obtain data on current level of lethality, access to means, and response to prior therapeutic interventions
- Assess client competence and act accordingly
- Do not rely on no-self-harm "contracts" or patient promises not to kill himself or herself
- Use a systematic approach to assess for suicide ideation (available in the literature)
- Write down specific patient comments in quotes
- Try to obtain releases to talk to collateral contacts, or document that you tried
- Obtain previous treatment records
- Document how hospitalization was offered or considered
- Document consultations with other professionals

According to Jacobs and Brewer (2004), the mental health professional should document the identified risk factors, alterations made to the treatment plan, and supporting reasons for making the alterations. In addition, documentation should be made on the availability of suicide methods and any intervention that has been completed to reduce the availability (Jacobs & Brewer, 2004). It is also at these times that the therapist needs to make himself or herself available to the client, call and check on the client, and extend himself or herself in a way that communicates extraordinary caring. The therapist may be the only lifeline at these times, and this does not end even if the client is hospitalized (Kitchener, 2000).

Safety Planning

Samantha is a 21-year-old Caucasian female who struggles with depression and feelings of hopelessness. She has a history of self-injurious behavior and suicide attempts and has been hospitalized twice over the past 3 years. When Samantha came in for her regularly scheduled outpatient therapy appointment, she presented with depressed mood and feelings of hopelessness. Samantha reported she had no plan of suicide and had not made any attempts at harming herself. The therapist was aware of Samantha's history of cutting and previous attempts, so the session focused on Samantha being able to keep herself safe.

> After thoroughly processing with Samantha, a safety contract was created in which Samantha reported she would call the crisis hotline or 911 if she felt like harming herself. Samantha also agreed to write down positive coping skills that would be helpful for her when she feels sad or feels like self-harming. A thorough understanding of this client's mental health history and the therapeutic alliance that had been already created allowed the therapist to work with the client to create a safety contract.

Historically, clinicians have relied on verbal and written no-suicide contracts as a staple of treating suicidal clients. Davidson and Range (2002) defined a no-suicide contract as an agreement between the mental health practitioner and client, which states that the client will not harm himself or herself accidentally or on purpose for a specified length of time. These contracts have also been referred to as no-harm contracts, safety contracts, and suicide prevention contracts. Typically these contracts include a statement or agreement from the client:

- Agreeing not to harm, attempt to kill, or to kill himself or herself (typically, for a specified amount of time).
- To rid his or her environment or to surrender means that he or she has thought about using to harm or kill self with.
- To call given crisis numbers or go to the nearest emergency room if suicidal thoughts become overwhelming.
- To seek support sources or utilize positive coping skills in order to deal with overwhelming feelings.
- Contingency plans if the client cannot keep the contract conditions.

It is vital that the no-suicide contract not be used in place of suicide assessment and clinical assessment (Simon, 2004). No-harm contracts are not empirically supported as a method for preventing suicide, and they do not prevent clinicians from malpractice litigation (Lewis, 2007). However, the no-harm contract can help to provide a safe environment for the client to share thoughts and concerns. In addition, the contract helps to foster a therapeutic alliance (Kelly & Knudson, 2000), to help explore concerns about safety, establish short-term goals, reduce anxiety, and identify positive coping skills (Range, Campbell, Kovac, & Marion-Jones, 2002).

Confidentiality

Confidentiality must be maintained and honored unless a client appears to be at risk of harm to himself or herself or others. According to Bongar (1992), it is recommended that mental health professionals be knowledgeable about the concerns surrounding the breaching of confidentiality, as well as establish guidelines for when to breach confidentiality, because breaching confidentiality can damage the existing relationship between the client and mental health practitioner (Isaacs & Stone, 2001).

Therefore, at the start of therapy, the practitioner needs to be very clear with clients under what conditions confidentiality will be broken (Linehan, 1999). This can be clearly stated in one's informed consent as well as the therapist's emergency procedures (Rudd, Joiner, Jobes, & King, 1999). A statement about the exception to confidentiality regarding suicidality can read something like the following:

> All information about clients is kept strictly confidential. Clients must give written consent for the release of any information. There are, however, a few legal exceptions to the therapist keeping therapy information confidential. Therapists are ethically and legally required to break confidentiality if a client threatens to harm himself or herself, if the therapist is obligated to seek hospitalization for him or her, or if it is necessary for the therapist to contact family members or other parties who can provide protection.

Ideally, the therapist can work with the client collaboratively to get permission to discuss the client's distress with others outside of therapy. Ultimately, the client and therapist can work together with whatever resources can be utilized to ensure client safety and get the client on the road to recovery. Confidentiality with minors warrants special consideration and is discussed in Chapter 4.

Therapists as Suicide Survivors

Litigation

Suicide accounts for a "comparatively large proportion of all lawsuits filed against mental health professionals" (Baerger, 2001, p. 359). According to Reamer (1995), when mental health professionals do not follow a professional *standard of care*, claims for malpractice will be founded. If a professional's standard of care was substandard, that means that it did not follow similar guidelines as other mental health professionals would have followed under the same set of conditions (Reamer, 1995). Mishna, Antle, and Regehr (2002) stated that professional standards of care regarding suicidal clients include performing assessments, providing appropriate treatments, and being knowledgeable in issues regarding the breaching of confidentiality (see Chapter 3, the section on "Exceptions to Confidentiality and Privileged Communication").

There are four guidelines courts follow in assessing whether or not negligence occurred. They are as follows: the mental health practitioner had a responsibility to the client; the responsibility between the mental health practitioner and the client was breached; causal evidence exists between the breach of responsibility and the client's sustained injury; and the client suffered damage or injury. The practitioner's malpractice insurance should be contacted immediately upon notification of intent of the client's family to pursue legal action.

The therapist will likely experience significant stress or even posttraumatic stressors following the death of a client (Chemtob et al., 1988a); it is wise for the therapist to seek professional help in the way of therapy. As stated in Chapter 10, it is a therapist's ethical responsibility to remain competent, and sometimes that includes self-care, including receiving external help. However, if a therapist has pending litigation, he or she faces some interesting ethical dilemmas. First, in most states, the client's confidentiality does not cease just because the client has died. So although the therapist has a right to receive therapy, he or she would likely need to discuss details of the case in order to process the dilemma at hand, thus violating confidentiality. Second, much like the issue Officer Mary Lu Redmond faced when she sought therapy from social worker Karen Beyer after an on-duty shooting (see Chapter 2), what the therapist says in therapy to his or her therapist (the therapist's therapist, as it were) could be subpoenaed to court to determine his or her thoughts about the suicide. This situation has not yet been litigated, so no precedent has been set. In addition, the therapist has likely been told by counsel not to discuss the case with anyone, thus further isolating him or her from any outside sources of support. At a time when support is greatly needed, the therapist is relegated to an emotional island with options that seem very limited in the face of the legal controversy surrounding him or her.

Summary

It is impossible to predict any suicide, but it is possible to be familiar with the risk factors of suicide, to be thorough in assessment and intervention, and to be vigilant in documenting one's response to suicide threats. Treatment of depression is an important method of staving off suicide and decreasing risk factors. Given that suicide has devastating consequences, it is important for therapists to provide the highest-quality standard of care. Family members can be particularly helpful when risk is high.

Suicide is one of the most devastating events that can occur in the career of a couple and family therapist. Suicide also brings with it particularly litigious sequelae, compounding feelings of grief, loss, and guilt. Therapists need to be well versed in suicide assessment and intervention and understand that clients are communicating their excruciating sense of pain, hoping the therapist will help them find a solution and ameliorate the darkness they feel within. Suicidal clients have more pain than they have coping resources; couple and family therapists can help them access the resources in their system to alleviate some of their pain and suffering to live a more fulfilling and happy life.

References

Baerger, D. R. (2001). Risk management with the suicidal patient: Lessons from case law. *Professional Psychology: Research and Practice, 32,* 359–366.

Blumenthal, S. (1988). Suicide: A guide to risk factors, assessment, and treatment of suicidal patients. *Medical Clinic of North America, 72,* 937–971.

Bongar, B. (1992). The ethical issues of competence in working with the suicidal patient. *Ethics and Behavior, 2,* 75–89.

Brown, G. K., Ten Have, T., Henriques, G. R., Xie, S. X., Hollander, J. E., & Beck, A. T. (2005). Cognitive therapy for the prevention of suicide attempts: A randomized controlled trial. *Journal of the American Medical Association, 294,* 563–570.

Carney, S. S., Rich, C. L., Burke, P. A., & Fowler, R. C. (1994). Suicide over 60: The San Diego study. *Journal of the American Geriatric Society, 42,* 174–180.

Centers for Disease Control and Prevention. (1995). Suicide among children, adolescents, and young adults—United States, 1980–1992. *Morbidity and Mortality Weekly Report, 44,* 289–291.

Centers for Disease Control and Prevention. (1998). Suicide among black youths, United States, 1980–1995. *Morbidity and Mortality Weekly Report, 47,* 193–196.

Chemtob, C. M., Hamada, R. S., Bauer, G. B., Torigoe, R. Y., & Kinney, B. (1988a). Patient suicide: Frequency and impact on psychologists. *Professional Psychology: Research and Practice, 19,* 421–425.

Chemtob, C. M., Hamada, R. S., Bauer, G., Kinney, B., & Torigoe, R. Y. (1988b). Patients' suicide: Frequency and impact on psychiatrists. *American Journal of Psychiatry, 145,* 224–228.

Davidson, M., & Range, L. M. (2000). Age appropriate no-suicide agreements: Professionals' ratings of appropriateness and effectiveness. *Education and Treatment of Children, 23,* 143–155.

Department of Health and Human Services. (2007, April 19). The Surgeon General's call to action to prevent suicide. Washington, DC: Department of Health and Human Services. Retrieved October 21, 2008, from: www.cdc.gov/ncipc/factsheets/suifacts.htm.

Henriksson, M. M., Aro, H. M., Marttunen, M. J., Heikkinen, M. E., Isometsä, E. T., Kuoppasalmi, K. I., et al. (1993). Mental disorders and comorbidity in suicide. *American Journal of Psychiatry, 150*, 935–940.

Hovey, J. D. (2000). Acculturative stress, depression, and suicidal ideation in Mexican immigrants. *Cultural Diversity and Ethnic Minority Psychology, 6*, 134–151.

Isaacs, M. L., & Stone, C. (2001). Confidentiality with minors: Mental health counselors' attitudes toward breaching or preserving confidentiality. *Journal of Mental Health Counseling, 23*, 342–350.

Jacobs, D., & Brewer, M. (2004). APA practice guideline provides recommendations for assessing and treating patients for suicidal behaviors. *Psychiatric Annals, 34*, 373–380.

Kelly, K. T., & Knudson, M. P. (2000). Are no-suicide contracts effective in preventing suicide in suicidal patients seen by primary care physicians? *Archives of Family Medicine, 9* (November/December), 1119–1121.

Kitchener, K. S. (2000). *Foundations of ethical practice, research, and teaching in psychology*. Mahwah, NJ: Lawrence Erlbaum Associates.

Lewis, L. M. (2007). No-harm contracts: A review of what we know. *Suicide and Life-Threatening Behavior, 37*, 50–57.

Linehan, M. M. (1999). Standard protocol for assessing and treating suicidal behaviors for patients in treatment. In D. Jacobs (Ed.), *The Harvard Medical School guide to suicide assessment and intervention*. San Francisco: Jossey-Bass.

Mishna, F., Antle, B. J., & Regehr, C. (2002). Social work with clients contemplating suicide: Complexity and ambiguity in the clinical, ethical, and legal considerations. *Clinical Social Work Journal, 30*, 265–280.

Range, L. M., Campbell, C., Kovac, S. H., & Marion-Jones, M. (2002). No-suicide contracts: An overview and recommendations. *Death Studies, 26*, 51–74.

Reamer, F. (1995). Malpractice claims against social workers: First facts. *Social Work, 40*, 595–600.

Rudd, M. D., Joiner, T. E., Jobes, D. A., & King, C. A. (1999). The outpatient treatment of suicidality: An integration of science and recognition of its limitations. *Professional Psychology: Research and Practice, 30*, 437–446.

Rudd, M. D., Joiner, T., & Rajab, M. H. (2001). *Treating suicidal behavior: An effective, time-limited approach*. New York: Guilford Press.

Simon, R. I. (2004). *Assessing and managing suicide risk*. Arlington, VA: American Psychiatric Publishing.

Simpson, S., & Stacy, M. (2004). Avoiding the malpractice snare: Documenting suicide risk assessment. *Journal of Psychiatric Practice, 10*, 1–5.

9

Managing Risk With Potentially Dangerous Clients

Kathleen Beck Kmitta and Michelle T. Mannino

> Bill is a 21-year-old male who was involved in a fistfight in a bar several months prior and is now seeking therapy by court order. Bill's therapist immediately notes Bill's gender, young age, substance use, and learns Bill has a violent past. The therapist realizes that Bill is at risk to be a danger to others. He is angry at his girlfriend and makes veiled threats to the girlfriend in session. Bill also shares that he keeps a gun in his car "just in case" he needs it.

Over the past 30 years, the role of couple and family therapists has evolved to focus on both clients and the good of the public at large. Although the responsibility to help the client is of primary concern, state statutes typically mandate that the therapist fulfill a twofold position as a licensed or certified practitioner; he or she has a responsibility to protect the client's confidentiality as well as a responsibility to protect any third parties who may be in potential danger from the actions of the client. This creates conflicting responsibilities for the therapist who wants to create a safe, trusting environment in which the client can share private thoughts, yet has a legal and ethical duty to ensure the safety of others. In the above scenario, Bill's therapist must balance fostering a trusting relationship and managing protecting Bill's girlfriend or any others from harm.

Couple and family therapists have the potential to encounter clients who may be a danger to themselves and others. It is important to be conscious of the types of danger that clients may pose to others (including the therapist), ways of assessing potential danger, and the specific ethical codes pertaining to one's area of expertise within the mental health field. In addition, it is essential for therapists to be proactive by structuring their practice in a way that reduces the risk of danger to the therapist, the client, and possible third parties. Despite the need for clarification regarding a therapist's duties, a specific standard of care for treating dangerous clients has not been established (Truscott, Evans, & Mansell, 1995). This chapter addresses risk management and screening for potentially violent clients outside of domestic violent or intimate partner violence (IPV) situations, though there is certain overlap in applicability. For more information on IPV, see Chapter 7.

Duty to Warn and Duty to Protect

The seminal case that defined the legal responsibility of therapists to warn and protect those who may be at risk of harm from clients is *Tarasoff v. the Regents of the University of California* (Doner Kagle & Kopels, 1994). The first court decision in 1974 determined that mental health providers have a duty to warn third parties. The second court decision in 1976 more specifically stated that mental health providers not only have a duty to warn but also a duty to protect (Chaimowitz, Glancy, & Blackburn, 2000; Costa & Altekruse, 1994).

The duty to warn has generally been understood and implemented by mental health professionals by informing the victim, and potentially family members or authorities who can restrain the client. The duty to protect, however, requires mental health professionals to go beyond warning others and utilize direct interventions. Chaimowitz and Glancy (2002) summarized the *Tarasoff* ruling by stating that

> The duty to protect carries broader implications and encompasses actions that lead to protecting potential victims. Unlike the duty to warn or inform, the duty to protect may be discharged without breaching confidentiality.... With the duty to protect we now have duties both to our patients and, flowing through them, to third parties. (p. 2)

Since the *Tarasoff* decision, three conditions named in the Supreme Court ruling have been used by therapists to evaluate their duty to warn or protect. These conditions include the existence of a *special relationship* (such as the inherent nature of the therapist–client relationship), a *foreseeable risk*—reasonable cause to believe that the client needs to be controlled—and an *anticipated victim* or group of victims.

It is important to note that the guidelines that stem from the *Tarasoff* decision apply only to California law (Vandecreek & Knapp, 1984). In spite of this fact, many mental health professionals use this decision to determine their responsibility for best practice. Each state has specific laws

governing the acceptability of breaches of confidentiality that are necessary when fulfilling the duty to warn or protect.

In addition, most mental health professionals consider the duties to
warn and protect to be ethical obligations. The *Code of Ethics* for the
American Association for Marriage and Family Therapy (AAMFT) (2001),
Principle 2.1 stated that

> Marriage and family therapists disclose to clients and other interested par-
> ties, as early as feasible in their professional contacts, the nature of confiden-
> tiality and possible limitations of the clients' right to confidentiality.... Thus,
> these exceptions to confidentiality should be clearly outlined in the therapist's
> informed consent. (see Chapter 13)

Courts usually sanction the confidentiality of clients' communications
with their therapists through the legal standard of privilege. "Privileged
communication protects a client from having his confidential and private
discussions revealed to the public during legal proceedings without his
permission" (Shah, 1969, p. 57). However, the court determined in the
case of *Tarasoff* (1976) that "protective privilege ends when the public peril
begins" (Costa & Altekruse, 1994, p. 346).

Assessment of Dangerous Clients

Client Risk Factors

Becoming familiar with the client's past is essential when assessing the client's potential to become violent. Researchers found that *past violent acts,
involvement with the justice system,* and *self-reported violence* are the most
predictive characteristics for future violent behavior (Otto, 2000; Truscott
et al., 1995). Researchers (Otto, 2000; Rueve & Welton, 2008; Truscott et
al., 1995) found the most predictive demographic and historical characteristics, outside of previous violence, that would indicate the client's potential to be violent are as follows:

- Gender (males are more likely to be violent)
- Age (younger adults are more likely to be violent)
- History of head trauma or neurological impairment
- History of substance abuse
- Lower intellectual functioning and education
- A history of child abuse or witnessing domestic violence

- Dissociative states
- History of military service
- Weapons training
- Diagnosis of a major mental illness
- Unstable employment history

It appears that males in their late teens through early twenties with low intellectual functioning, who also display any of the other previously mentioned characteristics, are most at risk for committing violent acts (Otto, 2000; Truscott et al., 1995).

It is important to be aware of the demographic and historical characteristics that may indicate violent behavior, but considering a variety of other factors is also necessary. These factors include stress level, lack of social support, weapon availability, victim availability, availability of substances, the presence of anger or rage, the level of impulsivity, and mental illness. It should be noted that for those clients who are diagnosed with a mental illness, no differences have been found regarding the sex of the client and the client's potential to be violent (Otto, 2000; Truscott et al., 1995).

There is not one specific diagnosis that is predictive of violent behavior, though substance abuse disorder vastly increases the risk of violence (Rueve & Welton, 2008). Many clinicians assume that a diagnosis of an antisocial personality disorder automatically increases the risk for violence. However, Hare (1993) found that it is not the diagnosis of antisocial personality disorder that is predictive, but rather the person meeting the criteria for psychopathy. The criteria for psychopathy are as follows: egocentricity; impulsivity; irresponsibility; shallow emotions; lack of empathy, guilt, or remorse; pathological lying; and manipulativeness (Hare, 1993). It has also often been assumed that delusions increase the risk of violence, but the large-scale project of the MacArthur Violence Risk Assessment Study found this not to be true (Appelbaum, Robbins, & Monahan, 2000). Persistent violent thoughts or voices commanding violent acts were associated with increased violence risk (MacArthur Violence Risk Assessment Study, n.d.). Researchers found personality and adjustment disorders were more likely to be associated with violence than a major mental disorder. Schizophrenics actually had a lower rate than those diagnosed with personality or adjustment disorders. Those with more than three psychiatric diagnoses were 2 to 4.5 times more likely to also report violence (Rueve & Welton, 2008). Having a psychiatric diagnosis *and* a substance abuse disorder was a *strong predictor* of violence (MacArthur Violence Risk Assessment Study, n.d.).

Assessment Questions

> Jim and Donna were coleading an anger management group in an inner-city agency. The group seemed to be at a standstill, and there appeared to be a "vibe" between the group members, but no one was talking. Jim and Donna had led previous groups, but this one was different. Their attempts to process the feelings fell on deaf ears. When they finally had an individual session with one of the group members, the member reported that two members were from rival gangs, and in previous times, one had tried to kill the other. Because they were both here on probation, the member they were interviewing thought all of the group members would be safe and that the gang members would not act out. The therapists had to act to protect the interests of all group members and removed the two group members from the group.

Violence risk assessment involves an ongoing process, the start of which is developing the relationship with clients and asking initial screening questions. The above clients were clearly not well screened. Otto (2000) recommended the following questions as part of the assessment process:

1. What kinds of things make you mad? What do you do when you get mad?
2. What is your temper like? What kinds of things make you lose your temper?
3. What is the most violent thing you have ever done, and how did it happen?
4. What is the closest you have ever come to being violent?
5. Have you ever used a weapon in a fight or to hurt someone?
6. What would have to happen in order for you to get so mad or angry that you would hurt someone?
7. Do you own weapons like guns or knives? Where are they now?*

In the event that the client reveals previous incidents of violent behavior, it would be important to gather more detailed information as part of the assessment. The following questions are suggested by Otto (2000).

---

* Otto, R. K. (2000). Assessing and managing violence risk in outpatient settings. *Journal of Clinical Psychology, 56*(10), 1252. (Copyright 2000, R. K. Otto. Reprinted with permission of John Wiley & Sons, Inc.)

Anamnestic Violence Risk Analysis: Detailed Questions Related to Specific Incidents

1. What kind of harm occurred?
2. Who were the victim(s) and/or target(s)?
3. In what setting or environment did the altercation(s) take place?
4. What do you think caused the violence?
5. What were you thinking and how were you feeling before, during, and after the altercation(s)?
6. Were you using alcohol or other drugs at or around the time of the altercation(s)?
7. Was the client experiencing psychotic symptoms?
8. Were you taking psychoactive medication at the time of the incident?
9. Can patterns or commonalities across this and other episodes be identified?[*]

Otto (2000) recommended screening all new clients and asking the questions neutrally within the initial interview.

A checklist is provided to the reader in Appendix 9.1 as a screening aid to help conduct an initial appraisal of the clients' potential for violence. The assessment lists both static and dynamic factors to consider when determining risk, with questions to solicit detailed information, and offers questions to ask in order to help determine if the therapist has reason to take further action with the client to prevent harm (i.e., duty to warn or protect). It can be followed up with formal assessment instruments.

Assessment Instruments

It is initially important to recognize signs that would indicate violence, and it is equally important to continually assess for the possibility of violent behavior throughout the course of therapy. Assessment instruments are available to aid in that process.

The HCR-20 by Webster, Douglas, Eaves, and Hart (1997) is a 20-item scale designed to assess risk for violence by assessing historical factors, clinical factors, and risk management factors. It is designed for clinical use but can also be coded for research purposes.

In their extensive comparison of anger scales, Eckhardt, Norlander, & Deffenbacher (2004) described the usefulness of measures designed to assess

---

[*] Otto, R. K. (2000). Assessing and managing violence risk in outpatient settings. *Journal of Clinical Psychology, 56*(10), 1252. (Copyright 2000, R. K. Otto. Reprinted with permission of John Wiley & Sons, Inc.)

anger and hostility. Specifically, three scales—the Anger Questionnaire (Buss & Perry, 1992), the Novaco Anger Scale (Novaco, 1994), and the State Trait Anger Expression Inventory (Spielberger, 1988)—were found to be effective in distinguishing between clinical and nonclinical populations. Although anger and hostility are not precise indicators of violent behavior, they provide a basis that could point toward the urgency for further assessment.

Relationship violence is a specific type of violence to be assessed for which is addressed in Chapter 7. The revised Conflict Tactic Scale 2 is widely used for this purpose (Straus, Hamby, Boney-McCoy, & Sugarman, 1996), as is the Spousal Assault Risk Assessment Guide (Kropp, Hart, Webster, & Eaves, 1994). Listed in Chapter 7 are additional scales regarding relationship violence.

Decision-Making Models

There are several decision-making models that can be used to determine a client's potential for violence. Truscott et al. (1995) presented a model that considers the level of risk for violence and the strength of the therapeutic alliance. The ultimate goal is to have a low risk of violence and a strong therapeutic alliance. It should be noted that there is no objective measure to determine the strength of the alliance between client and therapist. This leaves the therapist in a position to use good judgment and consult with other professionals to get a second opinion regarding his or her decision.

Laughran and Bakken (1984) suggested following a checklist of four questions to determine potentially violent behavior and the need for therapist action. In the event that there is a positive answer to two or more of the questions, the therapist should consider it his or her duty to warn and follow the procedure to appropriately break confidentiality and notify the appropriate outside sources:

1. Has the client expressed some specific intention to commit violence, as against transitory thoughts, or expressions of feelings?
    a. Has the client identified the kind of actions he or she intends?
    b. Does the client have the ability to carry out the action (e.g., weapon, proximity to the victim)?
2. Has the client identified an intended victim or plan of action?

3. Is the client unable to understand what he or she is doing and incapable of exercising self-control? (History of prior violence would be a negative indication.)
4. Is the client incapable of collaborating with the therapist in maintaining control of his or her behavior?[*]

These are two models to consider when making decisions about the danger that clients may pose to others. They are not empirically based, but they can serve as guides for therapists to make an ethical decision about their legal duty to warn and protect others.

Safety Plans and Hospitalization

The ideal solution when a client has a potential to be dangerous would involve the therapist and client creating a mutually agreed upon safety plan in which the client agrees to specific guidelines should he or she begin to feel violent urges or intent. The safety plan should stipulate that the client voluntarily submit to hospitalization. This would provide protection to the threatened third party and maintain the client's confidentiality and integrity.

When a client refuses to comply with the safety plan, therapists can arrange for the client to be hospitalized in a psychiatric facility for emergency detention. Hospitalization alone may not be sufficient to remove the threat of danger, because clients may refuse or not receive treatment; therapists need to work closely with the treating psychiatrist for optimal safety.

Special Considerations

Working with potentially dangerous clients requires the therapist to be proactive to protect the public, but the safety of the therapist is also a consideration that deserves attention.

Danger to the Therapist

Although most of this paper addresses clients who pose a danger to third parties or beginning therapists, it is suggested in the literature that even experienced therapists can be in danger when working with violent clients

---

[*] Laughran, W., & Bakken, G. (1984), The psychotherapist's responsibility toward third parties under current California law. *Western State University Law Review Association, 12,* 34. (Reprinted with permission.)

(Gately & Stabb, 2005). Gentile, Asamen, Harmell, and Weathers (2002) and Romans, Hays, and White (1996) make reference to incidents where clients stalk, threaten, or attack their therapists. Therefore, it is important to be aware of practices that ensure the safety of the therapist as well as others.

Beginning trainees or student therapists are least experienced in assessing and managing potentially dangerous clients. Gately and Stabb (2005) discussed the need to increase trainees' confidence levels in recognizing and interacting with clients who may pose a threat. They recommended that training programs provide more extensive assessment tools and resources to better prepare beginning therapists. The checklist found in Appendix 9.1 could be particularly beneficial to assist beginning therapists in determining a client's risk of becoming violent.

Protective Measures for Clinical Practice

Mental health professionals can protect themselves by explicitly stating rules and expectations for appropriate behavior during therapy within the informed consent for treatment. Examples could include not allowing firearms or other weapons on the premises, prohibiting clients from coming to session under the influence of substances, and notifying that police will be called immediately if behavior escalates during session.

The therapist should also be cognizant of office conditions that could cause clients to become irritable, such as long waiting times, high noise levels, lack of personal space (Gately & Stabb, 2005), overcrowding of clients, and unpleasant or polluted surroundings (Rueve & Welton, 2008). Tishler, Gordon, and Landry-Meyer (2000) recommended removing heavy objects or breakable light fixtures that can be used as potential weapons from the therapy room, particularly during assessment.

Additionally, therapists can evaluate the safety of their facility for themselves and their clients. This may include installing an alarm system or employing security personnel to deter dangerous behavior.

Therapists should be cautious not to disclose specific information that would allow clients to identify, for example, the child of the therapist, in the event a client may seek revenge if he or she is unhappy with his or her therapist. Therapists should avoid providing services in their home because this ultimately gives clients direct access to the therapist's family members and personal property. Therapists can limit the risk of being a victim by having an unlisted home address and telephone number (Gentile et al., 2002).

Summary

As a result of the *Tarasoff* ruling, literature has addressed a therapist's responsibility to warn and protect third parties when they are aware of a danger posed by a client. Clients may be a danger to others in a variety of ways, including threatening others, physically assaulting others, or killing an individual or group of people. Therapists should be aware of ways to screen, assess, and treat dangerous clients. The authors offered the handout in Appendix 9.1 as an initial assessment for violent behavior. Throughout the treatment process, therapists may face ethical and legal dilemmas that make it imperative to be aware of state and local laws. Therapists may also face personal risk while treating dangerous clients and should take precautions to ensure their own safety and the safety of others.

Appendix 9.1

Assessment for Risk Factors: Is This a Potentially Dangerous Client?

Static Factors: *Those factors that cannot be changed therapeutically.*

Age

Gender

* Past violent acts

    When did you become the angriest and what happened?

* Involvement with the justice system

    Have you ever been involved with the police or the courts?

* Past weapon use

    Have you ever used a weapon with the intent to harm another person?

* Low intelligence (possible indications may be length of time required to complete intake paperwork and questionnaires, speed of cognitive processes during conversations)

History of child abuse

Witnessed domestic violence

    Is there a history of domestic violence or battering within your family?

    What was the worst argument that you ever saw?

Note: An asterisk indicates very strong predictive characteristics for future violent behavior.

Dynamic Factors: *Those factors that can be changed therapeutically.*

Substance use

>   What is the frequency and quantity of your drug or alcohol use?

Psychotic symptomology

>   Do you have a history of psychiatric hospitalization or use psychotropic drugs? Are there any present violent thoughts or voices?

Stress level

>   Has there been a recent death in your family?

>   Are you currently unemployed?

>   (Consider Axis 4 in the *Diagnostic and Statistical Manual of Mental Disorders*, text revision [*DSM IV-TR*, 2000] for further questions.)

Screening Questions: To Determine If There Is a Duty to Warn or Protect

These questions were suggested by Laughran and Bakken (1984, p. 34):

1. Has the client expressed some specific intention to commit violence, as against transitory thoughts, or expressions of feelings?
    a. Identified the kind of actions he or she intends?
    b. Have the ability to carry out the action (e.g., weapon, proximity to the victim)?
2. Has the client identified an intended victim and/or plan of action?
3. Is the client unable to understand what he or she is doing and incapable of exercising self-control? (History of prior violence would be negative indication.)
4. Is the client incapable of collaborating with the therapist in maintaining control of his or her behavior?

References

American Association for Marriage and Family Therapy (AAMFT). (2001). *Code of ethics.* Alexandria, VA: Author.

Appelbaum, P. S., Robbins, P. C., & Monahan, J. (2000). Violence and delusions: Data from the MacArthur Violence Risk Assessment Study. *American Journal of Psychiatry, 157*(4), 566–572.

Buss, A. H., & Perry, M. (1992). The aggression questionnaire. *Journal of Personality and Social Psychology, 59*, 73–81.

Chaimowitz, G. A., & Glancy, G. D. (2002). CPA Position Paper (2002-42): The duty to protect. Retrieved August 3, 2009, from: http://wwl.cpa-apc.org:8080/Publications/Position_Papers/duty.asp.

Chaimowitz, G. A., Glancy, G. D., & Blackburn, J. (2000). The duty to warn and protect—Impact on practice. *Canadian Journal of Psychiatry, 45*(10), 899–904.

Costa, L., & Altekruse, M. (1994). Duty-to-warn guidelines for mental health counselors. *Journal of Counseling and Development, 72*(4), 346–350.

Davis, S. D., & Piercy, F. P. (2007). What clients of MFT model developers and their former students say about change, Part I: Model dependent common factors across three models. *Journal of Marital and Family Therapy, 33*, 318–343.

Doner Kagle, J., & Kopels, S. (1994). Confidentiality after Tarasoff. *Health and Social Work, 19*(3), 217–222.

Eckhardt, C., Norlander, B., & Deffenbacher, J. (2004). The assessment of anger and hostility: A critical review. *Aggression and Violent Behavior, 9*(1), 17–43.

Gately, L. A., & Stabb, S. D. (2005). Psychology students' training in the management of potentially violent clients. *Professional Psychology: Research and Practice, 36*(6), 681–687.

Gentile, S. R., Asamen, J. K., Harmell, P. H., & Weathers, R. (2002). The stalking of psychologists by their clients. *Professional Psychology: Research and Practice, 33*(5), 490–494.

Hare, R. D. (1993). *Without conscience: The disturbing world of the psychopaths among us.* New York: Pocket Books.

Kropp, P. R., Hart, S. D., Webster, C. D., & Eaves, D. (1994). *Manual for the spousal assault risk assessment guide.* Vancouver, British Columbia, Canada: The British Columbia Institute on Family Violence.

Laughran, W., & Bakken, G. (1984). The psychotherapist's responsibility toward third parties under current California law. *Western State University Law Review, 12*, 32–34.

MacArthur Violence Risk Assessment Study. (n.d.). Executive Summary. Retrieved September 23, 2007, from: www.macarthur.virginia.edu/risk.html.

Novaco, R. W. (1994). Anger as a risk factor for violence among the mentally disordered. In J. Monahan & H. Steadman (Eds.), *Violence and mental disorder: Developments in risk assessment* (pp. 21–60). Chicago: University of Chicago Press.

Otto, R. K. (2000). Assessing and managing violence risk in outpatient settings. *Journal of Clinical Psychology, 56*(10), 1239–1262.

Romans, J. S. C., Hays, J. R., & White, T. K. (1996). Stalking and related behaviors experienced by counseling center staff from current or former clients. *Professional Psychology: Research and Practice, 27*(6), 595–599.

Rueve, M. E., & Welton, R. S. (2008). Violence and mental illness. *Psychiatry, 5*(5), 35–48.

Shah, S. A. (1969). Privileged communications, confidentiality, and privacy: Privileged communications. *Professional Psychology, 1*, 56–69.

Spielberger, C. D. (1988). *State-trait anger expression inventory professional manual.* Odessa, FL: Psychological Assessment Resources.

Straus, M. A., Hamby, S. L., Boney-McCoy, S., & Sugarman, D. B. (1996). The revised Conflict Tactics Scales (CTS2): Development and preliminary psychometric data. *Journal of Family Issues, 17*, 283–316.

Tishler, C. L., Gordon, L. B., & Landry-Meyer, L. (2000). Managing the violent patient: A guide for psychologists and other mental health professionals. *Professional Psychology: Research and Practice, 31*(1), 34–41.

Truscott, D., Evans, J., & Mansell, S. (1995). Outpatient psychotherapy with dangerous clients: A model for clinical decision making. *Professional Psychology: Research and Practice, 26*(5), 484–490.

Vandecreek, L., & Knapp, S. (1984). Counselor, confidentiality, and life-endangering clients. *Counselor Education and Supervision, 24*(1), 51–57.

Webster, C. D., Douglas, K. S., Eaves, D., & Hart, S. D. (1997). *HCR-20: Assessing risk for violence (Version 2)*. Vancouver, British Columbia, Canada: Mental Health Law, and Policy Institute, Simon Fraser University.

10

The Self of the Therapist

Jared A. Durtschi and Melanie K. McClellan

"It is not possible to play a guitar when one or more of the strings are out of tune or missing."

Walter Lowe, Jr., Ph.D., L.M.F.T.

The self of the therapist is the instrument through which interventions and therapeutic models are provided to clients. If we think of the therapist as the guitar and one or more strings are out of tune or missing, the therapist may not be fully effective. The self of the therapist is important because therapists' values, morals, relationships, competence, education, and training all influence the procedure and outcome of therapy, just as strings on a guitar affect the quality of that instrument. The purpose of knowing about the self of the therapist is to make ethically sound and unbiased decisions in assessment and treatment. Recently, some have suggested that therapy is effective not simply due to the use of theory and interventions, but also in large part to other common factors of successful outcome, such as how the therapist uses himself or herself to build a therapeutic alliance and facilitate hope in clients (e.g., Sprenkle & Blow, 2004). Thus, the self of the therapist is a critical ingredient to the process of change and will be explored throughout this chapter.

Therapist and Client Values

The values of therapists and clients strongly influence the course of therapy. "Moral values refer to basic beliefs regarding what an individual, group, or society considers good and right; they represent the standards of appropriate behavior" (Becvar, 2001, p. 155). Jensen and Bergin (1988) described values as therapists' own beliefs about what is good or bad for clients. Values are deeply rooted in constituting who we are, what is important to us as individuals, and what directs our course of action throughout life. Values are the standard by which evaluations are made, and they inform the attitudes, decisions, and behaviors of individuals and systems (Rokeach, 1973). Therefore, values affect how people behave in every setting. Everyone has his or her own original value system for what is defined as important in his or her life. These differences in values are evidenced among those who have differing ethnic, religious, racial, sexual, and cultural backgrounds. Even within these differing groups, there is a wide variety of individual diversity in core values. Therapists may find themselves with clients of differing values, and both therapist and client may become cognizant of these inherent value clashes.

In order to gain integrity as a science, mental health disciplines historically tried to distance themselves from value issues by maintaining that therapeutic neutrality was both possible and optimal. However, a truly "value-free" therapy approach is not possible, and many have critiqued the ideal of purely objective clinical work, as values are always present in the therapeutic process. A fear of imposing values on clients can lead some therapists to sidestep value issues (Tjeltveit, 1986), and feeling unsure of how to address value issues with clients can lead to the ignoring of values (Fife & Whiting, 2007). Another common way to avoid the influence of values is for therapists to cite research to explain something to their clients that supports the therapist's personal values (Fife & Whiting).

Authors explored and scrutinized how values pervade couple and family therapy (e.g., Fife & Whiting, 2007; Melito, 2003). Becoming more reflective and conscientious about values will help therapists become increasingly effective (Fife & Whiting). It is clear that values affect therapy, but managing these issues is paramount in protecting against power abuse (Parrott, 1999). Clients tend to shift their value system to reflect those values of their therapists, and therapists' values are more stable than their clients. In addition, during therapy, clients' values converge over time with those of their therapist (Schwehn & Schau, 1990), and clients begin to verbally conceptualize their problems in the same way as their therapist (Davis & Piercy, 2007). These strengthened values of the client can help elicit and maintain positive changes for the client. On the contrary, there are possible dangers of the therapist abusing this power by covertly imposing the therapist's values onto his or her clients. Therapists must proceed with great sensitivity in projecting values onto the client. Often, conflicted value systems in therapy between client and therapist can generate emotional reactivity in the therapist, refocusing therapy away from the client's presenting problem and toward alleviation of the therapist's own anxiety. Instead, clients could be better served by therapists learning to identify and integrate their personal value system into their professional development (Brosi & Rolling, 2007).

Therapists must be skilled in successfully handling these sensitive issues regarding values. Fisher-Smith (1999) found that therapists handle values in session in one of two ways: trying to remain neutral or being explicit in sharing their values with clients. Jensen and Bergin (1988) encouraged therapists to be transparent in sharing their values with clients, although not pressuring clients to adopt the therapist's values. Others recommended not even to attempt to change a client's values unless the client requested that type of treatment (Lageman, 1993). Doherty (1995) recommended that discussions about client and therapist values in session may be a helpful tool in the progression of therapy. Further, Doherty suggested that the therapist should not evaluate values in his or her head about whether the client's values are good or bad, but should include that discussion in the dialogue of the session where those values can be explored in a nonjudgmental, noncoercive environment. Melito (2003) discussed further options of how to handle value conflicts in session through a variety of different theoretical lenses.

It is important that therapists do not make decisions regarding their clients' lives for them. Sometimes it may be difficult for therapists who harbor their own strong belief systems to not make decisions for clients. For example, if a couple who is cohabitating were attending therapy to discuss relationship problems, the therapist cannot encourage the couple to get married or to no longer cohabitate. If a therapist were to direct clients into making life decisions for them, that therapist is in direct violation of the American Association for Marriage and Family Therapy (AAMFT) *Code of Ethics*. Specifically, Subprinciple 1.8 of the AAMFT *Code of Ethics* (2001) stated:

> Marriage and family therapists respect the rights of clients to make decisions and help them understand the consequences of these decisions. Therapists clearly advise clients that they have the responsibility to make decisions regarding relationships such as cohabitation, marriage, divorce, separation, reconciliation, custody, and visitation.

Although therapists must not make life decisions for their clients, it is expected that therapists will help clients reach an appropriate outcome.

Sometimes therapists may find it difficult to separate their own values from those of the client, and this may interfere with the therapeutic process. For example, if a therapist's values are strongly against divorce, and clients want aid in ending their marriage, it would be inappropriate for the therapist to allow his or her values to be imposed on his or her clients by pushing them toward saving their marriage. Hence, it is pertinent for the therapist to ensure that the client is benefiting from therapy. The therapist must make every effort to support the client despite any value differences. Particularly, Subprinciple 1.9 of the AAMFT *Code of Ethics* (2001) stated that "Marriage and family therapists continue therapeutic relationships only so long as it is reasonably clear that clients are benefiting from the relationship." The therapist must always be cognizant of whether or not his or her clients are progressing, and specifically whether or not value differences between therapist and client are the reason behind therapy not progressing. It is helpful to evaluate these differences in light of ᵛMemes discussed in Chapter 2, and following the ethical decision-making model presented in Chapter 3.

The Therapist's Personal Life

> Keisha, a family therapist, has been seeing Tony on a weekly basis for approximately 9 months. Keisha developed a positive client–therapist relationship with Tony. Tony recently developed a terminal disease and has less than 2 months to live. Keisha comes home from therapy, feeling upset, and feels a need to process her feelings of sadness. Her husband notices that Keisha is visibly disturbed and asks what is on her mind. Keisha describes what is happening with her client, to her husband.

For a variety of personal reasons, therapists often inappropriately talk with friends and family about their clients. Similar to the example discussed above, a common breach of confidentiality that occurs for family therapists is when therapists share information with their own families (Baker & Patterson, 1990). Sharing clients' confidential information with family or friends is a critical ethical problem that goes largely unaddressed (Pope, Tabachnick, & Keith-Spiegel, 1987). Pope and colleagues (1987) found that three-fourths of the therapists in their study believed that it is unethical to disclose confidential information; however, almost two-thirds reported that they engaged in behaviors that imperiled their clients' confidentiality. Although only 8% of the psychotherapists discussed clients by name with friends, about three-fourths discussed clients (without names) with friends. Breaching confidentiality is widely considered as inappropriate by therapists; nevertheless, therapists commonly share stories (with or without names) that may put their client's confidentiality at risk (Pope et al., 1987).

Speaking freely about clients, like Keisha did with her husband in the previous case example, is a violation of the code of ethics, unless a waiver was previously obtained from the client(s) involved. This is explicitly stated in the AAMFT *Code of Ethics* (2001), Subprinciple 2.2: "Marriage and family therapists do not disclose client confidences except by client authorization or waiver, or where mandated or permitted by law. Verbal authorization will not be sufficient except in emergency situations, unless prohibited by law." A therapist does not disclose information outside the treatment context without a written authorization from each individual competent to execute a waiver in couple, family, or group treatment.

From an ethical perspective, the directing principle in this issue is the identifiability of the client from the information revealed. Baker and Patterson (1990) supported the position that a client's privacy should be preserved without question. They also suggested that the therapist may be able to discuss thoughts and feelings without revealing details that would identify the client. This option might be limited, however, in a small community.

Therapist Training and Education

Hardy and Laszloffy (1995) believed that when training a therapist, it is important for the training program to cultivate cultural competence. Hardy and Laszloffy (1995) suggested the cultural genogram as a training tool to help trainees increase their cultural competence by increasing cultural awareness and cultural sensitivity. Genograms help trainees understand their own personal, emotional, family-of-origin issues, and the goal of the cultural genogram is to promote cultural awareness and sensitivity by helping trainees to understand their cultural identities (Hardy & Laszloffy, 1995). To reach this goal, the cultural genogram illustrates and clarifies the influence that culture has on the family, assists trainees in identifying the groups that contribute to the formation of their cultural identity, encourages open discussions that reveal and challenge culturally based assumptions and stereotypes, aids trainees in discovering their culturally based emotional triggers, and supports trainees in exploring how their unique cultural identities may impact their therapeutic style and efficiency (Hardy & Laszloffy, 1995). Although originally designed for client assessment, White and Tyson-Rawson's (1995) gendergram can also be used as a training tool to increase therapist awareness and sensitivity to gender issues. Power and privilege may also be underlying these training issues surrounding culture and gender. (See Chapter 5 for a detailed discussion of this issue.)

The training of a couple and family therapist can have a substantial impact on the family of the therapist. Sori, Wetchler, Ray, and Niedner (1996) investigated the stressors and enhancers associated with being in marriage and family therapy (MFT) graduate programs for students and their families. MFT trainees' social lives and recreation time suffer, and often little time or energy is left for the trainee to relax (Sori et al., 1996). Scheinkman (1988) found that graduate school in general has a negative impact on student marriages; couples are at high risk for divorce, especially during transition points, such as graduation. There are also many stressors for the families of trainees, including a spouse getting angry at a trainee for increased independence, disagreement about the division of chores, and failure to resolve conflicts over role expectations (Sori et al.).

Many stressors affect the family of a marriage and family therapist trainee, and there are also numerous positive effects. The positive effects include personal challenge and growth for the trainee, focus on one's self-awareness, better overall functioning and emotional stability, and increased confidence leading to improved interpersonal relationships (Sori et al., 1996). In addition, Sori and colleagues found that students in MFT graduate programs and their spouses found their experience to be considerably more enhancing than stressing.

Difficulties in the personal lives of trainees affect their sensitivity and perspective with the problems presented by their clients (Catherall & Pinsoff, 1987). Therapist trainees are called to deal with their personal issues in relation to the therapy that they provide; therefore, they need training that both opens them up to themselves and teaches them vulnerability, discipline, and freedom within the relationship (Aponte, 1994). Therapists' social and familial relationships play a role in the therapy room. Because the person of the therapist is of crucial influence in the change process in therapy, attention to one's personal and family life is an important professional obligation.

Maintaining Competence

Competence broadly refers to the therapist's ability to promote positive client change (Shaw & Dobson, 1988). A therapist's competence is critical to providing a beneficial service to clients and is an essential facet of the therapist's ethical responsibility to clients. The therapist must promote beneficence (doing good on the client's behalf). Further, the therapist must be vigilant in assuring that he or she is maintaining individual competence as a professional in providing the highest quality of service to clients. Many contributing dynamics may lead to risk factors detrimentally affecting the therapist's professional abilities to provide beneficial service to clients, such as personal stresses, relationship problems, and family problems.

The clinician's first step in becoming competent is to obtain an education. Through training programs, therapists develop a primary level of expertise with therapeutic theory, clinical skills, the process of change, and human development. These basic skills were outlined by Figley and Nelson (1989) and Nelson and Figley (1990a, 1990b). This training is important for providing the framework from which the therapist will practice. Prior to graduation and licensure, a therapist will accumulate many hours of supervision while in the therapeutic training process. This supervision will provide the basic keys necessary to provide beneficial therapy to clients, while also strengthening the therapist's confidence, skill, and experience. Supervision is not limited to training programs only, but must be sought in any circumstance throughout one's career in which the therapist feels incompetent in providing helpful service to a specific population or problem. Of these three factors of gaining an education, supervision and experience are fundamental for beginning therapists in becoming competent clinicians. AAMFT developed the Marriage and Family Therapy Core Competencies (AAMFT, 2004) that reflect the minimal standards practicing MFTs should possess. These include six primary domains in which the therapist should be competent: admission to treatment; clinical assessment and diagnosis; treatment planning and case management; therapeutic intervention; legal issues, ethics, and standards; and research and program evaluation.

A great deal of emphasis has rightfully been placed upon training and experience in developing and maintaining competence, yet utilizing the therapist's own personal characteristics is also imperative in maintaining competence. Education and training alone are not enough to predict positive outcome in therapy. The role of the therapist is crucial in client change. There are "common factors" that contribute to therapeutic change irrespective of therapeutic modality (Hubble, Duncan, & Miller, 1999). Some of these include therapist behaviors such as alliance building, client engagement, hope and expectancy generation, and reframing, among others (Blow, Sprenkle, & Davis, 2007). In addition, the therapist should have knowledge of empirically based models, and the traditional models on which they are based. Blow, Sprenkle, and Davis (2007) advocated that therapists need to have knowledge of current "best practices" and be competent in other relevant nonclinical research information (p. 311). Research utilization is an essential aspect of therapist competence and will strengthen clinical work and our profession. The AAMFT *Code of Ethics* (2001) clarified this concern with Subprinciple 3.1: "Marriage and family therapists pursue knowledge of new developments and maintain competence in marriage and family therapy through education, training, or supervised experience." It is necessary for therapists to pursue knowledge of new developments in the field to be more effective as facilitators of change in clients. There is a growing movement toward evidence-based practice (EBP) in mental health (McCabe, 2006). The core of EBP is the "systematic preference for those clinical practices for which there has been some documented empirical effectiveness in promoting positive client outcomes" (Hardiman, Theriot, & Hodges, 2005, p. 105). Therapy success rates can improve if clinicians focused their interventions on empirically validated treatments rather than on potentially erroneous conceptions of what works.

Life Stress of the Therapist

> Howard, a couple and family therapist, graduated and obtained his license and started his own private practice. Howard is excited that he is finally done with graduate school and is relieved that he does not have to read any more research articles. Howard is currently working with a family that is not making any progress in therapy. Howard fears that his clients are not progressing due to his novice stature as a beginning therapist and his unfamiliarity with their problem; however, due to financial struggles he is facing (student loan payments, among others) he does not want to refer these clients elsewhere. Howard is also struggling with several other stressors in his personal life.

Other factors also affect the therapist's ability to maintain competence, such as personal life stresses and willingness to seek help. Despite the fact that therapists are professionals in helping others with personal and relational problems, they are not impervious to experiencing personal and relational problems in their own lives, and they may themselves require help. Similar to the above-mentioned case example, researchers found that beginning therapists experiencing severe personal life stress became distracted, were less observant, and were less effective in their therapy (Bischoff, Barton, Thober, & Hawley, 2002).

Deacon, Kirkpatrick, Wetchler, and Niedner (1999) found from a survey of 175 AAMFT clinical members that 95% of those clinicians seeking therapy expressed that their experience was at least somewhat successful, and 99.4% reported they would seek therapy again if necessary. Remaining competent to act as a proficient therapist remains the ultimate goal, and receiving therapy should be seen as a key ingredient to maintaining competence in the face of life stresses from work and personal life. Blow and colleagues (2007) noted that "Intense self of the therapist work is required that will bring to awareness the unresolved issues and biases that contribute to lack of effectiveness with clients, as well as therapist strengths and resources that can help the therapist be more effective" (p. 311). Students in training seem to agree that personal therapy is important (Patterson & Utesch, 1991). It is required of therapists to seek professional help in response to their own individual and relational problems that may impinge upon their work. As stated in the AAMFT *Code of Ethics* (2001), Subprinciple 3.3, "Marriage and family therapists seek appropriate professional assistance for their personal problems or conflicts that may impair work performance or clinical judgment." In addition, it may be helpful to consult a professional colleague about personal stressors that may arise. Therefore, in the case example discussed at the beginning of the section, it may have been helpful for Howard to receive therapy or other outside professional assistance for his personal concerns rather than jeopardize his client's mental health to help diminish his personal financial struggles.

Therapist Stressors and Self-Care

Stress is a mental, emotional, or physical strain caused, for example, by anxiety or overwork. Stress is an inevitable part of life that influences all people, including mental health workers, and it may reveal itself in a collection of negative reactions that may result in burnout if not handled wisely (Azar, 2000). Excessive exposure to stress and anxiety can leave a therapist feeling burned out. Maslach and Leiter (1997) identified three dimensions of burnout: emotional exhaustion, cynicism (e.g., an impersonal response to clients), and ineffectiveness. In such situations, one can feel an inadequate sense of personal achievement, reduced self-esteem, with a tendency to evaluate oneself negatively with regard to one's work (Vrendenburgh, Carlozzi, & Stein, 1999). Rosenberg and Pace (2006) reviewed some of the physical and emotional symptoms of burnout in couple and family therapists, including chronic fatigue, gastrointestinal problems, insomnia, headaches, hypertension, feelings of hopelessness, futility, boredom, anxiety, withdrawal, and irritability. Similarly, Azar (2000) addressed some common indications of burnout, which include becoming easily angered, frustrated, or irritated; crying often and having difficulty managing feelings; often engaging in risky situations; having substance abuse problems; showing extreme rigidity in thinking; displaying signs of depression; spending a great amount of time on tasks, but with decreased amounts of accomplishment; and living to work. The therapist must be sufficiently self-aware to be able to identify these burnout risk factors. These symptoms may be associated with conditions such as compassion fatigue, secondary traumatic stress, and vicarious traumatization through "reexperiencing" clients' trauma and emotional pain, which can also have negative effects on therapists' services.

Attributions for the origins of burnout typically include characteristics of the client, the practitioner, and the setting. Menniger (1990) surveyed 88 practicing psychotherapists regarding anxiety-provoking therapy situations. He found that suicide, violence, a difficult patient, clients challenging their competence, clients' anger, sexual issues in therapy, litigation, and testifying in court were among the most frequent causes of anxiety for the psychotherapist. Meeting with depressed, hostile, suicidal, borderline, and dependent clients on a regular basis can also have a detrimental impact on the emotional well-being of the therapist. In light of all these stressful work situations the therapist may encounter, it is possible that this level of demand can drain therapists of their emotional resources (Fishman & Lubetkin, 1991).

Burnout can occur in those therapists who have had many years of practice; however, it can also occur in beginning practitioners. With experienced therapists, burnout can occur when the therapist's sense of accomplishment and achievement is no longer adequate. Conversely, inexperienced therapists may experience stress or burnout because they are not psychologically prepared for the work (Shapiro, Brown, & Biegel, 2007). When beginning practitioners encounter unavoidable failures in treating clients or the client's needs exceed the therapist's skills, the beginning practitioner may experience feelings of ineptitude (Freudenberger, 1984) and diminished self-confidence (Lee, Eppler, Kendal, & Latty, 2001). A sample of psychologists reported up to 40% burnout levels, suggesting a substantial number of therapists are overstressed, resulting in a diminished quality of therapy (Fortener, 1999).

Preventing stress and burnout is essential to maintaining competence and keeping a positive outlook. Researchers Stevanovic and Ropuert (2004) found that of their sample of 286 psychologists, the highest-rated career-sustaining behaviors included spending time with one's partner or family, maintaining a balance between one's personal and professional life, and maintaining a sense of humor. Rosenberg and Pace (2006) reviewed many ideas for prevention and treatment of burnout, including engaging in physical exercise, eating a proper diet, taking regular vacations, participating in psychotherapy, setting limits and separating work and private lives, shortening work hours, allowing workday breaks, and improving relations with colleagues and staff members. For a rare resource on therapist self-care, see Baker (2003).

Despite the occurrence of burnout, many therapists find their clinical work to be highly fulfilling and growth inspiring. Linley and Joseph (2007) surveyed 156 therapists identifying factors that relate to increased levels of therapist well-being and personal growth. They found that those therapists who receive personal therapy experienced more personal growth, increased positive life changes, and less burnout. Also, even seasoned therapists who sought clinical supervision experienced more personal growth in their clinical career. Women reported more personal growth than men, and those therapists who reported a greater number of hours per week spent with clients reported more personal growth.

Summary

Ethics apply to the person of the therapist because he or she is an instrument by which therapy occurs, and the values of the therapist and client are an inherent part of the therapeutic process. Couple and family therapy is a challenging field, and clinicians must be prepared through education, training, and supervision to meet these challenges. There are many facets for the person of the therapist to consider throughout his or her professional career. Specifically, the therapist must keep within the AAMFT *Code of Ethics* (2001), be aware of value conflicts, maintain clients' confidentiality, gain an education, become a self-aware therapist, maintain competence, and take appropriate measures to prevent stress and burnout. The person of the therapist is an indispensable component to the outcome of therapy, and as such, therapists must constantly strive to ensure that all of the therapist's "strings" are in place and finely tuned.

References

American Association for Marriage and Family Therapy (AAMFT). (2001). *Code of ethics.* Alexandria, VA: Author.

American Association for Marriage and Family Therapy (AAMFT). (2004). *Marriage and family therapy core competencies.* Alexandria, VA: Author.

Aponte, H. J. (1994). How personal can training get? *Journal of Marital and Family Therapy, 20,* 3–15.

Azar, S. T. (2000). Preventing burnout in professionals and paraprofessionals who work with child abuse and neglect cases: A cognitive behavioral approach to supervision. *JCLP/In Session: Psychotherapy in Practice, 56,* 643–663.

Baker, E. K. (2003). *Caring for ourselves: A therapist's guide to personal and professional well-being.* Washington, DC: American Psychological Association.

Baker, L. C., & Patterson, J. E. (1990). The first to know: A systemic analysis of confidentiality and the therapist's family. *The American Journal of Family Therapy, 18,* 295–300.

Becvar, D. S. (2001). *Ethics in marriage and family therapy.* Washington, DC: The American Association for Marriage and Family Therapy.

Bischoff, R. J., Barton, M., Thober, J., & Hawley, R. (2002). Events and experiences impacting the development of clinical self confidence: A study of the first year of client contact. *Journal of Marital and Family Therapy, 28,* 371–382.

Blow, A. J., Sprenkle, D. H., & Davis, S. D. (2007). Is who delivers the treatment more important than the treatment itself? The role of the therapist in common factors. *Journal of Marital and Family Therapy, 33,* 298–317.

Brosi, M. W., & Rolling, E. S. (2007). The effect of value conflicts on therapists' work with abusive clients: Implications for the integration of feminist tenets. *Journal of Feminist Family Therapy, 19,* 63–89.

Catherall, D., & Pinsoff, W. (1987). The impact of the therapist's personal family life on the ability to establish viable therapeutic alliances in family and marital therapy. *Journal of Psychotherapy and the Family, 3,* 135–160.

Davis, S., & Piercy, F. (2007). What clients of couple therapy model developers and their former students say about change, Part I: Model dependent common factors across three models. *Journal of Marital and Family Therapy, 33*(3), 318–343.

Deacon, S., Kirkpatrick, D., Wetchler, J., & Niedner, D. (1999). Marriage and family therapists' problems and utilization of personal therapy. *American Journal of Family Therapy, 27*, 73–94.

Doherty, W. J. (1995). *Soul searching: Why psychotherapy must promote moral responsibility*. New York: Basic Books.

Fife, S. T., & Whiting, J. B. (2007). Values in family therapy practice and research: An invitation for reflection. *Contemporary Family Therapy, 29*, 71–86.

Figley, C. R., & Nelson, T. (1989). Basic family therapy skills: Conceptualization and initial findings. *Journal of Marital and Family Therapy, 16*, 225–240.

Fisher-Smith, A. M. (1999). From value neutrality to value inescapability: A qualitative inquiry into values management in psychotherapy. Unpublished doctoral dissertation. Brigham Young University, Provo, Utah.

Fishman, S. T., & Lubetkin, B. S. (1991). Professional practice. In M. Hersen, A. E. Kazdin, & A. S. Bellack (Eds.), *The clinical psychology handbook* (pp. 66–77). New York: Pergamon Press.

Fortener, R. G. (1999). Relationship between work setting, client prognosis, suicide ideation, and burnout in psychologists and counselors. Doctoral Dissertation. University of Toledo, OH.

Freudenberger, H. J. (1984). Impaired clinicians: Coping with "burnout". In P. A. Keller & L. L. Ritt (Eds.), *Innovations in clinical practice: A source book* (Vol. 3, pp. 221–228). Sarasota, FL: Professional Resource Exchange.

Hardiman, E. R., Theriot, M. T., & Hodges, J. Q. (2005). Evidence based practice in mental health: Important challenges for consumer run programs. *Best Practices in Mental Health, 1*, 105–124.

Hardy, K. V., & Laszloffy, T. A. (1995). The cultural genogram: Keys to training culturally competent family therapists. *Journal of Marital and Family Therapy, 21*, 227–237.

Hubble, M. A., Duncan, B. L., & Miller, S. (Eds.). (1999). *The heart and soul of change: What works in therapy. A meta-analysis*. Washington, DC: American Psychological Association.

Jensen, J. P., & Bergin, A. E. (1988). Mental health values of professional therapists: A national interdisciplinary survey. *Professional Psychology: Research and Practice, 19*, 290–297.

Lageman, A. G. (1993). *The moral dimensions of marriage and family therapy*. Lanham, MD: University Press of America.

Lee, R. E., Eppler, C., Kendal, N., & Latty, C. (2001). Critical incidents in the professional lives of first year MFT students. *Contemporary Family Therapy, 23*, 51–61.

Linley, P. A., & Joseph, S. (2007). Therapy work and therapists' positive and negative well-being. *Journal of Social and Clinical Psychology, 26*, 385–403.

Maslach, C., & Leiter, M. P. (1997). *The truth about burnout: How organizations cause personal stress and what to do about it*. New York: Jossey-Bass.

McCabe, O. L. (2006). Evidence based practice in mental health: Accessing, appraising, and adopting research data. *International Journal of Mental Health, 35*(2), 50–69.

Melito, R. (2003). Values in the role of the family therapist: Self determination and justice. *Journal of Marital and Family Therapy, 29,* 3–11.

Menniger, W. W. (1990). Anxiety in the psychotherapist. *Bulletin of the Menninger Clinic, 54,* 232–247.

Nelson, T., & Figley, C. R. (1990a). Basic family therapy skills: Brief and strategic schools of family therapy. *Journal of Family Psychology, 4,* 49–62.

Nelson, T., & Figley, C. R. (1990b). Basic family therapy skills II: Structural and strategic family therapies. *Journal of Marital and Family Therapy, 16,* 225–240.

Parrott, C. (1999). Towards an integration of science, art and morality: The role of values in psychology. *Counseling Psychology Quarterly, 12,* 5–20.

Patterson, J., & Utesch, W. E. (1991). Personal therapy for family therapy graduate students. *Contemporary Family Therapy, 13,* 333–343.

Pope, K. S., Tabachnick, B. G., & Keith-Spiegel, P. (1987). Ethics of practice: The beliefs and behaviors of psychologists as therapists. *American Psychologist, 42,* 993–1006.

Rokeach, M. (1973). *The nature of human values.* New York: Free Press.

Rosenberg, T., & Pace, M. (2006). Burnout among mental health professionals: Special considerations for the marriage and family therapist. *Journal of Marital and Family Therapy, 32,* 87–99.

Scheinkman, M. (1988). Graduate student marriage: An organizational/interactional view. *Family Process, 27,* 351–368.

Schwehn, J., & Schau, C. G. (1990). Psychotherapy as a process of value stabilization. *Counseling and Values, 35,* 24–30.

Shapiro, S. L., Brown, K. W., & Biegel, G. M. (2007). Teaching self-care to caregivers: Effects of mindfulness-based stress reduction on the mental health of therapists in training. *Training and Education in Professional Psychology, 1,* 105–115.

Shaw, B. F., & Dobson, K. S. (1988). Competency judgments in the training and evaluations of psychotherapists. *Journal of Consulting and Clinical Psychology, 56,* 666–672.

Sori, C. F., Wetchler, J. L., Ray, R. E., & Niedner, D. M. (1996). The impact of marriage and family therapy graduate training programs on married students and their families. *The American Journal of Family Therapy, 24,* 259–268.

Sprenkle, D. H., & Blow, A. J. (2004). Common factors and our sacred models. *Journal of Marital and Family Therapy, 30,* 113–129.

Stevanovic, P., & Ropuert, P. A. (2004). Career-sustaining behaviors, satisfactions, and stresses of professional psychologists. *Psychotherapy: Theory, Research, Practice, Training, 41,* 301–309.

Tjeltveit, A. C. (1986). The ethics of value conversion in psychotherapy: Appropriate and inappropriate therapist influence on client values. *Clinical Psychology Review, 6,* 515–537.

Vrendenburgh, L. D., Carlozzi, A. F., & Stein, L. B. (1999). Burnout in counseling psychologists and pertinent demographics. *Counseling Psychology Quarterly, 12,* 293–302.

White, M. B., & Tyson-Rawson, K. J. (1995). Assessing the dynamics of gender in couples and families: The gendergram. *Family Relations, 44,* 253–260.

11

Multicultural Issues, Spirituality and Religion

*Ryan N. Parsons-Rozycki and Jeffrey J. Ford**

Client: *Well, Dr. Sahib, what should I do? (He wrings his hands in a gesture of despair and looks imploringly at the therapist.)*

Therapist: (with a mask of neutrality over his expressionless face) What do you think you should do?

Client: *(rather peeved, even angry.) Every time I am asking you a question you are throwing the question back at me!*

Therapist: Oh, am I?

Client: *(exasperated) You have done it again! Look Dr. Sahib. You are the expert. I have come to you for help. If I knew how to help myself surely I would not come to see you.*

Therapist: (not in the least put out) Mr. Ahmed, it is really for you to decide what you should do, I cannot decide for you.

Client: *(acutely disturbed and even bewildered) I understand. But I am not asking you to decide for me, Doctor. I am asking your opinion; I have come to you for help. I don't understand why you should not help me. You should be guiding me. Helping me. Showing me the way. I am like a Bedouin, lost in the sand dunes of Arabia. But you don't want to help me to decide what I should do.*

Therapist: (defensively) That is not quite true.

Client: *When I go to see my GP (General Practioner), he tells me what I should do, what medicines I should take, how long for, and so on and then leaves it to me to decide whether I will take them or not. But you don't even tell me what I should do! (looks at the therapist) If you were a brain surgeon, would you be asking me to perform my own operation?*

---

* The second author prefers the term "marriage and family therapy" over "couple and family therapy" to stay consistent with his religious beliefs.

Therapist: (in spite of himself) No, of course not!

Client: What's the difference? So if you were a brain surgeon, you would perform brain surgery on me. You are a surgeon of the mind and yet you will not perform psychosurgery—which you can!

Therapist: (reluctantly gets drawn into an argument) It is not my role to tell you what you should do, or even what you ought to do. My role, as I see it, is to interpret, or throw some light on your problems, to help you to see your problems.*

This scenario is an illustration of a cultural crossroads that therapists may approach when working with clients of different ethnicities and cultures. The above scenario illuminates how important it is for therapists to assess the needs of clients within their worldview. For example, Mr. Ahmed lives in a world where his life is preordained. He also believes that his life is determined by Allah, and his role in life is to submit to this higher power. Whereas he worships Allah, he also believes that the therapist serves as an intermediary between Allah and himself. This belief system is characteristic of the Islamic religion. However, the therapist's worldview is obviously very different from that of Mr. Ahmed. The therapist does not believe that life is ordained or preordained, but rather through free will or agency, the client has control to bring about change. Therefore, the therapist's position is to provide guidance without imposing his own value system. In this example, a Muslim client expects the therapist to act as an intermediary to provide direct guidance for his problems but encounters a therapist who is only willing to act as a sounding board in therapy (Laungani, 2004). This brings a cultural disparity that puts both individuals at odds with each other as to what assistance should look like.

As evidenced by this example, it is clearly important for therapists to integrate the client's cultural beliefs into the therapy process. Through the therapist's understanding of the client's ethnic, cultural, spiritual, and religious background, he can begin to intervene in a way that is syntonic for the client. Mr. Ahmed's ideas about therapy are quite different from those of the therapist. The therapist will need to educate Mr. Ahmed about the nature and purpose of therapy as well as adjust the language of therapy to accommodate the client's worldview.

Multiculturalism is defined as multiple cultures coexisting with the ability of each individual culture to retain distinctive identities, including

---

* Laungani, P. (2004). Counseling and therapy in a multicultural setting *Counseling Psychology Quarterly*. (Reproduced with the permission of Taylor & Francis Ltd., www.informaworld.com.)

traditions, beliefs, and morals. Multicultural counseling is defined as "preparation practices that integrate multicultural and culture-specific awareness, knowledge and skills into counseling interactions" (Arredondo et. al., 1996, p. 1). Therapists who are aware of multiculturalism possess

> specific knowledge and information about the particular group that they are working with. They are aware of the life experiences, cultural heritage, and historical background of their culturally different clients. They are also aware of how race, culture, ethnicity and so forth may affect personality formation, vocational choices, manifestation, help seeking behavior, and appropriateness or inappropriateness of counseling approaches. (Sue, Arredondo, & McDavis, 1992, p. 78)

Another aspect of multiculturalism that receives much less attention within the field of marriage and family therapy is that of spirituality and religion (Hage, Hopson, Siegel, Payton. & DeFanti, 2006). About 90% of Americans believe in God or some universal spirit (Gallup, Inc., 2008), and 40% of psychologists have a belief in God or some higher power (Bergin, 1991). However, only 29% of mental health professionals view religious matters as important in the therapy process (Bergin, 1991; Bergin & Jensen, 1990). Additionally, 76% of marriage and family therapists do not feel that they have received adequate training relating to religious and spiritual issues (Carlson, Kirkpatrick, Hecker & Killmer, 2002). This inconsistency may be due to minimal or nonexistent training in spiritual or religious issues. Of 153 American Association for Marriage and Family Therapy (AAMFT) members surveyed by Carlson, Kirkpatrick, Hecker, and Killmer (2002), 76% did not feel that they received adequate training relating to religious and spiritual issues. This lack of training certainly may lead therapists to underutilize a potentially beneficial resource of strength in their clients' lives (Smith & Orlinsky, 2004). Taken as a whole and compared to other disciplines, marriage and family therapists are largely more religious than other types of therapists. When Bergin and Jensen (1990) asked respondents in their study to agree or disagree with the statement: "My whole approach to life is based on my religion," professionals who agreed or strongly agreed were broken down as follows: Clinical Psychologists 33%, Psychiatrists 39%, Clinical Social Workers 46%, and Marriage and Family Therapists 62%.

Important aspects of integrating spirituality and religion into couple and family therapy include health benefits as previously noted (Miller & Thorensen, 2003). In addition, individuals, couples, and families may appreciate the sense of support in therapy that they feel from a higher power. Clients whose lives are based on religion may have difficulty not discussing religion in therapy, and may feel fragmented by not being able to discuss their spiritual life in therapy. The integration of spirituality and religion is an important benefit to their wholeness (Wolf & Stevens, 2001). For others, religion is synonymous with their culture or ethnicity, and the therapist must respect and discuss the religion to have a cultural context for the client. In a time that cross-cultural sensitivity is frequently intergrated into therapy to improve efficacy, therapists may not be giving spirituality and religion the deserved attention in the therapy room. Watts (2001) wrote that "special populations cannot be understood at all without appreciating the history and centrality of religion in their community. It is a serious blind spot, then, not to understand or even ask about spirituality in our clients' lives" (p. 207). Even if issues of spirituality are not voiced by clients, it should not be assumed they are not important (Walsh, 2006). Therefore, spirituality and religion will be focused on in this chapter, as this part of the therapist is often an overlooked area of cultural competence.

Spirituality and Religion

Prest and Russell (1995) defined *spirituality* as referring to the human experience of discovering meaning, purpose, and values, which may or may not include the concept of a god or transcendent being (Prest & Russell, 1995). *Religion* is defined as "the formal institutional contexts for spiritual beliefs and practices" (Prest & Russell, 1995, p. 4). Further, as stated by Stewart and Gale (1994),

> Clients' religious orientations are as important a consideration in clinical work as race, ethnicity, social class, culture and gender because the *sine qua non* of all the various religions is their provision of worldviews, or interpretive lenses, through which believers apprehend and order their experience and reality (both moral and social). (p. 17)

The therapist can gain knowledge about a client's religion, spirituality, and culture by first asking and inquiring with the client in the session. The benefits of directly asking a client to educate the therapist about the client's own beliefs, is that it empowers the client, and it provides the therapist with the opportunity to obtain the client's perspective of how the client operates within his or her own culture.

> Marriage and family therapists adopting a collaborative approach with religious families may thus be less inclined to (a) mislabel religious issues as pathological, (b) misinterpret certain subtle religious issues as irrelevant to therapy, (c) inadvertently impose their view of religion upon the therapeutic process, while concurrently disallowing a much broader, deeper discussion of a family's religious and spiritual experience. (Joanides, 1996, p. 23)

A potential pitfall in asking a client to educate the therapist is that it might offend that person, because the client may feel it is not his or her responsibility to inform the therapist. This could lead to a decrease in trust and disclosure for the client (Adams, 1995; Sue, 1992).

Another way to attain important knowledge about a client's specific culture, religion, or spirituality, is to ask individuals within the community who are of the same culture. This will provide a therapist with an outlook on a client's culture that may give context to the client's concerns. However, a client may not affiliate with the particular group that the therapist learned about; therefore, the therapist's knowledge is misguided (Adams, 1995; Frame, 2000; Miller, 2002; Sue, 1992). It is best if therapists have a general overview of religions in order to have some cultural competence in all areas of religiosity. The therapist should educate himself or herself as much as possible about religions, though it is impossible to be fully informed about all religions.

It is also important for therapists, who are of the same culture and religion of the client, to not assume that the client will automatically feel comfortable with self-disclosure. In order to facilitate self-disclosure, a certain degree of congruency must exist between the belief systems or cultures of the client and therapist. This is because "the potential importance of mutual values and of interpersonal similarity would predict that the impact of therapist disclosure of religious values on intimacy of client disclosure would depend on the congruence between the client's faith and the religious beliefs disclosed by the therapist" (Chesner & Baumeister, 1985, p. 99).

Ethical Issues When Integrating Spirituality and Religion in Couple and Family Therapy

According to AAMFT *Code of Ethics* (2001), Principle 1.1: "Marriage and Family Therapists provide professional assistance to persons without discrimination on the basis of race, age, ethnicity, socioeconomic status, disability, gender, health status, religion, national origin, or sexual orientation." Thus, in order to decrease the chances of discrimination and increase therapist sensitivity, the following information will provide some of the most common ethical issues that therapists may encounter when working with different cultural and religious backgrounds.

Therapist Self-Awareness

Couple and family therapists should be cognizant and sensitive to their own spiritual and religious heritage and identities. This will allow them to become aware of congruencies they have with clients, which, in turn, may allow therapists and clients to become comfortable with differences between themselves regarding religion, race, spirituality, and culture (Sue, 1992; Toledano, 1996). Building a therapeutic alliance based on congruencies or similarities, between a client and therapist, provides a foundation of trust to work through differences when and if they occur. By understanding the impact of the therapist's self in therapy, the quality of interventions and level of power differential will be available for self-evaluation. One's openness to clients discussing spiritual and religious issues is an important factor; clients are often hesitant to bring up religion in therapy (Miller, 1992). Recent inclusion of spirituality in the COAAMFT (Commission of American Association for Marriage and Family Therapy) Standards of Accreditation for marriage and family therapy (MFT) training programs hopefully means that students are gaining training and cultural competence in spirituality and religion in working with couples and families (Hage et al., 2006).

Imposition of Therapist's Religious or Spiritual Values

> Sara is an Orthodox Jewish stay-at-home mother who recently had been struggling with depression. Her husband David expected, as was traditional in their religion, that Sara would stay at home with the children. Sara initiated therapy after some months of struggling with her depression; the therapist believed that seeking a part-time job might help alleviate her depression. Sara's husband was not in favor of the job; Sara was unsure but trusted her therapist.

Sara chose to be a stay-at-home caregiver based on her religious traditions. By encouraging an intervention that reflected the therapist's values, wherein which the adoption of egalitarian roles was encouraged between the client and her husband, the therapist risks unbalancing the marital relationship between Sara and David and perhaps deepening Sara's depression. The ethical concern is that the therapist risks promoting a type of egoism in conceptualizing cases so that the client believes that self is central to progress, and that the client's goals are created with reference to that which promotes his or her own self-interest (Roberts, 1997). The therapist's belief that there needs to be a career-related egalitarianism intervention in order to decrease depression would reflect a stereotypical view of the therapist, which may encumber therapy. Even though this may be a worthwhile topic to explore in therapy, it is not ethical, and it is not the therapist's responsibility to intervene in this manner. It is an ethically problematic situation when therapists try to bring about unwanted changes in clients' lives (Odell & Stewart, 1993).

For instance, a conservative Christian client attends therapy due to the tension of contemplating divorce. Another finds her way to therapy with guilt over same-sex attraction. The therapist should discuss the importance of religion in each of the above clients' lives, but not impose his or her own beliefs and values onto the clients. Therefore, after a thorough, heartfelt discussion in therapy, the first client may choose to stay married, and the second may choose to remain celibate in an attempt to adhere to his or her religious beliefs (Yarhouse, 1998; Yarhouse & VanOrman, 1999). Wolf and Stevens (2001) noted that it is unethical to proselytize, or make implicit or explicit judgments about clients' life choices with which the therapist may fundamentally disagree.

Tjelveit (1989) (as cited in Odell & Stewart, 1993) drew a distinction between moral values and mental health values. Mental health values are appropriate topics for therapists to solicit areas of change, but moral values should not be changed as a result of therapy. Mental health values are appropriate for therapists to engage in because they are within therapists' professionally and socially sanctioned area of expertise. The problem is in changing mental health values without touching on moral values (Odell & Stewart, 1993). The difficulty is when a therapist becomes invested in moral values over mental health values. Odell and Stewart (1993) referred to "therapists' guiding conceptions as to the optimal conditions of client functioning, particularly regarding moral, political, and spiritual values (e.g., a particular spiritual value form is *best*, etc.)" (p. 128). Even when a therapist does not have a moral agenda, he or she can get caught in an ethical conundrum between moral values and mental health values.

Rita presents for therapy with panic attacks. She is 29 years old and is caring for her elderly parents, as is the custom in her ethnic heritage. She is the youngest of eight children and has never married. She has given up the dream of college, and she suffers verbal abuse from her parents. Her siblings do not help out with the care of her parents. In her culture, sending her parents to a nursing home would be a disgrace. In examining her panic attacks, Rita always describes feeling "pressed in" and "suffocated." Rita's therapist wants Rita to work on emotional differentiation issues from her parents, but she believes Rita needs to move out of their house and have a life of her own in order to really thrive.

According to the American Psychological Association, "respecting clients' right to self-determination relative to personal values and beliefs and by realizing that theories and models of therapy carry certain value assumptions about life" (Becvar, 2001, p. 157). Therefore, it is imperative for the therapist to be nonjudgmental and sensitive to the client's religious, cultural, and spiritual values (Haug, 1998). Rita's therapist must curb her belief that Rita "needs" to behave in a certain way in order to cure herself. Her bias will have a negative effect on therapy and limit the options that are available for therapy.

Odell and Stewart (1993) recommended that therapists who provide values disclosure statements at the onset of therapy create and maintain a context in which clients can disagree with the therapist, consult with other professionals about values-sensitive issues, and continually take stock of one's personal and professional issues. They wrote that "Therapists should take great care to respect the values and choice of their clients and to address values of a moral, political, and religious nature only when explicitly requested to do so via the informed consent of the client, and most cautiously even then" (p. 132).

Agency Policies: Organization Standards

Therapists in state-funded settings should become aware of their agencies' policies and procedures (Wolf & Stevens, 2001). In light of the separation of church and state, it may be inappropriate to discuss certain aspects of spirituality or religion in therapy. Even though it may not be necessary to totally avoid a discussion of spirituality or religion (or possible as discussed above), the therapist may need to be careful to avoid religious intervention. Discussing a client's spirituality and religiosity as part of their personhood and culture would seem to be acceptable, though one would want to check their agencies' policies and procedures, especially in order to protect the client's autonomy (Wolf & Stevens, 2001).

Fees

Collecting fees for spiritual or religious-based therapy can be a problematic issue. Is a therapist justified in receiving financial reimbursement for spiritual and religious interventions when a client can receive the same service from an ecclesiastical leader (Chappelle, 2000)? Another potential concern occurs when a therapist who has provided spiritual intervention attempts to collect insurance reimbursement for psychological intervention (Tan, 2003).

Professional Boundaries

Throughout the process of therapy, a therapist must create appropriate boundaries with his or her client, which include not forming multiple relationships. A multiple relationship is defined as "a situation in which the family therapist functions in roles associated with a professional relationship and also assumes another definitive and intended role that is not inconsequential or a chance encounter" (Sonne, 1994, p. 336). For instance, a therapist may have two roles: one as therapist, and the other as a member of the client's local religious organization. Therefore, role confusion may develop with the blurring of social and professional boundaries. There may also be a conflict of interests, knowing too much about other individuals in the religious environment, and possible violations of privacy and confidentiality. A client may also overextend his or her expectations of the therapist, thus placing the therapist in uncomfortable or compromising situations (Frame, 2000; Miller, 2002; Tan, 2003).

However, when working with spirituality and religion in therapy, boundary issues may need to be handled carefully. For example, if a client wishes to see a therapist of the same faith as his or her own, there is a risk that the client will have a multiple relationship, because there are smaller numbers of people with whom he or she will interact in his or her social domain. It is simply more likely the client will run into his or her therapist at religious-sponsored events. Hill and Mamalakis (2001) noted that in some religions, it is antithetical to separate the therapeutic relationship from the community of the church; the community of the church is seen as central to the healing process.

Assessment of Readiness for Spirituality and Religion Intervention

Prior to using spiritual interventions with clientele, the therapist must determine, through assessment, whether or not the client feels that the presenting problem would be ameliorated with the utilization of spiritual interventions (Hathaway, Scott, & Garver, 2004). When spiritual interventions are used, their goal is generally to help the client grow spiritually and correct problematic thoughts, feelings, and behaviors that distance the client from God (that is, sin) (Chappelle, 2000). Standardized instruments the therapist may use to assess spirituality in the client's life are provided by Wolf and Stevens (2001). They include the Spiritual Well-Being Scale (Ellison, 1983), the Spiritual Experience Scale (Genia, 1994), and the Spiritual Assessment Inventory (Hall & Edwards, 1996). Another way therapists can assess spirituality in a client's life is by using spiritual genograms, which provide the therapist and the client with a visual presentation of their spiritual beliefs throughout multiple generations (Haug, 1998). This, for example, could have particular meaning to someone who practices Taoism, because Taoists revere their ancestors. Another visual technique that may be helpful is a spiritual ecomap (Hodge, 2000). Whether or not the therapist intervenes spiritually or religiously, spiritual genograms or ecomaps are wonderful tools to track important spiritual and religious history in families, and they may be used to find spiritual resources to augment couple and family therapy.

Tan (2003) noted that clinical integration of spiritual or religious values can be implicit or explicit. When the therapist's religious values are implicit, they are not overtly discussed, but they guide therapy. Spirituality or religion is discussed if initiated by the client. In explicit integration, religious issues are addressed throughout therapy, including the use of prayer or scripture or the referral of the client to clergy. One danger that Tan warned against when working with clients is that the therapist should not take on the role of ecclesiastical authority or argue over doctrine issues (2003); this would be an abuse of therapeutic power, and clients should instead be referred back to religious leaders for clarity on ecclesiastical issues. The therapist must differentiate the theological from psychological or relational issues and ideally know when to refer clients back to their religious leaders (Stander, Piercy, MacKinnon, & Helmeke, 1994). The therapist's approach should be explained to the client prior to therapy, using a thorough informed consent.

Informed Consent

After determining that the client desires to use spiritual or religious interventions, the therapist should obtain a written informed consent authorizing the implementation of such practices. This can be done throughout therapy or at the time of the initial informed consent. The benefit of using an informed consent in conjunction with spiritual interventions is that it safeguards the client and the therapist, because each knows what to expect from one another and the intervention. In addition, a thorough documentation of the promulgation of the intervention, justification, and how it relates to the problem should be included in the client's file. Most importantly, when implementing a spiritual intervention, it is imperative for the therapist to avoid harming the client through creating an unsafe environment (Becvar, 2001; Chappelle, 2000; McMinn & McRay, 1997; Miller, 2002). However, if a couple in therapy are of the same or different faith and are of differing levels of adherence to religious beliefs, the therapist may find it beneficial to discuss how and if spiritual or religious interventions will be used. Last, because integrating spiritual or religious interventions has the potential to invite multiple relationship issues, written informed consent can clarify the nature of the therapist–client relationship.

Therapist Competencies and Limitations

Once a client determines that he or she wants to incorporate spiritual interventions into therapy, the therapist must then evaluate his or her own competencies in utilizing these interventions. Hall and Hall (1997), as cited in Taylor (2000), noted that "prayer, use of biblical scriptures or other sacred texts, and referral to religious groups and clergy were the most common" ways that therapists explicitly integrated spirituality into therapy (p. 15). (There were many ways therapists implicitly integrated spirituality, as detailed earlier.) The explicit manner in which therapists integrate spiritual and religiosity as detailed here creates ethical concerns with regard to therapist competencies. Taylor (2000) noted that most therapists do not have training in the world religions that might be practiced by their clients, or may be unaware of more unorthodox practices. Therefore, the therapist should be cognizant of his or her own limitations, obtain additional training and education in the specialty area needed, not practice outside his or her area of competence (Taylor, 2000), and make appropriate referrals.

The therapist should seek supervision and possibly see an ecclesiastical leader of the client's religion (Bishop, 1992; Chappelle, 2000; Frame, 2000; McMinn & McRay, 1997; Tan, 2003; Yarhouse & VanOrman, 1999). Thus, "therapists must make sure that clients are referred appropriately and are helped to find alternative professional help that is suitable for them" (Becvar, 2001, p. 158).

Usurping Religious Authority

The final ethical issue about which the therapist should be aware is ensuring that he or she does not usurp religious authority (Tan, 2003). This is a particularly sensitive issue in regard to morality among certain religions and cultures. For example, a therapist would not want to advise a couple to engage in masturbation as a treatment for a sexual dysfunction when their religious and cultural beliefs prohibit this practice. A client in this situation may feel obligated to follow the therapists' instructions while at the same time violating his or her religious standard. This is an inappropriate position for the therapist to place his or her client in. When there are issues of authority, misunderstanding, or triangling, it can be beneficial for the couple and family therapist to collaborate with the clergy (Weaver, Koenig, & Larson, 1997) and work to find solutions together.

Summary

The therapy room represents a microcosm of the larger world, which has many religions, cultures, beliefs, and values. Therapists routinely walk the cultural crossroads whether they intersect with religion or spirituality. Ideally, clients will be able to walk with them. In order to work with clientele from diverse backgrounds, a therapist must broaden his or her knowledge and enhance his or her repertoire of skills. Therapists should also be aware of the ethical issues that may transpire when dealing with these multicultural issues, such as the importance of therapist self-awareness, not imposing the therapist's religious or spiritual beliefs and values onto the client, understanding agency policies with regard to the separation of church and state, and ethical and legal issues around collecting fees. Also of importance are professional boundaries, the assessment of readiness for spiritual and religious intervention, informed consent, therapist competence, and the usurping of religious authority. Given that spirituality and religion have generally been found to be associated with health (Tan, 2003), it is important to understand in what situations couple and family therapists can ethically integrate spirituality and religion into their therapy.

References

Adams, N. (1995). Spirituality, science and therapy. *Association of New Zealand Journal of Family Therapy, 16*, 201–208.

Arredondo, P., Toporek, R., Brown, S., Jones, J., Locke, D. C., Sanchez, J., et al. (1996). Operationalization of the multicultural counseling competencies AMCD professional standards and certification committee. Empowerment Workshops, Boston, MA.

Becvar, D. S. (2001). Moral values, spirituality, and sexuality. In Woody, R. H., & Woody J. D. (Eds.), *Ethics in marriage and family therapy* (pp.153–168). Washington, DC: American Association for Marriage and Family Therapy.

Bergin, A. (1991). Proposed agenda for a spiritual strategy in personality and psychotherapy. *Journal of Psychology and Christianity, 10*, 197–210.

Bergin, A. E., & Jensen, J. P. (1990). Religiosity of psychotherapists: A national survey. *Psychotherapy, 27*, 3–7.

Bishop, D. R. (1992). Religious values as cross-cultural issues. *Counseling and Values, 36*, 179–191.

Carlson, T. D., Kirkpatrick, D., Hecker, L., & Killmer, M. (2002). Religion, spirituality, and marriage and family therapy: A study of family therapists' beliefs about the appropriateness of addressing religious and spiritual issues in therapy. *The American Journal of Family Therapy, 30*, 157–171.

Chappelle, W. (2000). A series of progressive legal and ethical decision-making steps for using Christian spiritual interventions in psychotherapy. *Journal of Psychology and Theology, 28*, 43–53.

Chesner, S. P., & Baumeister, R. F. (1985). Effect of therapist's disclosure of religious beliefs on the intimacy of client self-disclosure. *Journal of Social and Clinical Psychology, 3*, 97–105.

Ellison, C. (1983). Spiritual well-being. Conceptualizations and measures. *Journal of Psychology and Theology, 11*, 330–340.

Frame, M. (2000). Spiritual and religious issues in counseling: Ethical considerations. *The Family Journal: Counseling and Therapy for Couples and Families, 8*, 72–74.

Gallup, Inc. (2008). Americans More Likely to Believe in God Than the Devil, Heaven More Than Hell. Retrieved October 31, 2008, from: www.gallup.com/poll/27877/Americans-More-Likely-Believe-God-Than-Devil-Heaven-More-Than-Hell.aspx.

Genia, V. (1994). Secular psychotherapy and religious clients: Professional considerations and recommendations. *Journal of Counseling and Development, 72*, 395–398.

Hage, S. M., Hopson, A., Siegel, M., Payton, G., & DeFanti, E. (2006). Multicultural training in spirituality: An interdisciplinary review. *Counseling and Values, 50,* 217–234.

Hall, M. L., & Hall, T. W. (1997). Integration in the therapy room: An overview of the literature. *Journal of Psychology and Theology, 25*(1), 86–101.

Hall, T. W., & Edwards, T. K. (1996). The initial development and factor analysis of the Spiritual Assessment Inventory. *Journal of Psychology and Theology, 24,* 233–246.

Hathaway, W. L., Scott, S. Y., & Garver, S. A. (2004). Assessing religious/spiritual functioning: A neglected domain in clinical practice? *Professional Psychology: Research and Practice, 35,* 97–104.

Haug, I. E. (1998). Including a spiritual dimension in family therapy: Ethical considerations. *Contemporary Family Therapy, 20,* 181–194.

Hill, M. R., & Mamalakis, P. M. (2001). Family therapists and religious communities, *Negotiating Dual Relationships, 50*(2), 199–208.

Hodge, D. R. (2000). Spiritual ecomaps: A new diagrammatic tool for assessing marital and family spirituality. *Journal of Marital and Family Therapy, 26(2),* 217–228.

Joanides, C. J. (1996). Collaborative family therapy with religious family systems. *Journal of Family Psychotherapy, 7,* 19–35.

Laungani, P. (2004). Counseling and therapy in a multi-cultural setting. *Counseling Psychology Quarterly, 17,* 195–207.

McMinn, M. R., & McRay, B. W. (1997). Spiritual disciplines and the practice of integration: Possibilities and challenges for Christian psychologists. *Journal of Psychology and Theology, 25,* 102–110.

Miller, G. (2002). Ethical issues. In Miller, G. (Ed.), *Incorporating spirituality in counseling and psychotherapy: Theory and technique.* (pp. 163–188). New York: John Wiley & Sons.

Miller, G. A. (1992). Integrating religion and psychology in therapy: Issues and recommendations. *Counseling and Values, 36*(2), 112–123.

Miller, W. R., & Thorenson, C. E. (2003). Spirituality, religion, and health: An emerging research field. *American Psychologist, 58,* 24–35.

Odell, M., & Stewart, S. P. (1993). Ethical issues associated with client values conversion and therapist value agendas in family therapy. *Family Relations, 42,* 128–133.

Prest, L. A., & Russell, R. (1995). *Spirituality in training, practice, and personal development.* Unpublished manuscript.

Roberts, R. C. (1997). Attachment: Bowlby and the Bible. In Roberts, R. C., & Talbot, M. R. (Eds.), *Limning the psyche* (pp. 206–228). Grand Rapids, MI: Eerdmans.

Sonne, J. L. (1994). Multiple relationships: Does the new ethics code answer the right questions? *Professional Psychology: Research and Practice, 25,* 336–343.

Smith, D. P., & Orlinsky, D. E. (2004). Religious and spiritual experience among psychotherapists. *Psychotherapy: Theory, Research, Practice, Training, 41,* 144–151.

Stander, V., Piercy, F. P., MacKinnon, D., & Helmeke, K. (1994). Spirituality, religion and family therapy: Competing or complementary worlds? *The American Journal of Family Therapy, 22*(1), 27–41.

Stewart, S. P., & Gale, J. E. (1994). On hallowed ground: Marital therapy with couples on the religious right. *Journal of Systemic Therapies, 13,* 16–25.

Sue, D. W. (1992). The challenge of multiculturalism: The road less traveled. *American, Counselor,* (Winter), 7–14.

Sue, D. W., Arredondo, P., & McDavis, R. J. (1992). Multicultural counseling, competencies, and standards: A call to the profession. *Journal of Multicultural Counseling and Development, 20,* 64–88.

Tan, S. (2003). Integrating spiritual direction into psychotherapy: Ethical issues and guidelines. *Journal of Psychology and Theology, 31,* 14–23.

Taylor, J. (2000). Clinical integration: Should religious and spiritual values be incorporated in therapy? *The Clinical Psychologist, 53*(4), 12–19.

Tjeltvelt, A. (1989). The transformation of the social bond: Images of individualism in the 1920s versus the 1970s. *Social Forces, 67,* 851–870.

Toledano, A. (1996). Issues arising from intra-cultural family therapy. *Journal of Family Therapy, 18,* 289–301.

Walsh, F. (2006). *Strengthening family resilience* (2nd ed.). New York: Guilford Press.

Watts, R. E. (2001). Addressing spiritual issues in a secular counseling and psychotherapy: Response to Helminiak's (2001) views. *Counseling and Values, 45,* 207–218.

Weaver, A. J., Koenig, H. G., & Larson, D. B. (1997). Marriage and family therapists and the clergy: A need for clinical collaboration, training, and research. *Journal of Marital and Family Therapy, 23*(1), 13–25.

Wolf, C. T., & Stevens, P. (2001). Integrating religion and spirituality in marriage and family counseling. *Counseling and Values, 46,* 66–75.

Yarhouse, M. A. (1998). When families present with concerns about an adolescent's experience of same-sex attraction. *The American Journal of Family Therapy, 26,* 321–330.

Yarhouse, M. A., & VanOrman, B. T. (1999). When psychologists work with religious clients: Applications of the general principles of ethical conduct. *Professional Psychology: Research and Practice, 30,* 557–562.

12

Ethics, Legal, and Professional Issues in Mediation and Parent Coordination

Julia M. Becerra, Nicole Manick, and Lorna L. Hecker

Parents who must encounter the legal system to end the legal status of their relationship can consequently transfer their relational life into an adversarial arena where conflicts between the couple can last for years. This conflict, in turn, can affect the parent–child relationship as well (Amato & Booth, 1996). Children suffer from parental conflict, and continued conflict after a divorce negatively affects children (Amato 2001; Ayoub, Deutsch, & Maraganorr, 1999; Kelly, 2000). Therapists can, and should, respond to the need to pull families from an adversarial stance to one of healing and successful transition to a postconflict family life, where both adults and children can thrive. Traditionally, family therapy theories were developed based on the norm of intact nuclear families; however, most family therapists see families in all states and forms. Although there is slight movement toward developing family therapy models to deal with high-conflict divorce disputes (cf. Lebow & Rekart, 2006), the models and techniques that couple and family therapists have learned in their formal training typically do not extend to couples undergoing divorce or custody conflicts. Alternative methods are needed.

Alternative dispute resolution (ADR) is a service typically offered through the legal system but is one that the couple and family therapist can, with appropriate training, practice. ADR is commonly seen in business practices as mediation or arbitration and has long been seen as a more amicable and cost-effective way to settle disputes. These alternatives are now being expanded into divorce settlements and child custody disputes. The legal issues need to be tended to by attorneys, but the emotional issues can best be resolved by couple and family therapists who understand the systemic nature of the conflict and can aid the couple in detangling from entrenched positions. Couple and family therapists can assist the court to reduce the amount of animosity between parents (Doty & Berman, 2004). In this chapter, two methods of ADR in which couple and family therapists can engage are discussed. Mediation and parent coordination are two areas that show promise for the profession of marriage and family therapy.

Mediation

Mediation is a process whereby dispute resolution is facilitated by a neutral third person who is selected by the two disputing parties. The mediator has no authority to settle the dispute but acts as a nonbinding alternative to the litigation system. Sullivan (2004) noted that judges delegate their decision-making power to an expert in "the best interest of the child." The process involves joint and separate meetings between the mediator and the parties to emphasize the strengths and weaknesses of the case and to reach a compromise; it is a legally binding process and often includes a parenting plan. The benefits of mediation can include the following:

- Participants can avoid taking adversarial positions or "battling" issues in court.
- Clients are saving time and money by avoiding litigation, thereby gaining an economic advantage.
- Clients learn to communicate such that it sets the tone for further dispute resolution (Saposnek, 1998).
- Parents formulate a joint set of parenting rules.
- Parents model positive adult behavior for their children.
- The two parties maintain decision-making power over their own circumstances (Gilchrist & Marshall, 1999).
- Parents experience a decrease in conflict, which can take children out of the middle of conflict.
- Clients experience an emotional advantage of compromise versus conflict.

Mediation begins with two disputing parties selecting a mediator for the facilitation of a resolution to their case. Often a judge will order mediation to attempt to resolve the dispute, or if both parties' attorneys know the judge will order this, they may suggest it themselves. Parties are usually at least somewhat willing to participate, as legal fees and missed work time for litigation readily accrue.

The first consideration the mediator should make is whether or not the mediator has had past contact with the parties. If the therapist has had social or professional contact with either party, it should be disclosed in writing to both parties (Goodman, 2004). This does not indicate that the therapist could not act as the mediator, but both parties must have knowledge of the prior contact and still agree that this mediator is appropriate. The mediator should then disclose his or her qualifications, how the process occurs, fees, and any other necessary arrangements that the mediator would need to facilitate a resolution of the dispute. The parties then sign a contract and usually pay a retainer for the mediator to begin to work on the dispute. Informed consent must be obtained from both parties to proceed with mediation, as with therapy.

Attorneys may or may not be present at the mediation. If one party has informed the mediator of the presence of an attorney, the mediator should let the other party know before the first session; this balances the power equally in the session. Mediation, unlike arbitration, is nonbinding, and *ex parte* (contact with only one party) is permitted. A mediator may ask for a caucus and speak confidentially with one party at a time to try to reach a settlement. It must be understood that the mediator can ask to speak to either party, with or without an attorney, or with an attorney alone to help reach a settlement or break an impasse.

Process of Mediation

The mediation begins with the opening statement by the mediator and those of the parties on their stance. All necessary paperwork (e.g., custody evaluation results, provisional custody order, and divorce decree) is reviewed in advance but may also be reviewed during the session as needed (Emery, 1994). Every part of the mediation should be brief, and summaries of documents are usually best. The parties should both be informed that they will be charged for time the mediator must spend reviewing documents.

Usually, the mediator then goes on to list the important issues of the case that require compromise. The needs of the child, the custody (referred to as parenting time within mediation), child support, and legal custody (referred to as academic decisions, religious decisions, and health decisions in mediation) must all be discussed within the family mediation process. Each issue must be explored from multiple angles so that both parties know and understand the settlement they are agreeing to in session.

The process of mediation ends when the couple agrees that no further decisions can be made. This happens in one of three ways. The couple may have compromised a solution to all important issues. The couple may have partial agreement on some of the issues but cannot agree on others. Finally, no resolutions may have been made, and an impasse is called by the mediator. Whatever the conclusion, the mediator writes the outcome down and has all parties sign that this is what was agreed upon in the meeting, even if that was that no agreement was reached. This could be a handwritten, numbered list of the resolved issues that includes payment by one party or the other, return of goods, restitution of funds, promises to perform certain conduct, and issues that were discussed and are no longer at issue. The mediator does not sign the agreement, as only the parties involved sign the document. This agreement document will suffice, but the parties may request that their attorney draft a more detailed document that is then signed by both parties (Goodman, 2004). If the couple has been court ordered, the judge will then receive a copy of the mediator's report and settle any issues that were unresolved in the mediation process.

Ethics

First, "the mediator has an ethical obligation to ascertain whether mediation is appropriate, whether it is safe, whether parties should be brought together in the same room, and who ought to be at the table" (Mayer, 2004, p. 40). As discussed above, the first order of business prior to mediation is to disclose any conflicts of interests. A contract that includes informed consent should be reviewed and signed.

When tensions rise or a party feels uncomfortable, it may be necessary to caucus and meet separately with each party to explore possible settlements. These discussions are also confidential, and information shared within caucus must not be shared with the other party, or the other party's lawyer. The mediator must ask the party exactly what settlement offer or issue can be communicated to the other party. The mediator also needs to make sure that he or she does not do counseling or give legal advice during mediation.

Within the context of mediation, one of the most important ethical considerations is confidentiality. Confidentiality should be discussed within the therapist's written disclosure or in the explanation of the process. Like therapist–client and attorney–client privilege, everything that is said within the session remains confidential. Only the parties and their attorneys are allowed to be present. If another person is necessary (e.g., a guardian ad litem), that person may also attend. Whether a mediator allows a friend or stepparent to be present is at the discretion of the mediator.

Another important ethical and legal consideration is that of noncoercion, or the right of the client to self-determination. It is important to educate clients and allow them to make their own choices, free from pressure from the mediator (Welsh, 2004). Even though a settlement is optimal, it should not be made at the expense of free will of the clients. Mediator bias is also a significant issue that can get in the way of a fair and ethical mediation. Mediators who find themselves unable to be neutral or bias free must excuse themselves from the case and make necessary referrals.

The mediator should be conscious of couples who have had violence in their relationship, as coercion or intimidation may be present but never overtly stated. Again, caucus can be used to ensure that these problems do not interfere with the process. The mediation process is voluntary, and no one can be forced to participate. Rules of the mediation sessions should also be explained during the initial session, and those clients who cannot adhere to the rules (no shouting, throwing things, and so forth) should also be asked to caucus. Mediation may be terminated in these instances. In any instance where a client is emotionally unable to effectively participate in mediation, it is an ethical responsibility of the mediator to suspend or terminate mediation (Welsh, 2004).

Aside from violence, there are other power imbalances of which the mediator needs to be aware in order to facilitate a fair settlement; the mediator has to walk a thin line between protecting a disempowered party from an unfair settlement and staying neutral. These include tangible disparities such as education and income differences, but also intangible factors such as "status, dominance, depression, self esteem, reward expectation, fear of achievement, and sex role ideology" (Walther, 2000, p. 95).

At times parents will make agreements on issues that may not be in the child's best interests. For example, the parents want to fly a 3-year-old across country alone for summer and holiday visits with the alternate parent. Most mediators ask questions to help parents understand the implications of their decision making (Mayer, 2004). This tends to be an effective way to get parents to understand the effects of their decision on the child and reconsider their options for a more child-focused solution. How the mediator raises concerns will affect the mediation relationship that should be bias free.

The mediator is there to control the process and suggest solutions. A mediator is facilitating a settlement discussion and should know that anything said during the process is inadmissible in court. The mediator may ask permission to take notes but may also communicate that those notes will leave with that mediator and be destroyed after the session (Goodman, 2004). Malpractice insurance is available through the Academy of Family Mediators, the Society of Professionals in Dispute Resolutions, and Association of Family and Conciliation Courts.

Role of the Couple and Family Therapist

When couple and family therapists see conflictual couples separately, they are often in the position to negotiate or facilitate the agreement of positions on issues. The mediator may have both parties remain in the same room and talk to each other to try to resolve some of the pending issues. If this becomes problematic, the mediator asks the parties to speak only to the mediator. The mediator will also write down all issues that have been agreed upon prior to the session, so that the clients' time is not wasted and so that both parties have concrete examples of compromises they have reached before. The sessions usually end when all issues are unsolvable and the mediator calls an impasse or the issues are resolved and the settlement is written up and signed by both parties. This is a binding contract that is submitted to a judge for approval.

State Standards

Every state has mediation as an ADR. It is being widely utilized as an alternative to litigation; in some states it is mandated. In many states, it is often used for those high-conflict cases that continually appear before the same judge. It can be a viable alternative to litigation for the modification of a custody arrangement. Many states allow the ADR rules, the American Bar Association Section of Dispute Resolution, and the Academy of Family Mediators to set the guidelines for ethical mediation practices. Some states, such as Florida and California, have Mediator Ethics Advisory Committees to set and ensure the ethical and moral standards to which the mediator complies.

In mediation, authority is earned through the appointment of the mediator, who also has to maintain many of the same qualities as a family therapist, such as listening skills, general communication skills, conflict management skills, and a desire to help others. Ideally, the mediator should be a licensed professional, have at least a master's degree, be trained in family issues and conflict management, and possess an understanding of child development, which all closely mirror the training of couple and family therapists. There are mediation training programs available on a state-by-state basis, which usually run between 3 and 7 days. Standards are set by rule or statute (Welsh, 2004), though there is no required certification at this time (Milne, Folberg, & Salem, 2004).

Couple and family therapists are uniquely qualified to serve the postdecree families in reducing conflict and coming together for the sake of the children. As a mediator, the therapist has experience necessary in decreasing tension in the room, reaching a compromise, and is also familiar with the general discussion format that both roles require.

Parent Coordination

Parent coordination is another ADR process available to facilitate the resolution of family issues. It is a child-focused process that is performed by a mental health professional or an attorney. The parent coordinator assists high-conflict parents in implementing their parenting plan by facilitating resolution to their disputes, educating parents about their children's needs, and making decisions within the scope of the court or appointment contract (Association of Family and Conciliation Courts [AFCC] Task Force on Parenting Coordination, 2005, p. 3).

Parent coordinators (also called special masters and custody commissioners), are a third party selected to act as arbitrators to settle the dispute for the parties when agreement cannot be reached. They can also be appointed prior to the divorce to help set up the parenting plan, or can be appointed years after the divorce to help execute the parenting plan and facilitate other decisions or day-to-day conflicts or trouble spots. Parent coordinators are trained mediators and problem solvers (Bartlett, 2004). In some states, parent coordinators are used in high-conflict situations with families where the parent education and mediation were unsuccessful. Parent coordinators are usually used for those high-conflict parents who demonstrated their longer-term inability or unwillingness to make parenting decisions on their own, to comply with parenting agreements and orders, to reduce their child-related conflicts, and to protect their children from the impact of the conflict (AFCC Task Force on Parenting Coordination, 2005, p. 3).

Parenting coordinators facilitate a discussion about the disputed issues by exploring possibilities for compromise, developing methods of compromise, identifying the most important concerns, and maintaining compliance with court guidelines, similar to the mediation process. They may map out in-depth parenting plans to avoid future conflict between parents. The parenting coordinator first makes every attempt to mediate decisions between both parents, and if it is not possible for both parties to make a decision, then the coordinator is allowed legal jurisdiction to make a decision for them. Parent coordination involves a means of resolving disputes for parents who are not good candidates for mediation and who need more intense, ongoing intervention. Typically parents are court referred. They have an assessment function (they gather information from all referring sources), they have an education function (they educate parents about child development and the impact of parental conflict), they perform a case management function between all involved parties, they provide conflict management, and if the parents cannot agree on a decision, they have the legal authority to make the decision for them (AFCC Task Force on Parenting Coordination, 2005).

Benefits of Parent Coordination

A parenting coordinator is helpful for families because they have the opportunity to make the decisions about the living arrangements of their children and are able to have a voice in these decisions. Other benefits include the following:

- It is less expensive to use a parenting coordinator than to go through the process in the court system. The court fees and the costs for attorneys are much more than the cost of hiring one parenting coordinator.
- For situations in which the parenting coordinator must make a decision, that person will have a greater understanding about the case than a judge due to the close contact with both parents. The coordinator can, therefore, make a more informed decision.
- Parent coordination is timelier than the potential drawn-out process in a divorce in which many delays may take place due to extensions or modifications in child custody.
- A successfully parent-coordinator–mediated case will be less likely to return to the courtroom for revisions at a later date, unlike the divorce litigation.
- Parent coordinators can help with day-to-day details in parenting conflict that courts are unable to litigate on an ongoing basis.

- Children may fare better in a parent-coordinator-mediated situation, because parents may be less likely to continue to carry on destructive behavior as a result of coming to joint decisions together.
- There can be regular contact with someone who is monitoring the family situation, and the family does not need to wait for court dates for intervention to occur.

Requirements for Parent Coordinators

The requirements of a parent coordinator differ from state to state; it is important to find out what requirements there are in one's jurisdiction and if there are any statutes used to appoint parent coordinators (Boyan & Termini, 2005). States that use parent coordinators include California, Florida, Georgia, Idaho, Kentucky, Oklahoma, Massachusetts, Michigan, New Jersey, North Carolina, Pennsylvania, and Texas. Parent coordinators in California are either Special Masters or Parent Coordinators. Special Masters are attorneys, whereas, parent coordinators are typically therapists (Boyan, 2000). Parent coordinators in Hawaii are called Custody Commissioners (Sullivan, 2004). Most states require applicants to go through a training program along with other various requirements. The AFCC Task Force on Parenting Coordination (2005) suggested training on the parent coordination process, family dynamics in separation and divorce, parent coordination techniques and issues, the court-specific parent coordination process, and domestic violence training. Some states require that parent coordinators have considerable training in the effects of abuse on victims in order to take on cases such as these (Bartlett, 2004).

Ethics

An informed consent is especially important to outline the role that the parent coordinator plays for the parents. In addition, the informed consent needs to clearly outline the limits to confidentiality and the fact that the coordinator is prone to being subpoenaed to court. Any conflicts of interests need to be explained. Fees (for in-session and out-of-session time spent) need to be divulged. This process is not confidential, because the clients are court mandated to participate; the limits of confidentiality need to be clearly outlined. There is no confidentiality for communications between the parents and their children and the parent coordinator. There is no confidentiality for communications between the parent coordinator and other relevant parties to the parent coordination process (e.g., guardian ad litem; attorneys) or for communication to the court (AFCC Task Force on Parenting Coordination, 2005, p. 8). Mandatory reporting guidelines also apply.

The role of the parent coordinator can easily be confusing for both the client and, at times, the coordinator. The coordinator must be careful to not perform therapy but to facilitate parenting without bias and to remain child-focused. Referrals should be made for any additional services needed, and never to any professional from which the therapist could profit from in some way (Boyan & Termini, 2005). The parent coordinator must clearly not serve multiple roles. The coordinator should not serve in sequential roles, such as becoming one party's therapist after parent coordination has terminated (AFCC Task Force on Parenting Coordination, 2005). As with mediation, the coordinator must also be sure not to give legal advice but may facilitate discussions in which one might consider what a judge might rule in that situation. He or she may also defer legal questions to each party's counsel for advice.

As in mediation, the parent coordinator must take care to remain impartial and provide effective parent coordination services to the dyad. He or she needs to be aware of any values or biases that may interfere with his or her ability to perform duties. There must be a commitment to assist all parties (AFCC Task Force on Parenting Coordination, 2005). If the parent coordinator is unable to do this, he or she should make a referral to a new parent coordinator, making sure to facilitate the transition to a new coordinator (Boyan & Termini, 2005). Also, like a mediator, the parent coordinator tries to maintain a stance of neutrality and to allow the clients the right of self-determination. However, when the parents choose options that are not in the best interest of the child, a parent coordinator may adjust parenting plans or take an arbitrator position and make a decision for the family.

Even though the parent coordinator regularly communicates with others involved in the case, the parent coordinator *does not* "engage in ex parte communication with the judge by telephone, e-mail, fax or in person" (Boyan & Termini, 2005, p. 332). Ex parte communication is communication with the judge without involving the attorneys of the involved parties. If it is specified in writing in the order of appointment, parent coordination agreement, or stipulation, the coordinator may communicate ex parte with each of the parties or their attorneys (AFCC Task Force on Parenting Coordination, 2005).

It is imperative that a parent coordinator be aware that he or she may be subpoenaed if the case were to go to court, and that he or she has no immunity from such situations. Therefore, he or she must be prepared to testify in cases involving his or her clients. Additionally, in allegations of child abuse, a parent coordinator has a duty to report and a duty to warn, and parent coordination may not be appropriate (Doty & Berman, 2004).

A parent coordinator is required to assess a family's dynamics and to refer parents who may need mental health assistance to an appropriate professional for care. They are expected to educate parents on coparenting techniques, the effects of parental conflict on children, and appropriate developmental issues (Bartlett, 2004). They are expected to connect with other professionals, including the children's school, therapists, attorneys, social services, extended family, and others (Boyan & Termini, 2005) to create a plan to resolve the conflict. They are instructed to do so by teaching empathy and respect for both partners to mimic in a parallel parenting relationship. Therapists in this role must also be certain not to act as a therapist as well as a parent coordinator (Boyan, 2000). They may refer parents to a therapist if psychotherapy is needed. Additionally, parent coordinators should not be as effusive as they might be in their role as a therapist. Parent coordinators must occasionally be authoritative and direct to further progress, to structure the session, and to limit what parents discuss. Parent coordinators have the authority to recommend additional services, use program discretion, send updates to counsel, make temporary visitation modifications, and, in some cases, they may be able to temporarily arbitrate parenting matters when an impasse is reached. Cases referred may include clients with Axis II disorders or substance abuse problems in which it is unethical and nonproductive for parent coordinators to treat them.

In domestic violence cases, it may be less productive or inappropriate to meet with both individuals together to make joint decisions, much like a mediation session. The abuse victim may feel too threatened to suggest or make decisions that could upset his or her previous partner. It is also suggested to use separate waiting areas, stagger arrival and departure times for both parties, consider the use of a caucus model, and take security precautions (Doty & Berman, 2004).

The AFCC is an international organization composed of family court and community professionals who work to resolve family disputes. They are committed to providing an interdisciplinary means for exchanging ideas and to the improvement of procedures in aiding families in disputes. More information can be found on their Web site at www.afccnet.org. AFCC can be a helpful resource for networking with other professionals to exchange information, expertise, and support. Seeking support is recommended to reduce burnout by communicating and networking with other parent coordinators (Boyan, 2000). The parent coordinator must protect himself or herself from professional burnout in order to keep efficacious. The work can be very rewarding but also tremendously challenging.

Comparing and Contrasting the Mediator and Parenting Coordinator Roles

The most pronounced difference between the mediator and the parent coordinator is the decision-making authority. In mediation, the two disputing parties maintain the choice to select what is appropriate for them. In the parenting coordinator's session, the parenting coordinator acts as an arbitrator and can make judgments if the two parties do not reach agreement. Mediators not only mediate child custody but are also certified to mediate property settlements.

Mediators help parents resolve disputes that arise during separation and after the divorce, and parent coordinators help divorcing parents implement parenting plans and make day-to-day decisions about the children (Jessani & James, 2006).

Parent coordinators have legal jurisdiction, whereas, mediators must call an impasse if final decisions cannot be reached. They may also make minor adjustments to temporary departures from the parenting plan. Parenting coordinators often determine when children are ready for increased visitation and can make sure that children receive items from one parent when with another in high-conflict cases. They are also able to speak with the child's therapist and the courts.

Anything shared in the mediation session is inadmissible in court, so there is no written record of the session (Goodman, 2004). The mediator may choose to use a dry-erase board, chalkboard, notepad, or large sketchpad to take notes on those topics that have been agreed upon, but nothing written in session, with the exception of the final settlement, is ever kept after the mediation. Goodman (2004) suggested that all notes from a mediation session be destroyed. It is important to note that one should only keep documents that support your fees and should maintain confidentiality in storing those documents. Confidentiality should be considered in the process of destroying documents. It is also important to inform the parties that you will not testify in court and that your documents may not be subpoenaed. In most states, the mediator has the same immunity as a judge from testifying in further proceedings (Gilchrist & Marshall, 1999). As previously stated, all documents and parenting coordination proceedings are admissible in court. A summary of differences between mediation and parent coordination is provided in Table 12.1.

TABLE 12.1   Mediation and Parent Coordination

Mediators	Parent Coordinators
Resolve disputes that arise during separation and after divorce.[a]	Help divorcing and divorced parents implement parenting plans and make daily decisions about children.[a]
Often voluntary process at all stages in divorce process; usually occurs in beginning of divorce process.[a]	Self-referral, attorney referral, court referral. Usually last resort.[a]
Confidential process.[a]	Not confidential.[a]
Must call impasse if parents do not agree	Can make decisions if parents do not agree.
No contact with judge.[a]	Typically referrals from court and can inform judge of recommendations.[a]
Nothing admissible in court.	Everything admissible in court.
No documentation.	Documentation.

[a] From Jessani, A. D., & James, L. (2006). Mediators and parent coordinators: 20 questions/40 answers. *American Journal of Family Law, 2*(3), 180–187.

Toward a National Standard

The American Bar Association Section of Dispute Resolution, the Academy of Family Mediators, and the AFCC all work to ensure that mediation and parent coordination sessions are working to resolve disputes in a fair and ethical way. Many state legislating bodies are also aware of mediators and parent coordinators and are working to get immunity rights for those who decide to practice in these fields if they do not already hold them (that is, protected from civil liability). A national standard would be a benefit to those states still litigating all domestic relations cases. The courts would be less inundated with familial issues that can be negotiated outside of the costly litigation process. Children could avoid having to testify or speak to a judge, and their interests could be more readily served.

Summary

Couple and family therapists are increasingly called upon to stretch beyond the realm of therapy to best serve families in need. Mediation and parent coordination are two areas in which family therapists, with additional training, can make a valuable contribution to parents and children suffering the ill effects of protracted parental conflict. Even when conflict is minor or nonexistent, therapists acting as mediators can help parents establish parenting plans and help parents stay out of the conflictual roles that can inadvertently develop out of the adversarial nature of the U.S. court system. Family therapists can use the skills they have in managing conflictual situations as a resource in parent coordination, and their systems training is immensely valuable in understanding the contextual underpinnings of the conflict at hand. It is incumbent upon family therapists to stretch outside of the therapy office into areas in which families are experiencing stress, anxiety, and transition, and help them navigate pain when they are in the most need.

References

AFCC Task Force on Parenting Coordination. (2005). Guidelines for parent coordination. Retrieved October 31, 2008, from: www.afccnet.org/pdfs/AFCCGuidelinesforParentingcoordinationnew.pdf.

Amato, P. R. (2001). Children and divorce in the 1990's: An update of the Amato and Keith (1991) meta-analysis. *Journal of Family Psychology, 15,* 355–370.

Amato, P. R., & Booth, A. (1996). A prospective study of divorce and parent–child relationships. *Journal of Marriage and the Family, 58,* 356–365.

Ayoub, C. C., Deutsch, R. M., & Maraganorr, A. (1999). Emotional distress in children of high-conflict divorce: The impact of marital conflict and violence. *Family Conciliation Courts Review, 37,* 297–314.

Bartlett, B. A. (2004). Parenting coordination: A new tool for assisting high conflict families. *The Oklahoma Bar Journal, 75*(6), 453.

Boyan, S. (2000). What is a parenting coordinator? Specialized therapists and mandated high conflict families. *Family Therapy News, AAMFT,* (June/July), 28–30.

Boyan, S. M., & Termini, A. M. (2005). *The Psychotherapist as Parent Coordinator in High Conflict Divorce: Strategies and Techniques.* New York: Haworth Press.

Doty, D. R., & Berman, W. B. (2004). Divorce Transition Services; Tulsa, Oklahoma, Parenting Coordination. (2004 AAMFT Conference).

Emery, R. (1994). *Renegotiating Family Relationships: Divorce, Child Custody, and Mediation.* New York: Guilford Press.

Gilchrist, C. A., & Marshall, C. L. (1999). Indiana Family Mediation. *Indiana Continuing Legal Education Forum*: Indianapolis, IN.

Goodman, A.H. (2004). *Basic Skills for the New Mediator* (2nd ed.). Rockville, MD: Solomon Publications.

Jessani, A. D., & James, L. (2006). Mediators and parent coordinators: 20 questions/40 answers. *American Journal of Family Law, 2*(3), 180–187.

Kelly, J. (2000). Children's adjustment in conflicted marriages and divorce: A decade review of research. *Journal of the American Academy of Child and Adolescent Psychiatry*, 963–973.

Lebow, J., & Rekart, K. N. (2006). Integrative family therapy for high-conflict divorce with disputes over child custody and visitation. *Family Process, 46*(1), 79–91.

Mayer, B. (2004). Facilitative mediation. In J. Folberg, A. L. Milne, & P. Salem (Eds.), *Divorce and family mediation*. New York: Guilford Press.

Milne, A. L., Folberg, J., & Salem, P. (2004). The evolution of divorce and family mediation: An overview. In J. Folberg, A. L. Milne, & P. Salem (Eds.), *Divorce and family mediation* (pp. 3–25). New York: Guilford Press.

Saposnek, D. T. (1998). *Mediating Child Custody Disputes: A Strategic Approach,* (rev. ed.) San Francisco: Jossey-Bass.

Sullivan, M. J. (2004). Ethical, legal, and professional practice issues involved as acting as a psychologist parenting coordinator in child custody cases. *Family Court Review, 42*(3) 576–582.

Walther, G. M. (2000). Power imbalances in divorce mediation. *American Journal of Family Law, 14*(2), 93–101.

Welsh, N. A. (2004). Reconciling self-determination, coercion, and settlement in court-connected mediation. In J. Folberg, A. L. Milne, & P. Salem (Eds.), *Divorce and family mediation* (pp. 420–446). New York: The Guilford Press.

13

Ethical Issues in Clinical Practice

Julie Ramisch

Literature regarding ethical issues of actual "nuts-and-bolts" practice of couple and family therapy is sparse, giving few sources for couple and family therapists to gain clarity of this process. Managed health care and managed care organizations (MCOs) have drastically changed the landscape of clinical practice of couple and family therapy. The development of preferred provider organizations (PPOs), health maintenance organizations (HMOs), and exclusive provider organizations (EPOs) has made payment for health care a complicated maze to navigate. Getting paid for therapeutic services is no longer between the therapist and the client but is between the therapist, the third-party payer, and the client. For therapists, being part of a panel, or being a preferred provider, for an MCO typically means that they provide therapeutic services for clients who belong to that specific organization at a reduced rate. Theoretically, a therapist would benefit from being part of an MCO in that in exchange for seeing clients at a reduced rate, presumably client volume would increase. Becoming an ethical provider for an MCO will be discussed later in this chapter.

Health Insurance Portability and Accountability Act

In 1996, the Health Insurance Portability and Accountability Act (HIPAA) was signed into law, affecting most therapists. Stemming from an increase in the use of MCOs and the electronic transmission of information, this law was meant to standardize storage and transmission of information in order to protect the privacy of clients and patients when they seek out different means of health care. Any health care provider who transmits client information electronically in order to receive payment, keeps electronic records, or employs a billing service is considered to be a provider that is covered by HIPAA law. The HIPAA law is also meant to guard client privacy and confidentiality from MCOs. For example, because of HIPAA law, these organizations may no longer request that a therapist disclose a client's psychotherapy notes. The difference between client records and psychotherapy notes is discussed further below along with other stipulations as mandated by HIPAA. It is imperative that therapists be knowledgeable about HIPAA standards and law in order to remain compliant with the privacy rules. For more information on HIPAA, see the Web site of the U.S. Department of Health and Human Services (2008).

Documentation: Developing and Managing Forms

Informed Consent Process

A crucial part of clinical practice is preparing the necessary documents that need to be discussed with clients prior to treatment. First is informed consent, which needs to, in clear language, explain the risks and benefits of therapy and give the client the option to decide whether or not to continue with therapy. Please see Appendix 13.1 for an example of an informed consent document. Informed consent, however, is not simply one document or conversation; it is a *process* that occurs throughout therapy. Although the American Association for Marriage and Family Therapy (AAMFT) *Code of Ethics* (2001) stated that this process should happen as early as possible in the therapeutic relationship, it is argued that it is not possible for it to happen in just one session (Pomerantz, 2005). Subprinciple 1.2 of the AAMFT *Code of Ethics* (2001) specifically mandated the following:

> Marriage and family therapists obtain appropriate informed consent to therapy or related procedures as early as feasible in the therapeutic relationship, and use language that is reasonable and understandable to clients. The content of informed consent may vary depending upon the client and treatment plan; however, informed consent generally necessitates that the client: a) has the capacity to consent; b) has been adequately informed of significant information concerning treatment processes and procedures; c) has been adequately informed of potential risks and benefits of treatments for which generally recognized standards do not yet exist; d) has freely and without undue influence expressed consent; and e) has provided consent that is appropriately documented. When persons, due to age or mental status, are legally incapable of giving informed consent, marriage and family therapists obtain informed permission from a legally authorized person, if such substitute consent is legally permissible.

In order for clients to make an informed decision about participating in therapy, they need to know to what they are agreeing. There is no publication that states the areas that have to be included in an informed consent (Haslam & Harris, 2004). Many states require *disclosure statements* that typically require disclosure of the therapist's education and qualifications, though they may legislate other disclosures as well (Hecker, 2003). It is evident that there needs to be more consistent standards put forth so that clients can understand the risks and benefits of couple and family therapy. The following list of what should be included has been compiled based on a comprehensive literature review.

The first section of an informed consent should introduce the therapist and include information about the therapist's credentials; theoretical orientation; procedures surrounding observation; any recording, consulting, or supervision of the sessions; the limits of confidentiality; and when confidentiality must be legally broken (Caudill, 2001). It is important that therapists be specific in these descriptions. For example, it is important to note any specific licenses and degrees of the therapist (Moline, Williams, & Austin, 1998).

Second, the rights of each individual client should be described. The informed consent should state that the client has access to his or her records, the right to choose the therapist and to be active in the treatment planning, the right to refuse counseling, the implication of refusing treatment, the right to ask additional questions about therapy, and the right to get questions answered in understandable language (Welfel, 2002). Third, the logistics section of the document should include the fees and billing practices, an estimate of the length of therapeutic services, procedures surrounding making and rescheduling appointments, what to do in an emergency, information about how long appointments will last, and how clients should address any grievances that should arise (Welfel, 2002). Fourth, risks and benefits of therapy should be clearly described. Risks to treatment, such as symptoms not getting better or in some cases getting worse, should be noted. Clients should be notified that therapy does not necessarily work for each person. The risks and benefits of procedures such as the use of cell phone communication should also be fully described and discussed with the client. Special consent will be needed if the therapist is going to use any controversial or experimental techniques. Controversial techniques are those that are often unusual, and experimental techniques are not used as often or are newer without much empirical support (Caudill, 2001).

Finally, there should be a section about privacy and third-party organizations. Each state has different standards, so therapists should be knowledgeable about their specific state's policies, procedures, and laws. A sample statement in compliance with HIPAA privacy policy standards can be found on the AAMFT Web site (American Association for Marriage and Family Therapy, 2002).

The AAMFT *Code of Ethics* (2001) does not specifically state that the informed consent document must be written. All of the necessary information could be communicated verbally. The only thing that needs to be included in the client's file is a signed document stating that the client agrees to the terms as set forth by the informed consent process (Woody & Woody, 2001). Although an oral discussion of informed consent may be preferred because it can be tailored to each specific client, there are also some drawbacks of using this method alone to obtain consent. For example, due to the stress that brought clients into therapy, they may forget what they hear (Welfel, 2002). If the informed consent material is given in written format, the therapist should remember that the material needs to be easily readable and understandable by any person that the therapist may see. Therapists also need to remember that a written document is not to replace a discussion about the contents of the document. Beahrs and Gutheil (2001) suggested that a compromise to the customized oral agreement and a written document would be a personalized written informed consent form that may also help to increase clinical rapport. The document stating that informed consent has been discussed with the client and that the client understands what was said to him or her should be signed and placed in the client's file prior to any therapy. If the informed consent has been given on paper, a copy should be made for the client.

This informed consent document should be updated and re-signed by the client if the treatment plan should change or should therapy take a different direction than originally thought (such as moving from individual to family therapy) (Woody & Woody, 2001). It is necessary that the client understands the differences about the therapy that he or she will be receiving. One of the most important things to discuss with clients when therapy changes includes changes in confidentiality and how they will be handled in the new therapeutic situation. For example, when a therapist begins seeing an individual and then moves to working with the individual and his or her partner, the therapist should discuss how secrets and things told individually to the therapist will be handled.

In the case of minor children, the therapist should make sure that consent is given by the custodial parent. If custody is legally divided, each parent should give consent for his or her child to attend therapy. "Joint legal custody" means that parents share the right and responsibility to make important decisions on behalf of their child. Whatever the custody situation is as told by the parent requesting therapy, therapists should require that parents bring in the most recent court order regarding each parent's right to consent on behalf of the child.

Assent should be gathered if consent is not legal. Assent means that clients are involved in decisions about therapy and agree to engage in therapy. Obtaining assent is not only an ethical matter, but also "as a practical matter, clients who do not understand counseling, and whose commitment to the enterprise is unknown, are unlikely to be cooperative clients who can work toward therapeutic goals. Without assent, they have little ownership of the goals that have been established" (Welfel, 2002, p. 117). Ultimately, even though children and people with disabilities are not often legally required to participate in the informed consent process, ethically they should be involved by therapists to the fullest extent possible (Ramisch & Franklin, 2008; Sori & Hecker, 2006).

Overall, therapists should remember that informed consent is about a process and a dialogue. It is not simply a piece of paper that is signed. As new treatments are used during the course of therapy, informed consent must be obtained for each new treatment. Clients must be given the chance to ask questions about the therapist and the therapy that they should expect to receive. Therapists should always remember to consult the AAMFT *Code of Ethics* (2001) about specific regulations and rules regarding informed consent. As the informed consent process is the basis for the therapeutic relationship between the therapist and the client, it is imperative that therapists be aware of both legal and ethical requirements in this area.

Record Keeping

Solid record keeping will not only benefit clients but will also benefit the therapist in the event that person must show evidence of his or her treatment. Subprinciple 3.6 of the AAMFT *Code of Ethics* (2001) mandated that "Marriage and family therapists maintain accurate and adequate clinical and financial records." Much like the research regarding the informed consent process, research regarding what constitutes adequate records is not explicit. The following are suggested guidelines for adequate, accurate, and ethical record keeping. This list has been compiled from marriage and family therapy literature as well as traditional psychotherapy and social work literature (Cameron & turtle-song, 2002; Caudill, 2001; Moline et al., 1998; Woody & Woody, 2001).

Identifying Information

Records should include basic information about the client such that anyone who might have access to the file can easily identify the client. This section should include the client's name, phone number, date of birth and age, marital status, occupation, school or education, people living in the same house, mental health insurance company, policy number, and phone number. It should be specific about how the therapist will get in touch with the client. Some clients choose to keep the fact that they are seeking therapy private from the other people that they live with, and thus, the therapist should be respectful of that. During the informed consent process, therapists should ask clients how they should introduce themselves when calling on the telephone. Additionally, therapists should ask clients about leaving messages, and if therapists should leave a message, how they should address themselves on the answering machine.

Informed Consent

As discussed above, at the very minimum the clients and the therapist should sign a document stating that the clients agree to the therapist's terms as set forth by the informed consent process. A summary of what was discussed should also be included. If a written informed consent document was used in this process, it should also be included in the case file. Whenever changes are made to the terms of therapy, the clients need to sign a new consent form. All updates need to be reflected in the informed consent document if one is being used or the summary that the therapist should provide which is kept in the client's file.

Diagnostic Testing and Assessment/Interview

This section should include the presenting complaints, results of the mental status evaluation (oriented to date, location, and who she or he is), and any significant history (past suicide attempts, substance use, or abuse).

Background and Historical Data

Information regarding the client's medical history, current problems (symptoms), social or personal history, developmental history, marital history, physical health, psychiatric and psychological history (inpatient services), medication history, family history, work history, sexual history, indication of a danger to self and others, and history of abuse should be gathered here. In case of any present suicidal or homicidal ideation, the therapist should make a detailed record of how the situation was handled.

Progress Notes/Therapy Notes
This area should include a descriptive summary of all contacts, observable data (appearance, behavior, mood), reactions of clients, reactions of parents/guardians, and significant events. Note the type of therapy (individual, group, couple, marital, or family) and the progress or lack of progress in relation to the treatment plan. These progress notes should be kept in a separate location from the rest of the file. The reasons for this are stated in the section about working with managed care organizations. This is a relatively new procedure that is reflective of the HIPAA privacy law.

Progress notes are the proof that sessions are being held and that sessions are continuing in the best interest of the client. Therapists should also keep in mind that clients have the right to see their own records. Therefore, therapists must take special care to write only what they are comfortable with the client reading. Certain things that should be left out of the notes are personal opinions that are not relevant to the client's progress (private notes should be kept in a journal), sensitive information such as sexual preferences or fantasies described by the client, and any past criminal behavior (Congress, 1999; Moline et al., 1998).

SOAP (subjective, objective, assessment, and plan) notes were developed by Weed (1964) and are meant to help clinicians effectively communicate with each other as well as have something with which to remember previous sessions accurately. SOAP notes also "provide an ongoing assessment of both the client's progress and the treatment interventions" (Cameron & turtle-song, 2002, p. 286). A summary of how to write a thorough case note using the SOAP method can be found in the article authored by Cameron and turtle-song (2002).

When writing a case note and an error is made,

> Never erase, obliterate, use correction fluid, or in any way attempt to obscure the mistake. Instead, the error should be noted by enclosing it in brackets, drawing a single line through the incorrect word(s), and writing the word 'error' above or to the side of the mistake. The counselor should follow this correction with her or his initials, the full date, and time of the correction. The mistake should still be readable, indicating the counselor is only attempting to clarify the mistake not cover it up. If not typed, all entries should be written in black ballpoint

pen, which allows for easy photocopying should the file be requested at a later date. (Cameron & turtle-song, 2002, p. 291)

Treatment Plan

This section should include an ongoing assessment of the client's progress and treatment success. All of the possible strategies and interventions to be used in therapy in order to help the client meet his or her short- and long-term goals should be described.

Material Given to the Therapist

Sometimes clients may give therapists a copy of what they wrote in their journal or poetry. The client may also send the therapist a greeting card or a letter in the mail. A copy of this material should be dated and included in the file. The therapist should also include a summary of what was discussed in reference to the material if there was a discussion. This summary should be included in the progress note.

Current Psychological/Psychiatric Evaluations/Consultations

There may be specific areas in which both the client and the therapist could benefit from a second opinion by another professional. As Moline et al. (1998) stated, "A second opinion provides you the assurance that you are working toward the client's benefit" (p. 43). If a therapist asks for a consultation from another therapist, the name of the therapist consulted, date of consultation, rationale for the consult, and what was stated should be noted in this section. Also, it is important for therapists to request that the results of any consultations or evaluations be put in writing and put in the client's file as well.

Subprinciple 2.6 stated that

> Marriage and family therapists, when consulting with colleagues or referral sources, do not share confidential information that could reasonably lead to the identification of a client, research participant, supervisee, or other person with whom they have a confidential relationship unless they have obtained the prior written consent of the client, research participant, supervisee, or other person with whom they have a confidential relationship. Information may be shared only to the extent necessary to achieve the purposes of the consultation.

When consulting with colleagues, it is important that therapists discuss only the necessary information. Precautions should be taken in order to ensure privacy and to keep the identity of the client private (Pope & Vasquez, 2001), or a release form is needed.

Current Medications
This section should include the name, dose, prescribing doctor, and possible side effects of all medications as stated by the client. If the therapist is unsure about any details, quick research can be done with the aid of the latest *Physician's Desk Reference* (2006) or through consultation with a psychiatrist. Any materials about the medications can be printed out and kept in clients' files for easy reference.

Diagnosis
As any diagnoses might be used for billing purposes, this section must be accurate and up to date. It may also be wise for therapists to consult the client about this area and inform him or her about diagnoses because other third parties such as a probation officer or a boss may have access to diagnoses.

Correspondence and Phone Calls
Any time that a client is contacted or an attempt for contact is made, a record should be kept about the date, time, reasons for, and what transpired during these phone conversations. When possible, therapists should make a point to use landline telephones, because the usage of a cell phone in an unsecured area may lead to a breach in confidentiality. Therapists should also keep copies of all signed letters that were mailed to the client along with the dates that the letters were mailed.

Suggestions/Directives
This section can be used as a diagnostic tool and can also be used as support for the therapist in the case of a legal suit. It is recommended that the therapist note all directions or homework assignments that were given and what the client's response was to those directions or assignments. Especially record instances when the client failed to follow through with directions, recommendations, or assignments.

Failed or Canceled Appointments
Like the previous section, this can also be used as a diagnostic tool. Therapists should record all sessions that the client failed to show up to or sessions that the client canceled. It may also be relevant to record sessions for which the client arrived late.

Supervision
Therapists should keep track of when they were supervised, what the supervisor requested of the therapist, and what suggestions the supervisor

made regarding each case. It is best to have the supervisor sign his or her name to the record after each supervision session.

Prognosis

This area is important to note and keep up to date for reasons important to third-party payers. Because many clients are not awarded unlimited therapy by insurance companies, this section is necessary to show that therapy is helpful and that the client is moving in a direction that indicates progress. This area might also be helpful for clients who are involved in litigation to show that they are meeting any legal requirements as deemed by a court.

Release of Information

It is a good idea to obtain previous treatment records, because this can help the therapist to avoid making the same recommendations as someone else. It might also be helpful for current therapists to get a summary of treatment from any past therapists and to find out the reasons for termination of the therapy. An official release of information document should be constructed by the therapist and should include the date, the name and address of the agency providing the information, the name and address of the agency receiving the information, information about what specific information is to be released, the time period of treatment covered by the release, the length of time the release is to be in effect, a provision that the information is not to be forwarded to a third party, and the signature of the client and a witness. Most often the witness is the therapist. When therapists are requested to send information about a client that she or he has previously seen, it is important that the therapist requests a copy of the release that was signed by the client. This can help the therapist to avoid any legal issues surrounding client confidentiality. In addition, the therapist should attempt to send a summary to an outside agency, rather than the entire case note, in order to help preserve confidentiality.

In the case of minor clients or clients who have legal guardians, it is important to obtain all necessary signatures (see Chapter 4). Ethically, it is also recommended to obtain the signature of the minor client or client with a legal guardian. Finally, therapists should remember that it is not legally allowed to release records that were obtained from another mental health practitioner. Only the original record keeper has the right to release those records.

Termination Notes

This section should include a brief note about how the decision to terminate therapy was made, what goals were attained that led to the termination, suggested referrals, the client's diagnosis at the time of termination, and the client's mental status. It is important to note any rationale for termination if the therapist made the decision to terminate.

Family/Marital/Couple Therapy

Therapists should keep separate progress notes on each spouse or partner or significant family member. Significant family members are those who are actively involved in treatment and do not attend on behalf of another family member. In the case of divorce, in conjoint therapy moving to individual therapy, or in any legal matters, the files can be easily separated. Information that is about the entire family can be copied and put in each person's file (Moline et al., 1998).

Even if separate progress notes are kept for each family member, if an individual's case records are requested to be released, it is imperative for the therapist to obtain written permission from all legal adults (in a release form) in order to release the records. The reason for this is that most likely information about all involved parties was documented on that individual's case notes when that individual was involved in family sessions.

Groups

If group members are always seen together, one record may be kept for the whole group. Therapists must take the appropriate steps to protect the confidentiality of the other individuals identified or discussed in such records (Congress, 1999). This can be done by using a coding system instead of using client names. If group members are ever seen individually, therapists should keep individual files for each member (Moline et al., 1998).

Keeping adequate and accurate records is vital to any practice of couple and family therapy. As described here, there are many pieces of a record that need to be assembled and kept up to date. Many of the items as just described are gathered during the first session. It is important for therapists to obtain as much of this information as possible and as quickly as possible. Therapists should regard the information gathered in the first

sessions essential to a quality therapeutic relationship just as being knowledgeable about policies and laws of practice are essential to a quality practice. Ethically, it is also important for therapists to follow state laws and
guidelines as set forth by the AAMFT *Code of Ethics* (2001) in order to
avoid legal troubles that may arise from inadequate record keeping.

Professional Practice

When thinking about starting to practice as a professional couple and
family therapist, there are many different areas that therapists must
consider. Policies and procedures for specific areas are outlined in the
AAMFT *Code of Ethics* (2001). Each therapist should obtain and read the
Code of Ethics thoroughly in order to establish his or her own policies for
practice. Below is a summary of the different areas and some guidelines to
get therapists thinking about how to handle different circumstances that
may arise during the course of practice.

Licensure or Certification Laws

"Licensure or certification laws for marriage and family therapists (MFTs)
provide a mechanism for the public and third-party payors to identify
qualified practitioners of marriage and family therapy. … All states
require a Master's or Doctoral degree and supervised clinical experience" (AAMFT, 2007, p. 1). Each state has its own summary of guidelines
that include educational requirements, supervision, and clinical hours
that must be obtained before a therapist can be licensed. The number
of required direct face-to-face postgraduation hours (graduation from a
master's degree program) typically ranges from 1,000 to 3,000 hours. The
state might also require that a specific number of those hours be with
couples and families. Additionally, states have guidelines about hours of
supervision. Most states require 200 total supervision hours, 100 of which
can be acquired during graduate studies. States might also have different
requirements of therapists that can count as a supervisor. It is imperative
that therapists check with the state with which they intend to get certified
or licensed and subsequently practice in before they get too far into the
process in order to be sure that they know how to properly document their
hours and the ultimate number of hours that they need. The number of
states regulating MFTs is 48 (plus the District of Columbia); specific Web

site links to state certification or licensure requirements can be found at the AAMFT Web site (American Association for Marriage and Family Therapy, 2007).

Working With Managed Care Organizations

In order to become a provider for most MCOs, therapists must select which MCOs they would like to provide for and then contact the company directly to ask for the proper application forms. Sometimes companies will close to new members and not allow any therapists to join. If denied access to the panels, clients who are members of the MCO can contact the organization (usually done by letter) or therapists can ask their professional association to ask that the panel be opened. When granted application forms, therapists will be asked to provide information such as relevant education, experience, vitae, copies of degrees, copies of license and certification, and a copy of liability insurance (Christensen & Miller, 2001). Hanson and Sheridan (1997) pointed out that when therapists are applying to be included as a managed care preferred provider, they have the power to negotiate specific terms of the contract. The contract should be specific and should state the terms of areas such as approval and rejection of proposed treatments, frequency of reviews, and what information is to be communicated to reviewers. Most importantly, through contract negotiations, therapists must fight to hold ultimate clinical judgment and decision making. "For instance, professionals must remain free to recommend specialized and sometimes more costly assessments...or interventions not typically covered" (Hanson & Sheridan, 1997, p. 239).

Small (2006) outlined the steps that therapists should take in order to ensure that they are paid for their services when dealing with MCOs. The first step is to verify that couple and family therapy is covered under the health plan of the individual. This can be done by calling the health organization or by asking the client to bring in his or her benefits booklet (or a member contract). The second step is to determine the parameters of working for the health organization by avoiding treatment of disorders that are not covered or that exceed the client's benefit limits. The parameters of the organization may also stipulate that therapists focus on symptom reduction and functional improvement rather than relationship or system dynamics. "Once treatment is authorized, individuals in the managed care organization determine which professionals the patient may see, what type of treatment he or she may receive, how frequently the patient may be seen, and for how long" (Cohen, 2003, p. 35). Finally, therapists must be able to demonstrate during reviews of notes and treatment plans that the primary purpose of therapy continues to be the treatment of one or more covered mental disorders.

To make sure that the services that therapists bill for are indeed needed and legitimate, a review process is utilized by these organizations. Often these organizations will request and inspect the records of the therapist in order to ensure that the therapy is benefiting the client and symptoms are being reduced. When doing reviews, MCOs usually request the general treatment notes that pertain to modalities and frequency of treatment, results of assessment or testing, diagnosis, symptoms, functional status, treatment plan, prognosis, and progress or lack thereof. They typically do not request the therapy notes that are protected by HIPAA regulations. Therapy notes, as defined by HIPAA, are notes that chart the content of therapy sessions or therapists' analyses of such content, and are separated from the rest of the chart by being in a separate section or in a different chart. The other information is considered general treatment notes and not therapy notes. If an MCO requests therapy notes, therapists need to remind the company that those notes are protected by HIPAA regulations. Therapists must take it upon themselves to learn about the privacy laws for their particular state. It is important for therapists to remember that they are to abide by the strictest law, or whichever law provides the individual the most privacy when it comes to disclosing private medical information. Additionally, before therapists send information to MCOs, it is ethical for therapists to notify clients of what information will be shared with their insurance company. A discussion about the limits of confidentiality in terms of once the information leaves the therapist's office needs to take place. Additionally, therapists must remember that they cannot promise unconditional confidentiality to clients. Clients may want to check with the providing company to ask any questions (Pope & Vasquez, 2001).

Getting paid from MCOs presents an ethical dilemma in that companies require therapists to give a *Diagnostic and Statistical Manual of Mental Disorders (DSM)* diagnosis in order to demonstrate medical necessity. Kielbasa, Pomerantz, Krohn, and Sullivan (2004) reported that clinicians were 10 times more likely to not assign a diagnosis when the client paid out of pocket versus when managed care paid for the client. For family therapists who give relational diagnoses (V-Codes), it might be beneficial to investigate MCOs that accept these diagnoses before becoming a preferred provider. If no MCO in an area accepts relational diagnoses, therapists may prefer to accept only clients who are willing to pay out of pocket rather than going through insurance companies that do not accept relational diagnoses.

Other ethical issues may arise when therapists seek payment from MCOs. Therapists must make sure that their billing procedures are accurate in that they are only charging for sessions that were held. Therapists may not bill MCOs for sessions that did not occur or for sessions of a family member. Finally, when using a sliding scale fee, it is unethical and also considered fraud by many MCOs to use different scales when sessions are paid by MCOs. One scale, in which session fees are determined by a client's financial condition, must be used for clients paying out of pocket and those who are represented by an MCO.

In the realm of managed care and insurance companies, the therapist must always remember that in the case of third-party sources, the primary allegiance of the therapist should be with the person receiving the services. Therapists should always explain to clients about the nature of having a third-party payer and the limits of therapy that will result. It ultimately should be up to the client if he or she would like to use his or her MCO. Just because the client and the therapist belong to the same organization does not mean that the client cannot choose to pay out of pocket to preserve his or her privacy.

Soundproofing the Office

When establishing a practice in an office building or a home that was not originally designed to be used as therapy offices, it is imperative that therapists spend the necessary money to guarantee client confidentiality by soundproofing the office. Sessions should not be heard in hallways, waiting rooms, or reception areas (Pope & Vasquez, 2001). Therapists should make every effort to keep private not only what the client says, but also the fact that the person is a client (Congress, 2001). This can be done by having one door for an entrance and a separate exit door that allows clients to exit a therapy session without being seen by clients waiting in the waiting room.

Confidentiality and Messages

Some therapists may choose to have clients leave messages on an answering machine or with an office staff member during business hours. Office staff should be instructed to keep phone messages with client's names on them out of the view of unauthorized individuals. If written messages are put a box for a therapist, this box should not be accessible by other people. Keep the messages locked in the same place with client files until the message can be returned and the paper message destroyed. Therapists should also invest in answering machines or services that record messages silently so they are not heard by other people who may be in the room. The use of answering machines that play messages out loud should be restricted as family members, friends, or other clients may be able to hear the message (Pope & Vasquez, 2001).

Confidentiality and Fax

Therapists should always make every effort to ensure that faxes sent and received keep confidential information protected. "Confidential or sensitive information should be faxed or e-mailed *only* if both sender and recipient have sufficient reason to be confident that the data will be protected both during transmission and once it arrives" (Pope & Vasquez, 2001, p. 239). A way to guarantee confidentiality is for therapists to make telephone contact before sending a fax when sending confidential information. This can ensure that an authorized person will be able to receive the fax. A phone call after the fax has been sent can also verify that the fax was received by an authorized person. A cover page should include a clear statement about the following confidential pages (Welfel, 2002).

Keeping Files Confidential

Therapists need to guard client confidentiality by being mindful about where files are placed and how files are labeled. When making files for clients, instead of using the client's name to label the file, a numbering or coding system can be used (Pope & Vasquez, 2001). These files should also never be left unattended and should be locked away when not in possession of the therapist. Information about clients should always be kept out of the view of people who are not authorized to see the information. Additionally, if a computer is used to write case notes or store information about clients, the information should be coded so that no identifying information is revealed.

Retention of Records

Subprinciple 2.4 stated that "Marriage and family therapists store, safeguard, and dispose of client records in ways that maintain confidentiality and in accord with applicable laws and professional standards." In order for therapists to determine the exact number of years that full records or summary of records need to be kept, they should look into the regulations for the state in which they live, as state laws vary. Some states require that records be kept for 3 years after the last appointment, and other states mandate that a summary be kept for 12 years (Pope & Vasquez, 2001).

Proper disposal of records is also imperative. As Moline et al. (1998) stated,

> When records are considered obsolete, you will need to shred, burn, recycle, or use some other means to destroy your records. You may contract with an outside company, but remember, if you have someone else destroy your clients' records, you are still responsible for maintaining confidentiality. If you have large volumes of records to be destroyed, consider investing in your own shredding machine. (p. 136)

It is very important that records be destroyed in a confidential manner. This is the only way that therapists can ensure that they are dealing with records ethically from the start of the file to the end when it is no longer needed or required.

Conclusion

In order to maintain an ethical practice of couple and family therapy in line with state and federal laws, it is essential that therapists maintain knowledge of standards of practice and continually update policies and procedures in their office. Informed consent, record keeping, and confidentiality are all areas about which therapists want to remain meticulous in order to maintain ethical practice and protect one's practice as much as possible from litigious interference. The different sections to be kept in the clients' records are identifying information, the informed consent document or a summary of what was discussed, a record of tests or assessments, background information, treatment plans, material that was given to the therapist by the client, current evaluations and consultations, current medications, diagnosis, correspondence and phone calls, suggestions, failed or canceled appointments, supervision, prognosis, permission for release of information, and termination notes. Progress notes should be kept in a separate file or location as mandated by privacy standards. Couple and family therapists dealing with third-party payers fall under HIPAA guidelines and must be cognitive of specific HIPAA privacy policies.

References

American Association for Marriage and Family Therapy (AAMFT). (2001). *Code of ethics.* Alexandria, VA: Author.

American Association for Marriage and Family Therapy (AAMFT). (2002). HIPAA resources. Retrieved October 14, 2008, from: www.aamft.org/members/Advocacy/HIPAAResources.asp.

American Association for Marriage and Family Therapy (AAMFT). (2007). Directory of MFT licensure and certification boards. Retrieved October 12, 2008, from: www.aamft.org/resources/Online_Directories/boardcontacts.asp.

Beahrs, J. O., & Gutheil, T. G. (2001). Informed consent in psychotherapy. *The American Journal of Psychiatry, 158,* 4–10.

Cameron, S., & turtle-song, i. (2002). Learning to write case notes using the SOAP format. *Journal of Counseling and Development, 80,* 286–292.

Caudill, O. B. (2001). Practice management: Integrating ethics into business. In R. H. Woody & J. D. Woody (Eds.), *Ethics in marriage and family therapy* (pp. 169–195). Alexandria, VA: American Association for Marriage and Family Therapy.

Christensen, L. L., & Miller, R. B. (2001). The practice of marriage and family therapists with managed care clients. *Contemporary Family Therapy, 23(2),* 169–180.

Cohen, J. A. (2003). Managed care and the evolving role of the clinical social worker in mental health. *Social Work, 48(1),* 34–43.

Congress, E. P. (1999). *Social work values and ethics: Identifying and resolving professional dilemmas.* Belmont, CA: Wadsworth Group.

Hanson, K. M., & Sheridan, K. (1997). Ethics and changing mental health care: Concerns and recommendations for practice. *Journal of Clinical Psychology in Medical Settings, 4(2),* 231–242.

Haslam, D. R., & Harris, S. M. (2004). Informed consent documents of marriage and family therapists in private practice: A qualitative analysis. *The American Journal of Family Therapy, 32,* 359–374.

Hecker, L. L. (2003). Ethical, legal, and professional issues in marriage and family therapy. In L. L. Hecker & J. L. Wetchler (Eds.), *An introduction to marriage and family therapy.* Binghamton, NY: Haworth Press.

Kielbasa, A. M., Pomerantz, A. M., Krohn, E. J., & Sullivan, B. F. (2004). How does clients' method of payment influence psychologists' diagnostic decisions? *Ethics and Behavior, 14(2),* 187–195.

Moline, M. E., Williams, G. T., & Austin, K. M. (1998). *Documenting psychotherapy: Essentials for mental health practitioners.* Thousand Oaks, CA: Sage.

Physician's Desk Reference. (2006). Montvale, NY: Author.

Pomerantz, A. M. (2005). Increasingly informed consent: Discussing distinct aspects of psychotherapy at different points in time. *Ethics and Behavior, 15(4),* 351–360.

Pope, K. S., & Vasquez, M. J. T. (2001). *Ethics in psychotherapy and counseling.* San Francisco, CA: Jossey-Bass.

Ramisch, J. R., & Franklin, D. (2008). Families with a member with mental retardation and the ethical implications of therapeutic treatment by marriage and family therapists. *The American Journal of Family Therapy, 36,* 1–11.

Small, R. H. (2006). Coverage of marital and family therapy by managed care and commercial health plans. *Getting Paid in Behavioral Healthcare, 11(4),* 1–4.

Sori, C. F., & Hecker, L. L. (2006). Ethical and legal considerations when counseling children and families. In C. F. Sori, *Engaging children in family therapy* (pp. 159–174). New York: Routledge.

U.S Department of Health and Human Services. (2004). Health care in America: Trends in utilization. National Center for Disease Control: Author. Retrieved October 14, 2008, from www.cdc.gov/nchs/data/misc/healthcare.pdf.

U.S. Department of Health and Human Services. (2008). Office for Civil Rights—HIPAA Medical Privacy—National Standards to Protect the Privacy of Personal Health Information. Retrieved October 31, 2008, from: www.hhs.gov/ocr/hipaa/.

Weed, L. L. (1964). Medical records, patient care and medical education. *Irish Journal of Medical Education, 6,* 271–282.

Welfel, E. R. (2002). *Ethics in counseling and psychotherapy: Standards, research, and emerging issues.* Pacific Grove, CA: Wadsworth Group.

Woody, J. D., & Woody, R. H. (2001). Protecting and benefiting the client: The therapeutic alliance, informed consent, and confidentiality. In R. H. Woody & J. D. Woody (Eds.), *Ethics in marriage and family therapy* (pp. 169–195). Alexandria, VA: American Association for Marriage and Family Therapy.

Appendix 13.1

*Informed Consent for Treatment**

Office of Mary F. Jones, L.M.F.T.

Please read the following information carefully; if you have questions regarding the content, please ask Ms. Jones for an explanation to your questions prior to signing the consent for treatment.

Information About Your Therapist and Therapy

Mary F. Jones graduated with her master's of science in marriage and family therapy from Purdue University Calumet. She is currently licensed to practice as a marriage and family therapist in the state of Indiana. She is dedicated to the treatment of family systems, including families, couples, children, and adult individuals. She primarily uses solution-focused therapy in her work with families and individuals; this type of therapy focuses on the resiliencies and strengths of people in order to aid them in solving the concerns they bring to therapy. Therapy will be held in sessions that typically last for 1 hour, once a week. These may occur more or less frequently depending on the situation and availability of the therapist. It is important that all therapy sessions be held in the therapy office. Because wireless systems are easily accessible by third parties, therapy sessions will not be held over the phone or the computer.

The therapist is available for sessions Monday through Friday from 10:30 A.M. to 9:00 P.M. Outside of these hours, or if the therapist or office staff is unable to answer the phone, a confidential voicemail box will be available for messages. An on-call person is available for emergencies outside of regular business hours by calling 555-555-4432. If you need *immediate* emergency services, please seek out your nearest hospital emergency room. If it is determined in our work that you need services beyond the capabilities of this office, a referral will be made.

Confidentiality

All information about clients is kept strictly confidential. Case notes and records are kept on a computer that is password protected by the therapist. In most cases, clients must give written consent for the release of any information. There are, however, a few legal exceptions to the therapist keeping therapy information confidential. Therapists are legally required to break confidentiality when the following situations occur:

1. If a client threatens to harm himself or herself, the therapist may be obligated to seek hospitalization for him or her, or to contact family members who can provide protection.
2. If a client threatens physical violence against another party, and has both the means and intent to commit violence, the therapist may have to disclose information in order to take protective action.

3. If the therapist has reasonable cause to suspect child abuse or neglect or elder abuse or neglect, the therapist is required to report this information to the proper authorities.

4. If a communication by you reveals the contemplation or commission of a crime or a serious harmful act, the therapist may need to disclose this information, if subpoenaed or required by law.

5. If a client files a lawsuit against a therapist, the therapist may disclose relevant information in order to defend himself or herself.

6. If a judge orders release of therapy information, the therapist is required to provide it, though therapists will attempt as best as they can to protect clients' confidentiality and legal right to privilege.

If individual family members choose to share secrets with the therapist, the therapist may ask the individual to share this information if it is important for therapy to progress. The therapist will discuss with the individual this information and how it is important for therapy first before it is brought up in family sessions.

Sometimes the therapist will need to consult with other therapists to ensure that he or she is providing the best therapy possible. In the case that identifying information needs to be revealed, you will have the opportunity to sign a statement agreeing to a release of your confidential information.

Cost

The fee for 50 minutes of therapy in the office with the therapist is $125 due at the end of each session. A client who carries insurance will be provided with a copy of his or her receipt that can be submitted to his or her insurance company for reimbursement if the client so chooses. It is your responsibility to verify the specifics of your coverage. If the therapist is required to attend a court hearing or other proceedings, you will be billed $200 an hour, including any waiting and travel time. A retainer is expected in these cases. If the session fee presents a hardship for you or your family, please feel free to discuss this with your therapist to investigate if anything can be done so you can continue with therapy. If you are not able to attend your scheduled session, please call within 1 business day prior to your session. Please call the office to speak to the office staff or leave a message after business hours. If you do not call, the therapist reserves the right to charge you for your missed session. All phone calls lasting longer than 20 minutes will also be billed to you at the hourly rate. The therapist accepts all forms of payment including cash, check, and credit, and your payment is due at the time of service. This office does not bill. There is a $25 fee for any returned checks.

Risks and Rights

Therapy is a highly collaborative process that involves both you and your therapist. At times, therapy may feel like it is challenging you and the way that you think or believe. Therapeutic work can be intensive and stressful. It may also be uncomfortable if it is necessary to bring up specific past memories or feelings. Resolutions of the issues that brought you into therapy may result in some changes that you never thought possible or intended to happen. These changes may happen quickly or slowly, and to one family member or to all family members. What is viewed as a positive change for one family member may be viewed negatively by another family member. There are no guarantees that therapy will have the results that you wish it to have.

You have the right to ask questions about your treatment at any time. You have the right to have input and say into your treatment goals and treatment plan. You have the right to ask about alternative treatments. If you wish to end therapy, you have the right to do so, though this decision is typically best made between you and the therapist together. You have the right to ask your therapist for the *Code of Ethics* of the American Association for Marriage and Family Therapy of which she is a Clinical Member.

Minors

Minors (children under 18 who are not emancipated) will not be seen in therapy unless there is permission from both parents, the court, or the legal guardian. In cases where minor children are seen individually, confidentiality will be maintained unless the therapist is required to break confidentiality (see above). However, the therapist may share general treatment themes and progress with the guardian. In cases where the minor child is seen individually with the therapist but is part of a client-family, the therapist may ask the child to share information with the parents or significant others in the family if it important for therapy to progress.

It is important that you agree not to call me as a witness or to attempt to subpoena records in the event you, as a parent (or parents), choose to pursue a divorce. Although a judge may overrule this agreement and issue a court order for information, your signature(s) below reflects your agreement not to call me as a witness or attempt to subpoena therapeutic records.

By signing below, I agree that I have read and understood the above information. My signature indicates that I give Mary Jones, L.M.F.T., consent to treat myself and any minor children that I may bring into therapy. If I have any questions, comments, or grievances, I agree to discuss these with my therapist.

_____   _____
Signature   Date

_____   _____
Signature   Date

_____   _____
Signature   Date

_____   _____
Witness Signature   Date

*Each state may have specific therapist disclosure requirements; therapists should check their own specific state laws. This form is also not HIPAA compliant.

14

Ethical Issues Endemic to Couple and Family Therapy

Sesen M. Negash and Lorna L. Hecker

When seeing more than one client as the unit of treatment, the dynamics of therapy transform, resulting in unique ethical and legal issues. Ethical issues endemic to the specific work of couple and family therapists include issues of multiconfidentiality, therapists' roles in defining marital status, using the *Diagnostic and Statistical Manual of Mental Disorders (DSM-IV-TR)* (American Psychiatric Association, 2000), and withholding services from families with nonattending members. Moreover, there are a number of additional issues that couple and family therapists must consider that will be addressed in this chapter, including working with culturally diverse clients, LGBT (lesbian, gay, bisexual, transgendered) people, sexual reorientation therapy, HIV-positive clients, and evidence-based practice.

Issues of Multiconfidentiality

> Dr. Lee met with Chad and Linda, an up-and-coming executive couple. When Chad was out of the room on a restroom break, Linda revealed to Dr. Lee that she had recently been chatting with a man she had formerly had an affair with. The affair had ended before Chad and Linda entered couple's therapy, but Linda revealed to Dr. Lee that she still had feelings for the man. Before Chad returned from the restroom, Linda asked Dr. Lee not to reveal their conversation to Chad.

According the the American Association for Marriage and Family Therapy (AAMFT) *Code of Ethics* (2001), Section 2.2:

> 2.2 Marriage and family therapists do not disclose client confidences except by written authorization or waiver, or where mandated or permitted by law. Verbal authorization will not be sufficient except in emergency situations, unless prohibited by law. When providing couple, family or group treatment, the therapist

does not disclose information outside the treatment context without a written authorization from each individual competent to execute a waiver. In the context of couple, family or group treatment, the therapist may not reveal any individual's confidences to others in the client unit without the prior written permission of that individual.

It is ethically very challenging for a couple and family therapist to decide a course of action when a family secret arises in therapy. What should Dr. Lee do? *Principle II* of the AAMFT *Code of Ethics* (2001) offers guidelines on how to responsibly and competently meet matters of confidentiality. Situations like this are not uncommon in relational therapy, especially in couple's therapy, where one partner withholds information that has an important bearing on the relationship and can even harm the relationship. In cases such as this, couple and family therapists may believe it is important that each family member's confidences be treated as though the member was in individual therapy, and others may adopt a written policy that runs counter to Principle 2.2 that requires clients to disclose secrets to other family members. In efforts to ethically maintain the confidences of both individuals and the overall trust of the family unit, couple and family therapists may also arrange individual sessions to actively encourage family members to share their secret with other family members, as well as help the withholding family members reveal a secret. Some couple and family therapists may believe that an existing secret is not benefiting and may even be harming the family unit but, regardless, are unwilling to break confidentiality. In such instances, when the therapist experiences decreased maneuverability, that person may decide to terminate services with the family, with appropriate referrals. Ordinarily, the use and regular update of a client's informed consent, writing case notes with germane information (Marsh, 1997), the promotion of honesty between family members, and implementing a no-secrets policy (Hines & Hare-Mustin, 1978), may minimize both the client's intrusion of privacy and the therapist's exposure to ethical violations.

Therapist Role in Defining Marital Status

The AAMFT *Code of Ethics* (2001) provides guidance as to the couple and family therapist's role in decisions about relationship status. Principle 1.8 stated the following:

Marriage and family therapists respect the rights of clients to make decisions and help them to understand the consequences of these decisions. Therapists clearly advise the clients that they have the responsibility to make decisions regarding relationships such as cohabitation, marriage, divorce, separation, reconciliation, custody, and visitation.

Clients ultimately need to make decisions whether to stay married or divorce, couple and family therapists are not often neutral on the issue itself or in their approach to therapy regarding the matter. In fact, relational ethics adopted by couple and family therapists may be the most challenging in cases where divorce is broached by clients in therapy. Here it may become necessary for couple and family therapists to carefully examine and maybe even temporarily redirect their attention away from the overall family unit so that they may focus more on the individual rights and conditions of individual family members. Conclusions from a study done by Wall, Needham, Browning, and James (1999) suggested that therapists confronted with possible divorce do not find it helpful to focus on individualism, but instead prefer actively preserving marriages. At the very least, therapists in this study used an individual framework while actively serving the best interests of the marital unit. Wall and associates (1999) also found that 33% of marriage and family therapists (MFTs) made strong moral claims of being committed to maintaining marriages and avoiding divorce whenever possible. In accordance, Brock and Coufal (1994) had similar findings, indicating that 49% of MFT participants reported that they encouraged clients to remain married at least on occasion. In that same study, 57% of MFTs believed that such recommendations were ethically appropriate at least sometimes. Even so, the majority of couple and family therapists do work to maintain a central ground between individualism and the preservation of the family unit. In order to maintain ethical integrity, couple and family therapists should work to prioritize the relationship between spouses by way of carefully assessing and working through the marital relationship (Wall et al., 1999) and allowing the couple to evaluate the marriage and make the decision to stay together or divorce.

The Use of the *Diagnostic and Statistical Manual of Mental Disorders* (*DSM-IV-TR*)

Case Scenario

Marty James, a licensed marriage and family therapist, completed an initial assessment with Leslie and Bob who complained of infidelity and financial hardship. However, the couple's insurance company would cover only the costs of mental disorders that fell under *DSM-IV* axis I and II. Considering the assessment, Marty was unable to recognize an identified patient and determined that neither partner showed symptoms of a mental disorder. Marty believed the couple's difficulties were engendered by their poor communication and work-related stresses. In a second session, Marty discovered that Bob had a family history of depression. As a result of the finding, Marty had Leslie and Bob complete depression assessments. Outcomes of the assessments suggested that Bob was experiencing moderate signs of depression, though both clients argued that Bob was more stressed than depressed.

This scenario illustrates the challenges that therapists face when implementing the *DSM-IV-TR*. Their dichotomous efforts to therapeutically depathologize clients and professionally obtain financial reimbursement may leave them straining to maintain their integrity. The *Diagnostic and Statistical Manual of Mental Disorders* (*DSM-IV-TR*) (American Psychiatric Association, 2000) is a mainstay in mental health treatment and reimbursement. However, it poses a dilemma for couple and family therapists: In order to get reimbursed, they must accept the medical model of individual diagnosis, which runs counter to systems theory on which couple and family therapy is built. The linear, pathologizing description of an individual runs counter to a relationally based systems theory that exercises circular causality and assesses the role of the family in creating and maintaining the identified patient's (IP) condition. Many couple and family therapists may find that using an individual diagnosis such as those provided in the *DSM-IV-TR* in therapy perpetuates the dysfunctional system. It pinpoints and focuses on the individual IP as the problem, leaving the other family members unwilling or unmotivated to change.

Accordingly, the identification of one person as the problem for insurance claims while providing services with the focus on the overall family units' problem raises an ethical question of whether couple and family therapists are misrepresenting diagnoses to third-party financiers. Gladding, Remley, and Huber (2001) suggested that some family therapists may not see misinterpretation as a cause of ethical concern. However, others may not view it as deceptive, or what Packer (1988) called "insurance diagnosis" (p. 19). In addition, labeling one person as the identified patient may have lifelong ramifications for that individual.

In efforts to minimize their risk of ethical violation in making a *DSM-IV-TR* diagnosis, couple and family therapists should refer to Subprinciple 3.11 of the AAMFT ethics code, which specifies that "Marriage and family therapists do not diagnose, treat, or advise on problems outside the recognized boundaries of their competencies" (AAMFT, 2001). Denton (1989)

suggested that family therapists become well versed with the *DSM* to identify and treat individual symptoms ethically and effectively. Benson, Long,
and Sporakowski (1992) suggested that an individual who has been labeled
by the diagnosis can proceed to work within a systems model; thus, the
family therapist need not discard systems theory in order to work within
the framework of the *DSM-IV-TR*. Moreover, Kaslow (1996) noted that
current awareness and examination into family systems along with our
curtailed understanding of difficult clinical disorders limit has opened up
the diagnostic system to include the adaptation of relational and systemic
ideology. Using the relational diagnosis, couple and family therapists may
integrate the biopsychological approach with varying relational models to
offer clients a wider gamut of treatment options. In the above scenario, the
therapist explored the couple's past and discovered a history of depression,
which prompted the therapist to assess the couple further. Conclusions
from the assessment in accordance with the client's inability to cope with
stressors gives the therapist enough information to diagnose the client
as depressed and therefore meets the criteria of the couple's insurance
policy.

Treating the Entire Family Unit or Withholding Services

One controversial issue in the history of marriage and family therapy
has been some therapists' refusal to work with only part of the family unit. It is a tactic some believe collides with therapists' therapeutic relational values and with that of clients' rights to autonomy and
self-determination. As such, the acceptance of the practice calls into
question the issue of voluntary participation. The practice may be considered coercive, overly strategic, and in direct violation of an ethical commitment as a helping professional (Margolin, 1982). Is refusing
to work with a motivated family member caring behavior (Teismann,
1980)? Huber (1994) suggested that an ethical problem exists in that
by withholding service from motivated family members, the therapist
may be creating an implicit alliance with the nonparticipating members of a family.

A number of alternatives have been suggested as to how to minimize
ethical violations associated with *all or nothing* practices. Huber and
Baruth (1987) recommended that therapists should encourage the participation of all significant family members in the initial stages of therapy.
Wilcoxon and Fenell (1983) also recommended that marital therapists

provide resistant clients with researched findings that promote the participation of marital therapy, as well as a formal invitation to attend therapy. Tesimann (1980) suggested the following:

> (a) brief sessions with the attending members that only focus on a plan for engaging nonparticipants, (b) an agreement between the non-attenders and the counselor for a single, private session in return for a conjoint session, (c) audio or videotaping segments of sessions for non-attenders, and (d) an agreement for short-term counseling for the attending member. (Cited in Beamish, Navin, & Davidson, 1994, p. 133)

Therapists who insist on working with the entire family unit are recommended to provide appropriate referral services to other providers (Margolin, 1982), preferably providers who they know are flexible about working with parts of or whole family units.

Featured Issues in Couple and Family Therapy

Working With Culturally Diverse Clients

Critical to the ethical, legal, and moral development of couple and family therapists is their awareness and understanding of cultural diversity. Unfortunately, many therapists are unaware of their own cultural assumptions. A general assumption held by our society is that just because we live in a culturally rich and diverse nation, we interact as such. In reality, we remain highly segregated by culture, race, politics, and class (McGoldrick, Giordano, & Garcia-Preto, 2006). A nation divided by cultural identity inevitably influences the foundation and stamina of the therapeutic relationship.

It is only through a thorough understanding of our own cultural identity that couple and family therapists may become sensitive to that of others. Therapists must also become attuned to their own negative cultural attitudes and behaviors. In order to effectively engage couples and families in culturally sensitive and competent relationships, therapists must accept that they are never completely immune from the exercise of bias, stereotyping, and ignorance. It is vital that therapists' understanding and use of cultural perspective not be on retainer, but instead, be a permanent fixture in all facets of the therapeutic process. Throughout the years, therapists have engaged in a therapeutic relationship with couples and families from culturally diverse backgrounds without a clear sense of their beliefs and customs and, as a result, exercised poor assessment practices and unethical therapeutic interventions (Kurilla, 1998).

Understanding the cultural context in which a behavior or attitude manifests or is perpetuated can offer the therapist beneficial information as to what the problem is. At times, the problem may lie within the context, not the family. Other times, the cultural context is important to understanding the presenting issues, as well as the search for family strengths and solutions. Concerns and strengths can arise due to cultural idiosyncrasies. For example, Italians may be more sensitive to issues regarding loyalty; Anglos may express anxiety about having to express emotion or exercising dependence on others, and Chinese may hold harmony as exceedingly important (McGoldrick et al., 2006). In addition, couple and family therapists work with clients challenged by family life-cycle transitions. Various cultural groups place different emphasis and value on the various life-cycle stages. Accordingly, in efforts to meet the needs of couples and families from culturally diverse backgrounds, the therapist must identify the cultural context the client is utilizing to work through the life-cycle dilemma. Additionally, as the number of multiracial couples and families continues to grow in the United States, couple and family therapists are challenged to maintain cultural neutrality. Therapists must be careful not to inadvertently build an alliance with the partner or family member whose cultural beliefs are closer to their own.

Working With the LGBT Community

The ethical and educational standards in marriage and family therapy reflect a set of shared values among couple and family therapists regarding their commitment to nondiscriminatory practices toward same-sex orientation clients (Hotvedt, 2004). According to Subprinciple 1.1. of the AAMFT *Code of Ethics,* MFTs are mandated to "provide professional assistance to clients without discrimination on the basis of race, age, ethnicity, socioeconomic status, disability, gender, health, status, religion, national origin, or sexual orientation." Moreover, the Commission on Accreditation for Marriage and Family Therapy Education (COAMFTE) requires MFT programs to incorporate power- and privilege-related issues, including gender, race, and sexual orientation into their curriculum and training. Even with what many may consider to be ethically clear outlines for how to work with LGBT (lesbian, gay, bisexual, transgendered) clients, there still seems to be confusion and even opposition over the matter.

Hermann and Herlihy (2006) noted that in cases of a religious therapist refusing to treat a same-sex client requesting help with relationship issues, the following moral principles should be examined: justice, beneficence, nonmaleficence, and respect for autonomy. With regard to *justice* (the belief that all people should be treated fairly), they noted that "While it may be challenging for counselors to work with clients who hold values different from their own, counselors must respect these differing values of clients and not impose their values on the counseling relationship" (Hermann & Herlihy, 2006, p. 416). For therapists who have clients with values or religious beliefs inconsistent with their own, it is incumbent upon the therapist to treat the client with sensitivity and overcome his or her predisposition toward the client. Couple and family therapists seek to work within the *client's* expressed value structure.

Beneficence refers to actions intended to do good for others. The therapist must be committed to the client's welfare, and refusing to counsel the client on certain issues can have a negative influence on the client (Hermann & Herlihy, 2006). *Nonmaleficence* refers to doing no harm. A therapist who refuses to counsel a homosexual client can harm the client due to the judgmental nature of the refusal and the previous discrimination and marginalization the client has experienced. The therapist is also responsible for getting education about the needs of LGBT clients (Subprinciple 3.1 of the AAMFT *Code of Ethics*), and being able to help competently. Last, probably the most important principle that needs to be examined when reviewing this issue is that of *autonomy*. Autonomy refers to respecting the individual and his or her right to make decisions with regard to his or her own health and well-being. It is not up to the therapist to decide what issues a client can and cannot address in therapy (Hermann & Herlihy, 2006). This type of paternalism infringes upon the client's right to autonomous decision making.

Legally, it is also becoming clear that the therapist's values need to be separated from the client's values. For example, a counselor by the name of Sandra Bruff was dismissed from her job at North Mississippi Health Services. The dismissal was a consequence of Bruff's refusal to counsel a lesbian regarding the client's relationship issues, because it conflicted with her religious beliefs. In 2001 a federal appeals court upheld the job termination. According to the court, providing counseling only on issues that do not conflict with a counselor's religious beliefs is an inflexible position not protected by the law (Hermann & Herlihy, 2006, p. 416). Growing intolerance of discriminatory practices against the LGBT community from mental health organizations and the judicial system speaks to the incontrovertible fact that LGBT clients should be provided the same level of services as heterosexual individuals.

Sexual Reorientation Therapy

Sexual reorientation therapy, also referred to as conversion or reparative therapy, is therapy aimed at changing an individual's dominant sexual orientation from homosexual to heterosexual. It grew due to the pathological view of homosexuality (Halpert, 2000). Since the American Psychiatric Association removed homosexuality as a psychiatric illness in 1973, and subsequent depathologizing of homosexuality has occurred, many professional health organizations have adopted an oppositional stance against the use of reorientation therapy (Halpert, 2000). The American Academy of Pediatrics, the American Counseling Association, the American Psychiatric Association, the American Psychological Association, the National Association of School Psychologists, and the National Association of Social Workers affirm the position that homosexuality is not a mental disorder or disease; thus, there is no need for a "cure" (American Psychological Association, 2007), as does AAMFT. In spite of the shift in consensus, reorientation therapies continue.

Therapists must use caution when addressing client values and evaluate their clients' desired goals and whether or not they can isolate their own moral agenda so that they may help clients meet their goals. Nystrom (1997) found that 46% of gay, lesbian, and bisexual clients experienced a homophobic therapist, and 34% experienced a therapist who either referred to their sexual orientation as temporary or disregarded it all together. Findings such as this suggest that those who refer to reorientation therapy may not be helping clients make autonomous decisions regarding their values, beliefs, and relationships. When therapists' own agenda impedes clients from meeting their desired goals, ethical violations become increasingly probable (recall that Subprinciple 1.7 in the AAMFT of ethics proscribes therapists from using their professional position to further their own interests).

Clients who request reorientation therapy must have their autonomy honored. However, when a client requests reorientation therapy, Serovich et al. (2008) noted that the therapist must ask the question: "Should we be conducting a type of therapy that is not clinically sanctioned by professional organizations and whose underpinning research is not clinically sound?" (p. 235). Empirical studies fail to show consistent results for reorientation therapy. Although some studies demonstrated efficacy for reorientation therapy (e.g., Nicolosi, Byrd, & Potts, 2000), others suggested it can be harmful (Schroeder & Shidlo, 2001; Shidlo & Schroeder, 2002) and futile (Shidlo & Schroeder, 2002). Serovich et al. (2008) noted a lack of rigor in general in studies evaluating reorientation therapy. The American Counseling Association's (2006) Ethics Committee makes recommendations about informing clients about their options with regard to reorientation therapy. First, they recommend that clients should be educated that homosexuality is not a mental disorder that needs a cure, and anyone providing it is practicing within the scope of some other profession (such as a Christian counselor). Second, the client should be educated that reorientation therapy is a religious practice, not a psychologically based practice. Third, research does not support conversion therapy, and there is potential for harm from it. Last, there are treatments available endorsed by the Association for Gay, Lesbian, and Bisexual Issues in Counseling (ACA, 2006). It is suggested that therapists who refer to reorientation therapy provide them with proficient information as to the risks and benefits of the particular treatment. Therapists who do not adhere to such provisions risk providing ethically and professionally irresponsible services that may potentially cause harm to clients.

Working With HIV-Positive Clients

> Dr. Lorian had counseled Dennis, who is seropositive, after his recent divorce. Dennis had started a new romantic relationship with Maria, and they had been dating for several weeks. Dennis has not yet informed Maria of his HIV status because he feared she would end the relationship. Dennis related to Dr. Lorian that he needed more time to get up the courage to tell Maria of his seropositive status. Dr. Lorian told Dennis that she respected his decision and would help him work toward dealing with the revelation of the diagnosis. Toward the end of the session, Dr. Lorian respectfully asked Dennis whether or not he was going to engage in any sexual activity prior to informing Maria. The client appeared offended and stated that he had no intention of engaging in any sexual contact. Realizing that she had upset Dennis, Dr. Lorian apologized for her seemingly offensive question and reassured him that she only meant to protect both he and Maria.

Clients who are HIV positive warrant several considerations for couple and family therapists wishing to maintain ethical practice. When dealing with HIV-positive clients, at minimum, a heightened emphasis on confidentiality is warranted. Serovich and Mosack (2000) noted that a therapist must be aware that documenting the HIV status of a client may make him or her vulnerable to losing benefits if the therapist is contacted by a third-party provider. Suicide or assisted suicide may also be an issue at hand with clients who are HIV positive. When a client refuses to tell his or her partner(s) about the seropositive status, it may trigger the therapist to act on his or her duty to protect (see Chapter 2). Ethical decision making must be made to weigh out the autonomous needs of the client *and* the needs of his or her partner(s). The therapist must make the ethical decision as to whether to break client confidence to protect the unknowing partner(s) if the client refuses to inform his or her partner(s). In the case scenario described above, the therapist acted responsibly when asking the client about his intent regarding his sexual behavior. However, if Dr. Lorian grew to become suspicious of Dennis's honesty regarding his sexual contact, her actions would need to be reconsidered.

When clients who are seropositive put their partners at risk, the therapist is faced with an ethical dilemma with legal consequences. Factors for therapists to consider when considering duty to warn and HIV include the following:

- Does my state have a duty to warn law?
- Does my state have a law that prohibits a licensed mental health professional from revealing a client's HIV status?
- Does my state have mandatory partner notification programs that anonymously inform at-risk partners of their exposed risk to an HIV partner (Serovich & Mosack, 2000)?
- Is it illegal for an individual who is HIV positive not to disclose in my state (Landau & Clements, 1997)?
- The mandate to apply duty to protect clients who are HIV positive who knowingly endanger the health of another has not been established by law.
- The American Psychological Association (1991) has taken the position that no legal duty to warn should be posed. Should states start to impose a duty to warn regarding HIV transmission, they recommend the following:
  - The therapist knows of an identifiable third party whom the therapist has compelling reason to believe is at significant risk for infection.
  - The therapist has a reasonable belief that the third party has no reason to suspect that he or she is at risk.
  - The client has been urged to inform the third party and has either refused or is considered unreliable in his or her willingness to notify the third party.

General guidelines include the following:

Offer to discuss the HIV with the partner or include the partner in therapy. This obviates the need for consent.

Have the client disclose. Discuss with the client the reasons that the other persons need to know. For example, let the client know that the other person will need to know his or her status so he or she can get tested and, if needed, commence treatment. The therapist can note that there are severe criminal and civil penalties for knowingly exposing another to HIV.

Have the client consent to disclosure. Some clients will not want to disclose for fear of repercussions. These clients can have the option to report the contact to the state's Department of Public Health (DPH). The DPH will notify the contact that he or she has been exposed and should be tested. This will be done anonymously without mention of the client's name.

Exercise duty to warn. In many states, it is illegal to have sex when you are HIV positive without informing the partner of your status (whether you use a condom or not), and it is also illegal to share needles when you are HIV positive without informing your partner(s) of your status. If the partners know the HIV-positive status and still opt to engage in risky behavior, it is their prerogative. If the behavior is not illegal in the state, the behavior is legally permissible. Schlossberger and Hecker (1996) argued that clients should not be denied their right to behaviors that are permissible by law. Ethically, however, it is most beneficial to work with clients to disclose their status to partners, as in the examples above. When there is no legal guidance, duty to warn remains a gray area. In states where it is illegal to knowingly expose others to HIV, when other methods fail to get the client to disclose his or her status, the therapist can take action to notify the state Department of Public Health. In most states, the Department of Public Health can anonymously warn the intended victim (after they confirm the diagnosis by a physician).

Evidence-Based Practice

Marriage and family therapy has had many charismatic leaders, and clinical research has historically been undervalued. Yet with the managed care movement, the need for empirically supported treatments gave rise to evidence-based practice. This refers to using research to make clinical decisions to meet the individual needs of each client (Patterson, Miller, Carnes, & Wilson, 2004). In efforts to protect the welfare of clients, greater emphasis toward establishing efficacious quality assurance modalities and accountability has been founded (Denton & Walsh, 2001). Quality assurance policies set forth in many sectors of the health care system are another reason why evidence-based practices have gained greater attention and use. McCabe (2006) outlined the steps of evidence-based practice that clinicians can follow to bridge the gap between research and practice:

1. What is the *problem*? Is there a disorder or diagnosis at hand?
2. Next, a *literature search* is conducted based on this disorder or diagnosis. These include studies, syntheses, and synopses.
3. The next stage is the appraisal of evidence stage, where one *evaluates the merit of the literature and data*. There are five levels of merit, starting with the strongest level:
   a. Level I: Evidence from True Experimental Designs
   b. Level II: Quasi-Experimental Designs
   c. Level III: Expert Consensus
   d. Level IV: Qualitative Literature
   e. Level V: Anecdotal Literature
4. An adopting evidence stage takes place to *implement the relevant findings* on a trial basis.
5. Next, a systematic assessment of results is conducted.
6. Then, adjustments are made to the trial intervention modified for maximum treatment effect and safety.

These stages can be applied to any type of issue seen by a couple and family therapist and will increase the efficacy of treatment. McCabe (2006) also listed the myriad of databases available to search for the existing research. A shift toward evidence-based practices would also require training programs to implement more quantitatively based curriculum and provide trainees with a working knowledge of statistical methodology. Notwithstanding the success of systemic-based theoretical rationales, couple and family therapists have entered a time when it has become increasingly necessary to utilize empirically supported models of therapy, so that they may stay viable and competitive in the mental health system. Though it is proposed that evidence-based practices shield clients from futile or possibly harmful interventions, it is important to understand that there exist limitations as to what science can explain and provide. Accordingly, increased scrutiny of existing clinical models and evidence-based practices will continue to be debated and yield questions as to what standards should be invoked among couple and family therapists.

Summary

The solutions to varying ethical challenges require couple and family therapists to carefully evaluate the context and conditions in which they operate. The systemic framework in which couple and family therapists operate creates unique ethical challenges. For example, confidentiality with multiple members remains a complex issue that couple and family therapists face every day. Therapists' values continue to influence defining relationships. The *DSM-IV-TR* still reigns; couple and family therapists have further to go with societal acceptance of relational diagnoses.

Some of the issues discussed in this chapter represent new trends in the field of marriage and family therapy. Multiculturalism has become increasingly highlighted and valued within the therapeutic setting. LGBT issues remain at the forefront. Some advocates for conversion therapy continue to be at odds with the mental health establishment. In a small number of cases when seeing clients who are HIV positive, the thorny issue of duty to warn may occur. Furthermore, increased state and federal health care regulations call for couple and family therapists to provide evidence-based practices to substantiate their legitimacy and significance within the mental health community. Family therapy continues to be a dynamic field with unique issues that stem from involvement of multiple family members in therapy.

References

American Association for Marriage and Family Therapy (AAMFT). (2001). *Code of ethics*. Alexandria, VA: Author.
American Counseling Association. (2006). Ethical issues related to conversion or reparative therapy. Retrieved October 31, 2008, from: www.counseling. org/PressRoom/NewsReleases.aspx?AGuid=b68aba97-2f08-40c2-a400-0630765f72f.

American Psychiatric Association. (2000). *Diagnostic and Statistical Manual of Mental Disorders DSM-IV-TR* (Rev. 4th ed.). Washington, DC: Author.

American Psychological Association. (1991). *Legal liability related to confidentiality and the prevention of HIV transmission.* Washington, DC: APA Council of Representatives.

American Psychological Association. (2007). Lesbian, gay, bisexual, and transgender concerns. Retrieved October 31, 2008, from: www.apa.org/pi/lgbc/publications/justthefacts.html#2.

Beamish, P. M., Navin, S. L., & Davidson, P. (1994). Ethical dilemmas in marriage and family therapy: Implications for training. *Journal of Mental Health Counseling, 16,* 129–142.

Benson, M. J., Long, J. K., & Sporakowski, M. J. (1992). Teaching psychopathology and the *DSM III R* from a family systems perspective. *Family Relations, 41,* 135–140.

Denton, W. (1989). DSM-III-R and the family therapists: Ethical consideration. *Journal of Marital and Family Therapy, 15,* 367–377.

Denton, W. H., & Walsh, S. R. (2001). Competency and integrity: Ethical challenges for today and the future. In R. H. Woody and J. D. Woody (Eds.), *Ethics in marriage and family therapy* (pp. 125–152). Washington, DC: American Association for Marriage and Family Therapy.

Gladding, S. T., Remley, T. P., & Huber, C. H. (2001). *Ethical, legal and professional issues in the practice of marriage and family therapy* (3rd ed.). Upper Saddle River, NJ: Prentice Hall.

Halpert, S. C. (2000). "If it ain't broke, don't fix it": Ethical considerations regarding conversion therapies. *International Journal of Sexuality and Gender Studies, 5,* 19–35.

Hermann, M. A., & Herlihy, B. R. (2006). Legal and ethical implications of refusing to counsel homosexual clients. *Journal of Counseling and Development, 84,* 414–418.

Hines, P. M., & Hare-Mustin, R. T. (1978). Ethical concerns in family therapy. *Professional Psychology, 9,* 165–171.

Hotvedt, M. (2004, September). Marriage, Politics, and the AAMFT. Plenary presented at the American Association for Marriage and Family Therapy Annual Conference. Atlanta, GA.

Huber, C. H. (1994). *Ethical, legal, and professional issues in the practice of marriage and family therapy.* New Jersey: Merrill.

Huber, C. H., & Baruth, L. G. (1987). *Ethical, legal and professional issues in the practice of marriage and family therapy.* Columbus, OH: Merrill.

Kaslow, F. W. (Ed.). (1996). *Handbook of relational diagnosis and dysfunctional family patterns.* New York: John Wiley and Sons.

Kurilla, V. (1998). Multicultural counseling perspectives: Cultural specialty and implications in family therapy. *Family Counseling: Counseling and Therapy for Couples and Families, 6,* 207–211.

Landau, J., & Clements, C. D. (1997). AIDS update for family therapists. *Family Therapy News, 28*, 16–26.

Margolin, G. (1982). Ethical and legal considerations in marital and family therapy. *American Psychologist, 37*, 788–794.

Marsh, D. T. (1997). Ethical issues in professional practice with families. In D. T. Marsh and R. D. Magee (Eds.), *Ethical and legal issues in professional practice with families* (pp. 3–26). New York: John Wiley & Sons.

McCabe, O. L. (2006). Evidence-based practice in mental health: Accessing, appraising, and adopting research data. *International Journal of Mental Health, 35*(2), 50–69.

McGoldrick, M., Giordano, J., & Garcia-Preto, N. (2006). Overview: Ethnicity and family therapy. In M. McGoldrick, J. Giordano, & N. Garcia-Preto (Eds.), *Ethnicity and Family Therapy.* New York: Guilford Press.

Nicolosi, J., Byrd, D., & Potts, R. W. (2000). Retrospective self-reports of changes in homosexual orientation: A consumer survey of conversion therapy clients. *Psychological Reports, 86*, 1071–1088.

Nystrom, N. M. (1997). Oppression by mental health providers: A report by gay men and lesbians about their treatment. *Dissertation Abstracts International, 58*-06A, 2394–2528.

Packer, P. (1988, October 3). Let's put a stop to the insurance diagnosis. *Medical Economics*, 19–28.

Patterson, J. E., Miller, R. B., Carnes, S., & Wilson, S. (2004). Evidence-based practice for marriage and family therapists. *Journal of Marital and Family Therapy, 30*(2), 183–195.

Schlossberger, E., & Hecker, L. (1996). HIV and family therapists' duty to warn: A legal and ethical analysis. *Journal of Marital and Family Therapy, 22*(1), 27–40.

Schroeder, M., & Shidlo, A. (2001). Ethical issues in sexual orientation conversion therapies: An empirical study of consumers. *Journal of Gay and Lesbian Psychotherapy, 5*, 131–166.

Serovich, J. M., Craft, S. M., Toviessi, P., Gangamma, R., McDowell, T., & Grafsky, E. L. (2008). A systematic review of the research base on sexual reorientation therapies. *Journal of Marital and Family Therapy, 34*(2), 227–238.

Serovich, J. M., & Mosack, K. E. (2000). Training issues for supervisors of marriage and family therapists working with persons living with HIV. *Journal of Marital and Family Therapy, 26*, 103–111.

Shidlo, A., & Schroeder, M. (2002). Changing sexual orientation: A consumer's report. *Professional Psychology: Research and Practice, 33*, 249–259.

Teismann, M. (1980). Convening strategies in family therapy. *Family Process, 19*, 393–400.

Wall, J., Needham, T., Browning, D. S., & James, S. (1999) The ethics of relationality: The moral views of therapists engaged in marital and family therapy. *Family Relations, 48,* 139–149.

Wilcoxon, A., & Fenell, D. (1983). Engaging the non-attending spouse in marital therapy through the use of therapist-initiated written communication. *Journal of Marital and Family Therapy, 9,* 199–203.

15

E-Therapy
Developing an Ethical Online Practice

Chad A. Graff and Lorna L. Hecker

There are over one billion Internet users worldwide, with that number expected to reach two billion users by 2011 (Etforecasts, 2007; Internet World Stats, 2008). The Internet has sparked a social revolution enabling rapid global communication that transcends limitations of time and geography. A study evaluating the Internet's impact on online health information seekers reported 52 million American adults or 55% of Internet users had accessed the Web to get health or medical information (Hsiung, 2002).

Many mental health professionals agree that Internet technologies are changing the way clinicians approach the practice of therapy (Blair, 2001; Derrig-Palumbo, 2002; Haberstroh, Duffey, Evans, Gee, & Trepal, 2007; Rochlen, Land, & Wong, 2004). Laszlo, Esterman, and Zabko (1999) suggested e-therapy as a viable alternative to providing individuals, families, and groups with mental health services. Others (Caudill, 2000; VandenBos & Williams, 2000) expect that the routine use of Internet and satellite technology for clinical purposes will continue to increase as the technology becomes more accessible and regularly used. Maheu, Pulier, Wilhelm, McMenamin, and Brown-Connolly (2005) reported that computer-mediated therapy is fast acquiring the status of a psychotherapeutic subspecialty. In fact, a growing percentage of clinicians offer psychotherapy online by telephone, videophone, instant messaging, or e-mail (Elleven & Allen, 2004).

E-therapy should be regarded as an experimental treatment with uncertain risks and benefits. Evidence-based research on its effectiveness is just beginning to emerge. Clinicians considering the practice of e-therapy must be cognizant of the potential ethical, legal, and practical issues (Houser, Wilczenski, & Ham, 2006; Maheu et al., 2005; Manhal-Baugus, 2001;

McCarty & Clancy, 2002). This chapter provides a primer of such issues and offers resources for helping clinicians develop an ethical online practice.

E-Therapy Types

Internet technology is undoubtedly changing the way people get help. As early as the 1980s, people accessed online self-help support groups. As Internet technology advanced in the mid-1990s, e-mail, chat rooms, online discussion groups, and computer-mediated services emerged. So, what is e-therapy? Manhal-Baugus (2001) described e-therapy as "the process of interacting with a therapist online in ongoing conversations over time when the client and therapist are in separate or remote locations and utilize electronic means to communicate with each other" (p. 551).

Over the past decade, e-therapy has gained popularity as a viable modality for helping people find solutions to their problems. Anonymity and accessibility also make e-therapy attractive to those who are in need of mental health services but are unable to access them or who might not otherwise seek out therapy. For example, adolescents; people with special needs (e.g., the deaf, physically disabled, and so forth); agoraphobics; people in rural or remote locations; people with time constraints; people who experience stress or stigma with traditional therapy; or diverse ethnic and cultural populations (e.g., lower class and middle class).

These individuals are often referred to as e-clients or e-patients. Most e-clients prefer to use home-based computer systems for psychotherapy. For the most part, "being online" is the norm for most e-clients. E-clients tend to prefer nonvisual, nonvoice, low-tech options. E-clients also tend to be more willing to disclose personal information online than in person, and they tend to enjoy insight and reflection via e-mail. This form of e-therapy is similar to journaling and is particularly desirable for people who enjoy and even excel in writing. However, it is important to keep in mind that not everyone can write fluently or communicate their ideas through text effectively (Fenichel, 2000). Consequently, e-therapy may be limited to those who are reasonably educated writers and readers: middle- to upper-class individuals.

In regard to e-therapists, all too often clinicians start using the technology before they understand how it works (Harder, 2002). One way to understand how technology works is to understand the language used to describe it. Some of the most common terms found in the e-therapy literature are briefly described below. Such terms are often described as modalities of online therapy.

- *Synchronous Communication*: This type of communication is described by Suler (2000) as a client and a therapist sitting down at their computers and interacting with each other at that moment. Online modalities that fit this type of communication are text-only chat, avatar chat, Internet telephoning, voice over Internet Protocol (VoIP), and audio- or videoconferencing.
- *Asynchronous Communication*: The opposite of synchronous communication. The biggest difference is the time delay. Online modalities that fit this type of communication are text-only (like e-mail, newsgroups or bulletin boards) or delayed viewing of multimedia recordings (Suler, 2000).
- *Sensory* modalities enhance some types of synchronous and asynchronous communication through the inclusion of sights, images, and sounds (e.g., audio- or videoconferencing).
- *Live Online Chat (LOC)*: Synchronous. LOC is synonymous with chat therapy.
- *E-mail Therapy*: Asynchronous. Clients exchange e-mails with a therapist over a period of time. This type of communication allows clients time to reflect on a therapist's responses and vice versa (Sharpe, 2000).
- *Audio- or Videoconferencing*: Can be either synchronous or asynchronous. A client talks with a therapist via a webcam (e.g., web conferencing) connected to a computer. This is the closest modality in comparison to face-to-face (f2f) therapy. Internet telephoning and VoIP are examples of Internet audio technologies.
- *Online Group Counseling*: Synchronous. Several clients participate in a live online chat or Web conference with a therapist.
- *Discussion Groups*: Either synchronous or asynchronous. Clients chat online with each other, sometimes with therapists as moderators. Discussion groups are similar to online support groups.
- *Computer-Mediated Therapy*: Clients may work independently without having contact with a therapist (Castelnuovo, Gaggioli, Mantovani, & Riva, 2003a; Lange, van de Ven, Schrieken, & Emmelkamp, 2001).
- *Computer-Assisted Psychotherapy*: Clients answer a series of computer-generated questions and get feedback from a computer. Automated. No live therapist is involved. It is the same as computer-guided therapy (Lange et al., 2001).

This list of terms is not at all comprehensive, but it can serve as a good starting point. See Elleven and Allen (2004), Maheu et al. (2005), or the National Board for Certified Counselors (2007) for more comprehensive lists. For simplicity, the terms *E-therapy, online counseling/*

therapy, Internet psychotherapy, cybertherapy, cybercounseling, Internet-based counseling/therapy, online counseling, and *virtual therapy* are used interchangeably.

Benefits of E-Therapy

One of the major benefits of e-therapy is that of convenience (Bischoff, 2004). E-therapy provides access to mental health services for those not previously accessible, such as those who live in remote geographical locations, are physically disabled, or may be too sick to travel. E-therapy also expands the list of potential referrals for those who live in inaccessible areas (Kenny & McEachern, 2004). Travel costs can be decreased or eliminated (Bischoff, 2004). Oftentimes, no appointment is needed, and it may be less expensive than traditional therapy. Others, too busy to keep scheduled appointments or work odd hours, may find e-therapy beneficial.

Manhal-Baugus (2001) asserted that one of the biggest contributing factors in choice of online psychotherapy is client anonymity. There is a "disinhibition effect whereby people say things online that they would not say face to face" (Alleman, 2002, p. 3). Greater depth in self-disclosure may lead to greater depth in therapeutic work. An advantage for clients utilizing asynchronous modes of communication is that they acquire more time to reflect on therapist feedback. In addition, Suler (2000) recognized that e-therapy offers multiple types of therapeutic relationships based on the different modes of communication it offers. He suggested that e-therapy could be an initial step of what could become an ongoing, in-person therapeutic relationship.

Ethical Considerations

Currently, technological advances are developing more rapidly than ethical or legal regulatory bodies can accommodate them (Maheu & Gordon, 2000; Rosik, 2001). A common misconception with e-therapy is that the basic rules of therapy are suspended when practicing it (Derrig-Palumbo, 2002; Harder, 2002). That is not the case. Many mental health professionals advocating e-therapy agree to the fact that ethical risks exist (Caudill, 2000; Derrig-Palumbo, 2002; Harder, 2002; Houser et al., 2006; Maheu &

Gordon, 2000; Maheu, Whitten, & Allen, 2001; McCarty & Clancy, 2002; Reed et al., 2001; Rosik, 2001). Clinicians considering e-therapy should be aware of the ethical issues engrossing it. As a general rule, clinicians who practice e-therapy must adhere to every professional and ethical principle pertaining to traditional, in-office care of clients (Kraus, Zack, & Stricker, 2004). What follows is a discussion of potential ethical considerations and standards issued by states and professional boards.

Informed Consent

What constitutes informed consent when e-therapy occurs between the therapist and client? How can e-therapists "adequately inform" their clients? Traditional ethics surrounding informed consent apply to e-therapy. Informed consent for e-therapy should include the following:

- Disclosures of the therapist's education (International Society for Mental Health Online [ISMHO], 2007), license and certification, and any additional special training or expertise (ISMHO, 2000) (A hyperlink on your Web site to your state licensing credentials is also helpful.)
- The limits of confidentiality, due to both the technology and the law (Houser et al., 2006; Maheu et al., 2005)
- Issues of safety, confidentiality, and privacy (ISMHO, 2000; Maheu & Gordon, 2000)
- The benefits and risks of e-therapy, and safeguards against those risks, and alternative treatments (ISMHO, 2000) (Include a statement about the stage of development of e-therapy and the limited outcome research available to support its efficacy and effectiveness.)
- Procedures and process, such as turnaround time for asynchronous communication, fees, level of security, and procedures for technical problems (ISMHO, 2000)
- The Web site for your professional society's code of ethics
- Payment information and any issues regarding third-party reimbursement involvement
- Record keeping procedures, including whether you will be keeping transcripts or summaries of sessions
- Procedures in the event of technological failure
- Written notice of privacy practices if therapists are covered entities under Health Insurance Portability and Accountability Act of 1996 (HIPAA) (www.hhs.gov.ocr/privacy/hipaa/understanding/coveredentities/)

Privacy and Confidentiality

McCarty and Clancy (2002) advised that clients should be informed about the potential risk of unauthorized access of information being transmitted, stored, or retrieved during the process of e-therapy. Encryption programs should be discussed, as well as the threat of hackers. Therapists can subscribe to a "SEAL" program (Secure Electronic Authenticated Link) which is a free program that helps ensure clients that they are accessing a secure framework. An example of a "SEAL" program is available at www. TRUSTe.org, which is an organization that certifies that your Web site is trustworthy and reliable and arbitrates any problems with the consumer. The therapist's privacy is also a consideration.

Liability and Risk Issues

Many legal issues arise with e-therapy. A prominent issue is whether or not providing e-therapy or telephone therapy to someone across state lines constitutes unlicensed practice in another state (Caudill, 2000). Likewise, the therapist would need to be clear whether malpractice insurance purchased in one state transfers across state lines.

E-therapy defies all state, national, and global boundaries. Moreover, state and case laws that differ create incongruent criteria for the burden of liability. However, malpractice insurers provide coverage for the services that fall within what is "generally accepted" by the profession (Koocher & Morray, 2000). Insurers may deny that e-therapy has won general acceptability within the profession.

Identification is a liability issue. The identification of the client is an issue with e-therapy. The lure of anonymity brings many potential pitfalls to therapy should the therapist allow clients anonymity. Issues around crisis intervention, suicide, or duty to warn arise when clients are granted anonymity. In addition, when clients desire anonymity, it puts e-therapists at a disadvantage in attempting to identify whether a client is of appropriate mental capacity or legal age. This does not allow for an adequate informed consent process, or it may put the therapist out of compliance with state statutes.

Blair (2001) confirmed others' concerns and suggested another issue, the verification of therapist credentials. Clients are at risk when the therapist's credentials cannot be verified. A hyperlink on the therapist's Web site to the therapist's professional licensing board's Web site can alleviate this concern.

Client misunderstandings are also possible because the paralinguistic cues are often missing with e-therapy. The typical nonverbal information gathered during therapy helps with assessment, diagnosis, and treatment planning. The absence of this information may thwart treatment efforts in some specific instances.

E-therapy may also reinforce maladaptive behavior, such as social phobia (Fisher & Fried, 2003) or agoraphobia. These behaviors may never come to the attention of the therapist, because the client is never driven out of his or her comfort zone to attend therapy.

Client technology competence may also be an issue. There may be a tendency to allow the challenges posed by the technology to become the main focus of discussion, or a technology-challenged client may receive inferior services. On the other hand, a therapist who is not technologically savvy may deliver poorer services. E-therapy requires the acquisition of a specific set of online communication skills. An absence of appropriate training in e-therapy skills limits the clinical competence of therapists providing such services. Technology failure is always a risk as well (Fenichel, 2000).

Another risk is adverse contact posttermination. Some clients may use the Internet to bother, stalk, or harass former therapists (Childress & Grohol, 2000). For example, one therapist who had limited e-therapy contact with a client was harassed by the client on her "MySpace" page.

Professional Practice

E-therapists are not immune from their professional codes of practice (Harder, 2002). The three most significant barriers to the development of e-therapy practices are reimbursement, uniform state licensure, and uniform confidentiality (McCarty & Clancy, 2002). In 2004, the American Medical Association added a new CPT code 0074T that allows physicians in the United States to receive reimbursement for online consults (Kraus, 2004). Despite this, many reimbursement issues remain. For example, Caudill (2000) was concerned that billings inappropriately submitted to insurance carriers could be interpreted as "fraudulent or misleading." Nonetheless, therapists are encouraged to document and research the effectiveness of their approaches to e-therapy.

Maheu and Gordon (2000) encouraged therapists who use e-mail to maintain high levels of "electronic security" through the use of encryption software. They also encouraged therapists to print out all e-mail exchanges and place them in the clients' case records. For a more detailed review of the ethical, legal, and practical issues in e-therapy, see Houser et al. (2006), Maheu et al. (2001), and Manhal-Baugus (2001).

E-Therapy Services

E-therapists typically offer several options for clients to engage and contract for services. One type of service offered online is an e-mail "education" session. Online education may be more effective for meeting the majority of people needing help than anything else. Diagnosis and treatment are typically not a part of an educational session, but advice or consultation may be. Other online services include online coaching, consulting, and psychoeducation. Additional information about services offered online can be found by visiting the following Web sites:

- Metanoia: www.metanoia.org
- ISMHO: www.ismho.org
- HealthyPlace.com: www.healthyplace.com
- eTherapyWeb.Com: www.etherapyweb.com
- OnlineClinics.com: www.onlineclinics.com

Finally, some e-therapists use virtual office space to conduct their online practices. Others offer their services via their own Web sites. The following Web sites offer virtual office space for e-therapists:

- myTHERAPYnet.com—Confidential online therapy for an evolving world: www.mytherapynet.com
- Online therapy and online counseling at HelpHorizons: www.helphorizons.com

Guidelines for E-Therapists

Establishing an ethical online practice can be a daunting task if you are not aware of some of the common guidelines. These guidelines have been compiled from various sources (e.g., American Psychological Association, 2007; Clinical Social Work Federation, 2001; ISMHO, 2000; National

Board of Certified Counselors, n.d.; Reed et al., 2000) and offer a brief overview of how to practice e-therapy (Elleven & Allen, 2004):

Know your technology. Be sure you are familiar with the technology you are using, your encryption software, and how you can guarantee your client's confidentiality so that you can communicate it to the client. Have security mechanisms in place. Explain to your clients the level of security you have in place. Describe your encryption software. Does your Internet service provider monitor transmission? Describe established procedures for technical problems to clients.

Define your scope of online practice for your client. Clearly outline your scope of practice. Disclose what you do, how you do it, how long you anticipate therapy will last, what services are charged for, and so on. For example, once therapy is done, may clients e-mail you?

Understand your organization's code of ethics, and practice accordingly. If your organization has not yet issued codes on Internet technology, familiarize yourself with the codes of ethics of other organizations (e.g., American Association for Marriage and Family Therapy, 2001; American Psychological Association, 2002; ISMHO, 2000; National Board of Certified Counselors, 2007).

Practice within the scope of your license, and only take clients who live within your state. Until laws regarding e-therapy are established, it is prudent to take only clients who are in the same jurisdiction as your license.

Assess a client's suitability for e-therapy. Some clients may not be suitable for e-therapy. The ISMHO (2007) developed guidelines for assessing client suitability. These guidelines are not intended to be exhaustive or definitive. When assessing client suitability, you should consider the following questions (ISMHO, 2007):

- What communication methods are adequate or preferable for assessing the client?
- How might the person's computer skills, knowledge, platform, and Internet access affect the therapy?
- How knowledgeable is the person about online communication and relationships?
- How well is the person suited for the reading and writing involved in text communication (e-mail, chat)?
- How might previous and concurrent mental health treatment affect online therapy?
- How might personality type, presenting complaint, and diagnosis influence the person's suitability for online therapy?
- How might physical and medical factors affect online therapy?
- How might cross-cultural issues affect the therapy?

- What other online resources might be appropriate to incorporate into a treatment package?
- Do potential clients understand the liabilities and risks involved with e-therapy?

Be sure that you have a verifiable name, phone number, and street address for your client. Clients may prefer anonymity, but you still have an obligation to intervene should there be duty to warn or intervene in the case of an emergency. In addition, you need to be sure you are treating an adult or have parent permission to treat a minor.

Get an informed consent (as detailed above). The informed consent should detail the risks and benefits of treatment and the alternative treatments available to the client. The procedures for therapy, including the nuances of the electronic media, should be clearly outlined.

Establish emergency/crisis intervention procedures. Establish detailed procedures for long-distance emergencies. Mental health and medical emergencies should be considered thoroughly, and referral sources will be needed. Emergencies may include suicidal clients, physical and sexual abuse, threats to harm others, and hospitalizations (Childress & Grohol, 2000).

Keep good documentation. Maintain clear records and good billing practices. Archive any electronic records (i.e., e-mails, chat sessions, etc.) according to your professional standard of practice.

Therapists who are seriously considering an online practice are strongly encouraged to acquaint themselves with the following books: *Online Counseling: A Handbook for Mental Health Professionals* by Kraus, Zack, and Stricker (2004); *Online Therapy: A Therapist's Guide to Expanding Your Practice* by Derrig-Palumbo and Zeine (2005); and *The Mental Health Professional and New Technologies: A Handbook for Practice Today* by Maheu et al. (2005). These books offer practical insight into how therapists can translate their traditional practice to an online medium.

Summary

Not all therapists will become e-therapy enthusiasts, but many therapists will find themselves using technology in some way to boost their practices. For example, intake information and assessment instruments can be downloaded prior to a first session, completed, and sent back to the therapist via electronic file transfer. Computer-assisted instruction can be used with homework assignments. Couple or family therapy might be available via video counseling when the couple cannot attend together due to distance or scheduling concerns (Sampson, Koldinsky, & Greeno, 1997). Some therapists communicate with clients via e-mail. There are many configurations in which e-therapy can augment practice. More research is needed to evaluate the effectiveness of e-therapy.

Finally, e-therapy offers many promising and innovative approaches to helping others struggling with mental health and relational issues. The convenience, affordability, and unique applications of e-therapy will continue to draw the attention of both clinicians and potential clients.

References

Alleman, J. R. (2002). Online counseling: The Internet and mental health treatment. *Psychotherapy: Theory, Research, Practice and Training, 32*(2), 199–209.

American Association for Marriage and Family Therapy (AAMFT). (2001). AAMFT Board of Directors. Alexandria, VA: Author.

American Psychological Association (APA). (1997). *APA statement on services by telephone, teleconferencing, and Internet.* Retrieved September 28, 2008, from: www.apa.org/ethics/stmnt01.html.

American Psychological Association (APA). (2002). *Ethical principles of psychologists and code of conduct.* Retrieved September 28, 2008, from: www.apa.org/ethics/code2002.html.

Bischoff, R. J. (2004). Considerations in the use of telecommunications as a primary treatment medium: The application of behavioral telehealth to marriage and family therapy. *The American Journal of Family Therapy, 32,* 173–187.

Blair, R. (2001). Psychotherapy online. *Health Management Technology, 22(2),* 24–27.

Castelnuovo, G., Gaggioli, A., Mantovani, F., & Riva, G. (2003a). From psychotherapy to e-therapy: The integration of traditional techniques and new communication tools in clinical settings. *CyberPsychology and Behavior, 6*(4), 375–382.

Castelnuovo, G., Gaggioli, A., Mantovani, F., & Riva, G. (2003b). New and old tools in psychotherapy: The use of technology for the integration of traditional clinical treatments. *Psychotherapy: Theory, Research, Practice, Training, 40*(1–2), 33–44.

Caudill, O. B. (2000). *Let your fingers do the walking to the courthouse: Long distance liability.* September 28, 2008, from: www.aamft.org/members/Resources/LRM_Plan/Legal/lgl_DistLiability.htm.

Childress, C. A., & Grohol, J. (2000). Ethical issues in providing online psychotherapeutic interventions. *Journal of Medical Internet Research, 2*(1), 5.

Clinical Social Work Federation (CSWF). (2001). *CSWF position paper on Internet text-based therapy*. Retrieved September 28, 2008, from: www.association-sites.com/page.cfm?usr=cswa&pageid=3670.

Derrig-Palumbo, K. (2002). Online therapy: The marriage between technology and a healing art. *Family Therapy Magazine, 1*(5), 20–23.

Derrig-Palumbo, K., & Zeine, F. (2005). *Online therapy: A therapist's guide to expanding your practice*. New York: W. W. Norton.

Elleven, R. K., & Allen, J. (2004). Applying technology to online counseling: Suggestions for the beginning e-therapist. *Journal of Instructional Psychology, 31*(3), 223–227.

Etforecasts. (2007). Internet user forecast by country. Retrieved September 28, 2008, from: www.etforecasts.com/products/ES_intusersv2.htm#1.0.

Fenichel, M. (2000). *Online psychotherapy: technical difficulties, formulations, and processes*. Retrieved September 28, 2008, from: www.fenichel.com/technical.shtml.

Fisher, C. B., & Fried, A. L. (2003). Internet-mediated psychological services and the American Psychological Association ethics code. *Psychotherapy: Theory, Research, Practice, Training. 40*(1–2), 103–111.

Haberstroh, S., Duffey, T., Evans, M., Gee, R., & Trepal, H. (2007). The experience of online counseling. *Journal of Mental Health Counseling, 29*(3), 269–282.

Harder, H. G. (2002). Technically ethical. *Family Therapy Magazine, 1*(5), 24–26.

Houser, R., Wilczenski, F. L., & Ham, M. (2006). *Culturally relevant ethical decision-making in counseling*. Thousand Oaks, CA: Sage.

Hsiung, R. C. (2002). *E-therapy: Case studies, guiding principles, and the clinical potential of the Internet*. New York: W. W. Norton.

International Society for Mental Health Online (ISMHO). (2000). *ISMHO/PSI suggested principles for the online provision of mental health services* [version 3.11]. Retrieved July 28, 2009, from: www.ismho.org/suggestions.asp.

International Society for Mental Health Online (ISMHO). (2007). *Assessing a person's suitability for online therapy*. Retrieved July 28, 2009, from: http://www.ismho.org/therapy_suitability_assessment.asp.

Internet World Stats. (2008). *World Internet usage and population stats*. Retrieved September 28, 2008, from: www.internetworldstats.com/stats.htm.

Kenny, M. C., & McEachern, A. G. (2004). Telephone counseling: Are offices becoming obsolete? *Journal of Counseling and Development, 82*(2), 199–202.

Koocher, G. P., & Morray, E. (2000). Regulation of telepsychology: A survey of state attorneys general. *Professional Psychology: Research and Practice, 31*(5), 503–508.

Kraus, R. (2004). CPT code 0074T for online consultation—A revolution in healthcare delivery? Retrieved September 28, 2008, from: www.onlineclinics.com/pages/content.asp?iglobalid=44.

Kraus, R., Zack, J., & Stricker, G. (2004). *Online counseling: A handbook for mental health professionals*. San Diego, CA: Elsevier Academic Press.

Lange, A., van de Ven, J. P., Schrieken, B., & Emmelkamp, P. M. G. (2001). Interapy. Treatment of posttraumatic stress through the Internet: A controlled trial. *Journal of Behavior Therapy and Experimental Psychiatry, 32,* 73–90.

Laszlo, J. V., Esterman, G., & Zabko, S. (1999). Therapy over the Internet? Theory, research, and finances. *Cyberpsychology and Behavior, 2*(4), 293–307.

Maheu, M. M., & Gordon, B. L. (2000). Counseling and therapy on the Internet. *Professional Psychology: Research and Practice, 31*(5), 484–489.

Maheu, M., Pulier, M. L., Wilhelm, F. H., McMenamin, J. P., & Brown-Connolly, N. E. (2005). *The mental health professional and new technologies: A handbook for practice today.* New York: Routledge.

Maheu, M., Whitten, P., & Allen, A. (2001). *E-Health, telehealth, and telemedicine: A guide to start-up and success.* San Francisco: Jossey-Bass/Pfeiffer.

Manhal-Baugus, M. (2001). E-therapy: Practical, ethical, and legal issues. *Cyberpsychology and Behavior, 4*(5), 551–563.

McCarty, D., & Clancy, C. (2002). Telehealth: Implications for social work practice. *Social Work, 47*(2), 153–162.

National Board for Certified Counselors (NBCC). (n.d.). *The practice of Internet counseling.* Retrieved July 29, 2009, from: http://www.nbcc.org/AssetManagerFiles/ethics/internetCounseling.pdf.

Reed, G. M., McLaughlin, C. J., & Milholland, K. (2000). Ten interdisciplinary principles for professional practice in telehealth: Implications for psychology. *Professional Psychology: Research and Practice, 31*(2), 170–178.

Rochlen, A. B., Land, L. N., & Wong, Y. J. (2004). Male restrictive emotionality and evaluations of online versus face-to-face counseling. *Psychology of Men and Masculinity, 5*(2), 190–200.

Rosik, C. H. (2001). Professional use of the internet: Legal and ethical issues in a member care environment. *Journal of Psychology and Theology, 29*(2), 106–121.

Sampson, J. P. Jr., Kolodinsky, R. W., & Greeno, B. P. (1997). Counseling on the information highway: Future possibilities and potential problems. *Journal of Counseling and Development, 75,* 203–212.

Sharpe, R. (2000). The virtual couch. *Business Week, 3699,* 134–138.

Suler, J. R. (2000). Psychotherapy in cyberspace: A five-dimensional model of online and computer-mediated psychotherapy. *Cyberpsychology and Behavior, 3*(2), 151–159.

VandenBos, G. R., & Williams, S. (2000). The Internet versus the telephone: What is telehealth anyway? *Professional Psychology: Research and Practice, 31*(5), 490–492.

Appendix

American Association for Marriage and Family Therapy
(AAMFT) *Code of Ethics* (Effective July 1, 2001)

Preamble

The Board of Directors of the American Association for Marriage and Family Therapy (AAMFT) hereby promulgates, pursuant to Article 2, Section 2.013 of the Association's Bylaws, the Revised AAMFT *Code of Ethics*, effective July 1, 2001.

The AAMFT strives to honor the public trust in marriage and family therapists by setting standards for ethical practice as described in this Code. The ethical standards define professional expectations and are enforced by the AAMFT Ethics Committee. The absence of an explicit reference to a specific behavior or situation in the Code does not mean that the behavior is ethical or unethical. The standards are not exhaustive. Marriage and family therapists who are uncertain about the ethics of a particular course of action are encouraged to seek counsel from consultants, attorneys, supervisors, colleagues, or other appropriate authorities.

Both law and ethics govern the practice of marriage and family therapy. When making decisions regarding professional behavior, marriage and family therapists must consider the AAMFT *Code of Ethics* and applicable laws and regulations. If the AAMFT *Code of Ethics* prescribes a standard higher than that required by law, marriage and family therapists must meet the higher standard of the AAMFT *Code of Ethics*. Marriage and family therapists comply with the mandates of law, but make known their commitment to the AAMFT *Code of Ethics* and take steps to resolve the conflict in a responsible manner. The AAMFT supports legal mandates for reporting of alleged unethical conduct.

The AAMFT *Code of Ethics* is binding on Members of AAMFT in all membership categories, AAMFT-Approved Supervisors, and applicants for membership and the Approved Supervisor designation (hereafter, AAMFT Member). AAMFT members have an obligation to be familiar with the AAMFT *Code of Ethics* and its application to their professional services. Lack of awareness or misunderstanding of an ethical standard is not a defense to a charge of unethical conduct.

The process for filing, investigating, and resolving complaints of unethical conduct is described in the current Procedures for Handling Ethical Matters of the AAMFT Ethics Committee. Persons accused are considered innocent by the Ethics Committee until proven guilty, except as otherwise provided, and are entitled to due process. If an AAMFT Member resigns in anticipation of, or during the course of, an ethics investigation, the Ethics Committee will complete its investigation. Any publication of action taken by the Association will include the fact that the Member attempted to resign during the investigation.

Contents

1. Responsibility to clients
2. Confidentiality
3. Professional competence and integrity
4. Responsibility to students and supervisees
5. Responsibility to research participants
6. Responsibility to the profession
7. Financial arrangements
8. Advertising

Principle I: Responsibility to Clients

Marriage and family therapists advance the welfare of families and individuals. They respect the rights of those persons seeking their assistance, and make reasonable efforts to ensure that their services are used appropriately.

1.1. Marriage and family therapists provide professional assistance to persons without discrimination on the basis of race, age, ethnicity, socio-economic status, disability, gender, health status, religion, national origin, or sexual orientation.

1.2 Marriage and family therapists obtain appropriate informed consent to therapy or related procedures as early as feasible in the therapeutic relationship, and use language that is reasonably understandable to clients. The content of informed consent may vary depending upon the client and treatment plan; however, informed consent generally necessitates that the client: (a) has the capacity to consent; (b) has been adequately informed of significant information concerning treatment processes and procedures; (c) has been adequately informed of potential risks and benefits of treatments for which generally recognized standards do not yet exist; (d) has freely and without undue influence expressed consent; and (e) has provided consent that is appropriately documented. When persons, due to age or mental status, are legally incapable of giving informed consent, marriage and family therapists obtain informed permission from a legally authorized person, if such substitute consent is legally permissible.

1.3 Marriage and family therapists are aware of their influential positions with respect to clients, and they avoid exploiting the trust and dependency of such persons. Therapists, therefore, make every effort to avoid conditions and multiple relationships with clients that could impair professional judgment or increase the risk of exploitation. Such relationships include, but are not limited to, business or close personal relationships with a client or the client's immediate family. When the risk of impairment or exploitation exists due to conditions or multiple roles, therapists take appropriate precautions.

1.4 Sexual intimacy with clients is prohibited.

1.5 Sexual intimacy with former clients is likely to be harmful and is therefore prohibited for two years following the termination of therapy or last professional contact. In an effort to avoid exploiting the trust and dependency of clients, marriage and family therapists should not engage in sexual intimacy with former clients after the two years following termination or last professional contact. Should therapists engage in sexual intimacy with former clients following two years after termination or last professional contact, the burden shifts to the therapist to demonstrate that there has been no exploitation or injury to the former client or to the client's immediate family.

1.6 Marriage and family therapists comply with applicable laws regarding the reporting of alleged unethical conduct.

1.7 Marriage and family therapists do not use their professional relationships with clients to further their own interests.

1.8 Marriage and family therapists respect the rights of clients to make decisions and help them to understand the consequences of these decisions. Therapists clearly advise the clients that they have the responsibility to make decisions regarding relationships such as cohabitation, marriage, divorce, separation, reconciliation, custody, and visitation.

1.9 Marriage and family therapists continue therapeutic relationships only so long as it is reasonably clear that clients are benefiting from the relationship.

1.10 Marriage and family therapists assist persons in obtaining other therapeutic services if the therapist is unable or unwilling, for appropriate reasons, to provide professional help.

1.11 Marriage and family therapists do not abandon or neglect clients in treatment without making reasonable arrangements for the continuation of such treatment.

1.12 Marriage and family therapists obtain written informed consent from clients before videotaping, audio recording, or permitting third-party observation.

1.13 Marriage and family therapists, upon agreeing to provide services to a person or entity at the request of a third party, clarify, to the extent feasible and at the outset of the service, the nature of the relationship with each party and the limits of confidentiality.

Principle II: Confidentiality

Marriage and family therapists have unique confidentiality concerns because the client in a therapeutic relationship may be more than one person. Therapists respect and guard the confidences of each individual client.

2.1 Marriage and family therapists disclose to clients and other interested parties, as early as feasible in their professional contacts, the nature of confidentiality and possible limitations of the clients' right to confidentiality. Therapists review with clients the circumstances where confidential information may be requested and where disclosure of confidential information may be legally required. Circumstances may necessitate repeated disclosures.

2.2 Marriage and family therapists do not disclose client confidences except by written authorization or waiver, or where mandated or permitted by law. Verbal authorization will not be sufficient except in emergency situations, unless prohibited by law. When providing couple, family, or group treatment, the therapist does not disclose information outside the treatment context without a written authorization from each individual competent to execute a waiver. In the context of couple, family, or group treatment, the therapist may not reveal any individual's confidences to others in the client unit without the prior written permission of that individual.

2.3 Marriage and family therapists use client and/or clinical materials in teaching, writing, consulting, research, and public presentations only if a written waiver has been obtained in accordance with Subprinciple 2.2, or when appropriate steps have been taken to protect client identity and confidentiality.

2.4 Marriage and family therapists store, safeguard, and dispose of client records in ways that maintain confidentiality and in accord with applicable laws and professional standards.

2.5 Subsequent to the therapist moving from the area, closing the practice, or upon the death of the therapist, a marriage and family therapist arranges for the storage, transfer, or disposal of client records in ways that maintain confidentiality and safeguard the welfare of clients.

2.6 Marriage and family therapists, when consulting with colleagues or referral sources, do not share confidential information that could reasonably lead to the identification of a client, research participant, supervisee, or other person with whom they have a confidential relationship unless they have obtained the prior written consent of the client, research participant, supervisee, or other person with whom they have a confidential relationship. Information may be shared only to the extent necessary to achieve the purposes of the consultation.

Principle III: Professional Competence and Integrity

Marriage and family therapists maintain high standards of professional competence and integrity.

3.1 Marriage and family therapists pursue knowledge of new developments and maintain competence in marriage and family therapy through education, training, or supervised experience.

3.2 Marriage and family therapists maintain adequate knowledge of and adhere to applicable laws, ethics, and professional standards.

3.3 Marriage and family therapists seek appropriate professional assistance for their personal problems or conflicts that may impair work performance or clinical judgment.

3.4 Marriage and family therapists do not provide services that create a conflict of interest that may impair work performance or clinical judgment.

3.5 Marriage and family therapists, as presenters, teachers, supervisors, consultants and researchers, are dedicated to high standards of scholarship, present accurate information, and disclose potential conflicts of interest.

3.6 Marriage and family therapists maintain accurate and adequate clinical and financial records.

3.7 While developing new skills in specialty areas, marriage and family therapists take steps to ensure the competence of their work and to protect clients from possible harm. Marriage and family therapists practice in specialty areas new to them only after appropriate education, training, or supervised experience.

3.8 Marriage and family therapists do not engage in sexual or other forms of harassment of clients, students, trainees, supervisees, employees, colleagues, or research subjects.

3.9 Marriage and family therapists do not engage in the exploitation of clients, students, trainees, supervisees, employees, colleagues, or research subjects.

3.10 Marriage and family therapists do not give to or receive from clients (a) gifts of substantial value or (b) gifts that impair the integrity or efficacy of the therapeutic relationship.

3.11 Marriage and family therapists do not diagnose, treat, or advise on problems outside the recognized boundaries of their competencies.

3.12 Marriage and family therapists make efforts to prevent the distortion or misuse of their clinical and research findings.

3.13 Marriage and family therapists, because of their ability to influence and alter the lives of others, exercise special care when making public their professional recommendations and opinions through testimony or other public statements.

3.14 To avoid a conflict of interests, marriage and family therapists who treat minors or adults involved in custody or visitation actions may not also perform forensic evaluations for custody, residence, or visitation of the minor. The marriage and family therapist who treats the minor may provide the court or mental health professional performing the evaluation with information about the minor from the marriage and family therapist's perspective as a treating marriage and family therapist, so long as the marriage and family therapist does not violate confidentiality.

3.15 Marriage and family therapists are in violation of this Code and subject to termination of membership or other appropriate action if they: (a) are convicted of any felony; (b) are convicted of a misdemeanor related to their qualifications or functions; (c) engage in conduct which could lead to conviction of a felony, or a misdemeanor related to their qualifications or functions; (d) are expelled from or disciplined by other professional organizations; (e) have their licenses or certificates suspended or revoked or are otherwise disciplined by regulatory bodies; (f) continue to practice marriage and family therapy while no longer competent to do so because they are impaired by physical or mental causes or the abuse of alcohol or other substances; or (g) fail to cooperate with the Association at any point from the inception of an ethical complaint through the completion of all proceedings regarding that complaint.

Principle IV: Responsibility to Students and Supervisees

Marriage and family therapists do not exploit the trust and dependency of students and supervisees.

4.1 Marriage and family therapists are aware of their influential positions with respect to students and supervisees, and they avoid exploiting the trust and dependency of such persons. Therapists, therefore, make every effort to avoid conditions and multiple relationships that could impair professional objectivity or increase the risk of exploitation. When the risk of impairment or exploitation exists due to conditions or multiple roles, therapists take appropriate precautions.

4.2 Marriage and family therapists do not provide therapy to current students or supervisees.

4.3 Marriage and family therapists do not engage in sexual intimacy with students or supervisees during the evaluative or training relationship between the therapist and student or supervisee. Should a supervisor engage in sexual activity with a former supervisee, the burden of proof shifts to the supervisor to demonstrate that there has been no exploitation or injury to the supervisee.

4.4 Marriage and family therapists do not permit students or supervisees to perform or to hold themselves out as competent to perform professional services beyond their training, level of experience, and competence.

4.5 Marriage and family therapists take reasonable measures to ensure that services provided by supervisees are professional.

4.6 Marriage and family therapists avoid accepting as supervisees or students those individuals with whom a prior or existing relationship could compromise the therapist's objectivity. When such situations cannot be avoided, therapists take appropriate precautions to maintain objectivity. Examples of such relationships include, but are not limited to, those individuals with whom the therapist has a current or prior sexual, close personal, immediate familial, or therapeutic relationship.

4.7 Marriage and family therapists do not disclose supervisee confidences except by written authorization or waiver, or when mandated or permitted by law. In educational or training settings where there are multiple supervisors, disclosures are permitted only to other professional colleagues, administrators, or employers who share responsibility for training of the supervisee. Verbal authorization will not be sufficient except in emergency situations, unless prohibited by law.

Principle V: Responsibility to Research Participants

Investigators respect the dignity and protect the welfare of research participants, and are aware of applicable laws and regulations and professional standards governing the conduct of research.

    5.1 Investigators are responsible for making careful examinations of ethical acceptability in planning studies. To the extent that services to research participants may be compromised by participation in research, investigators seek the ethical advice of qualified professionals not directly involved in the investigation and observe safeguards to protect the rights of research participants.

    5.2 Investigators requesting participant involvement in research inform participants of the aspects of the research that might reasonably be expected to influence willingness to participate. Investigators are especially sensitive to the possibility of diminished consent when participants are also receiving clinical services, or have impairments which limit understanding and/or communication, or when participants are children.

    5.3 Investigators respect each participant's freedom to decline participation in or to withdraw from a research study at any time. This obligation requires special thought and consideration when investigators or other members of the research team are in positions of authority or influence over participants. Marriage and family therapists, therefore, make every effort to avoid multiple relationships with research participants that could impair professional judgment or increase the risk of exploitation.

    5.4 Information obtained about a research participant during the course of an investigation is confidential unless there is a waiver previously obtained in writing. When the possibility exists that others, including family members, may obtain access to such information, this possibility, together with the plan for protecting confidentiality, is explained as part of the procedure for obtaining informed consent.

Principle VI: Responsibility to the Profession

Marriage and family therapists respect the rights and responsibilities of professional colleagues and participate in activities that advance the goals of the profession.

6.1 Marriage and family therapists remain accountable to the standards of the profession when acting as members or employees of organizations. If the mandates of an organization with which a marriage and family therapist is affiliated, through employment, contract or otherwise, conflict with the AAMFT *Code of Ethics*, marriage and family therapists make known to the organization their commitment to the AAMFT *Code of Ethics* and attempt to resolve the conflict in a way that allows the fullest adherence to the *Code of Ethics*.

6.2 Marriage and family therapists assign publication credit to those who have contributed to a publication in proportion to their contributions and in accordance with customary professional publication practices.

6.3 Marriage and family therapists do not accept or require authorship credit for a publication based on research from a student's program, unless the therapist made a substantial contribution beyond being a faculty advisor or research committee member. Coauthorship on a student thesis, dissertation, or project should be determined in accordance with principles of fairness and justice.

6.4 Marriage and family therapists who are the authors of books or other materials that are published or distributed do not plagiarize or fail to cite persons to whom credit for original ideas or work is due.

6.5 Marriage and family therapists who are the authors of books or other materials published or distributed by an organization take reasonable precautions to ensure that the organization promotes and advertises the materials accurately and factually.

6.6 Marriage and family therapists participate in activities that contribute to a better community and society, including devoting a portion of their professional activity to services for which there is little or no financial return.

6.7 Marriage and family therapists are concerned with developing laws and regulations pertaining to marriage and family therapy that serve the public interest, and with altering such laws and regulations that are not in the public interest.

6.8 Marriage and family therapists encourage public participation in the design and delivery of professional services and in the regulation of practitioners.

Principle VII: Financial Arrangements

Marriage and family therapists make financial arrangements with clients, third-party payors, and supervisees that are reasonably understandable and conform to accepted professional practices.

7.1 Marriage and family therapists do not offer or accept kickbacks, rebates, bonuses, or other remuneration for referrals; fee-for-service arrangements are not prohibited.

7.2 Prior to entering into the therapeutic or supervisory relationship, marriage and family therapists clearly disclose and explain to clients and supervisees: (a) all financial arrangements and fees related to professional services, including charges for canceled or missed appointments; (b) the use of collection agencies or legal measures for nonpayment; and (c) the procedure for obtaining payment from the client, to the extent allowed by law, if payment is denied by the third-party payor. Once services have begun, therapists provide reasonable notice of any changes in fees or other charges.

7.3 Marriage and family therapists give reasonable notice to clients with unpaid balances of their intent to seek collection by agency or legal recourse. When such action is taken, therapists will not disclose clinical information.

7.4 Marriage and family therapists represent facts truthfully to clients, third-party payors, and supervisees regarding services rendered.

7.5 Marriage and family therapists ordinarily refrain from accepting goods and services from clients in return for services rendered. Bartering for professional services may be conducted only if: (a) the supervisee or client requests it, (b) the relationship is not exploitative, (c) the professional relationship is not distorted, and (d) a clear written contract is established.

7.6 Marriage and family therapists may not withhold records under their immediate control that are requested and needed for a client's treatment solely because payment has not been received for past services, except as otherwise provided by law.

Principle VIII: Advertising

Marriage and family therapists engage in appropriate informational activities, including those that enable the public, referral sources, or others to choose professional services on an informed basis.

8.1 Marriage and family therapists accurately represent their competencies, education, training, and experience relevant to their practice of marriage and family therapy.

8.2 Marriage and family therapists ensure that advertisements and publications in any media (such as directories, announcements, business cards, newspapers, radio, television, Internet, and facsimiles) convey information that is necessary for the public to make an appropriate selection of professional services. Information could include: (a) office information, such as name, address, telephone number, credit card acceptability, fees, languages spoken, and office hours; (b) qualifying clinical degree (see Subprinciple 8.5); (c) other earned degrees (see subprinciple 8.5) and state or provincial licensures and/or certifications; (d) AAMFT clinical member status; and (e) description of practice.

8.3 Marriage and family therapists do not use names that could mislead the public concerning the identity, responsibility, source, and status of those practicing under that name, and do not hold themselves out as being partners or associates of a firm if they are not.

8.4 Marriage and family therapists do not use any professional identification (such as a business card, office sign, letterhead, Internet, or telephone or association directory listing) if it includes a statement or claim that is false, fraudulent, misleading, or deceptive.

8.5 In representing their educational qualifications, marriage and family therapists list and claim as evidence only those earned degrees: (a) from institutions accredited by regional accreditation sources recognized by the United States Department of Education, (b) from institutions recognized by states or provinces that license or certify marriage and family therapists, or (c) from equivalent foreign institutions.

8.6 Marriage and family therapists correct, wherever possible, false, misleading, or inaccurate information and representations made by others concerning the therapist's qualifications, services, or products.

8.7 Marriage and family therapists make certain that the qualifications of their employees or supervisees are represented in a manner that is not false, misleading, or deceptive.

8.8 Marriage and family therapists do not represent themselves as providing specialized services unless they have the appropriate education, training, or supervised experience.

This Code is published by: American Association for Marriage and Family Therapy, 112 South Alfred Street, Alexandria, VA 22314; Phone: (703) 838-9808; Fax: (703) 838-9805; www.aamft.org. (© Copyright 2001 by the AAMFT. Reprinted with permission of the American Association for Marriage and Family Therapy.)

Index